The Coming
Church Revolution

Other books by Carl F. George

Prepare Your Church for the Future (Revell 1991)

by Carl F. George and Robert E. Logan
Leading and Managing Your Church (Revell 1987)

by Carl F. George with Warren Bird
How to Break Growth Barriers (Baker 1993)

by C. Peter Wagner (editor) and Carl F. George (contributor)
Church Growth: The State of the Art (Tyndale 1986)

by James D. Berkley (editor) and Carl F. George
with Warren Bird (contributor)
Leadership Handbook of Practical Theology, Vol. 2
(Baker 1993)

***

"*The Coming Church Revolution* is definitely revolutionary! The book
is challenging but realistic to fit a church desiring to be the answer to
the modern-day needs of a challenging community!"

David Yonggi Cho, Senior Pastor
Yoido Full Gospel Church
Seoul, Korea

The Coming Church Revolution

*Empowering Leaders
for the Future*

Carl F. George
with
Warren Bird

Fleming H. Revell
A Division of Baker Book House
Grand Rapids, Michigan 49516

Published by Fleming H. Revell
a division of Baker Book House Company
P.O. Box 6287, Grand Rapids, Michigan 49516-6287
All rights reserved.

Third printing, May 1997

Printed in the United States of America

Library of Congress Cataloging-in-Publication Data

George, Carl F.
    The coming church revolution : empowering leaders for the future / Carl F.
George with Warren Bird.
        p.   cm.
    Includes bibliographical references and index.
    ISBN: 0-8007-5528-6
    1. Christian leadership.   2. Pastoral theology.   3. Small groups.
4. Christianity—Forecasting.   I. Bird, Warren   II. Title.
BV652.1.G45   1994
253—dc20   94-16616

For current information about all releases from Baker Book House, visit our web site:
http://www.bakerbooks.com

Contents

Part 3: Transitioning Wisely from "Here" to "There"

Part 4: Sharing the Ministry

List of Figures

2

The Importance
of Raising Up Leaders

The limiting resource on your church's part of the harvest is, in all probability, the lack of trained leaders.

Which of the following best defines the "irreducible minimum" of a leader?

Are church leaders people who are . . .

- elected or appointed to certain offices?
- present every time the church's doors are open?
- the quickest to volunteer when workers are needed?
- the chief financial underwriters of a church's programs?
- highly visible as "emcees" of a meeting?
- longest-term members at that church?
- able to influence others to meet with them?

Many commonly accepted definitions of *leader* do not describe a person who can help a church grow! Why? A leader, in many people's eyes, is someone who shows up regularly or gets elected to office, not someone who can produce an attendance or following.

From a functional point of view, the starting point for being a leader is the final item in the checklist above: Are followers present

List of Case Studies

Foreword

The Crow Wing Power and Light Company is headquartered in Baxter, Minnesota, serving small towns and rural areas. Inside the front cover of the employees' handbook is printed, "People Don't Care How Much You Know; People Care How Much You Care."

This slogan is an overstatement. Obviously, customers expect CWP&L to have the necessary technical knowledge about electricity, power lines, circuits, and monthly statements. But technical information is not enough. Customers want to be treated as people with needs, wants, and feelings. They want to know that they are more than meters. They want care.

A revolution has already begun in North American culture and churches making care far more important. An earlier generation asked the churches for knowledge. Local churches were chosen because of denominational labels and the attractiveness of preaching. Once the selection was made, relationships usually followed.

Increasingly, relationships come first. The new generation has been left hungry for love and care. Tens of millions of North Americans have grown up in dysfunctional families, have experienced broken relationships, live far from grandparents, or otherwise feel deprived of love, intimacy, and community. In a word, they just want someone to care. Who should care for them more than Christians? Where should they experience love more than from the church?

This is not to say that biblical knowledge and orthodox Christian faith are less important. Obviously they are essentially important. The church is not the church without truth any more than the power company is a power company without electricity. For Christians there is no choice between truth and love. Both are essential.

If North American Christians and churches seize the opportunity, present and future generations will be incorporated into the church of Jesus Christ through relationships. With those relationships they will become Christians, learn the Bible, and develop as obedient disciples of the Lord. If we do not seize the opportunity, they will be lost. The loss may be to caring relationships that are not Christian and have not truth.

Carl George has seen the revolution and wants to win it for Jesus Christ and his church. He follows in the tradition of Jesus, whose strategy was to empower leaders for the future. Dream with Carl George of a changed church for the twenty-first century where Jesus Christ is Lord, the Holy Spirit controls, care is normative, evangelism is relational, leaders are multiplying, lay people do ministry, and God's truth is lived out in everyday life.

—Leith Anderson

Acknowledgments

This book has been a team effort and would not be possible without the gracious experiences of the almost three hundred different pastors and churches cited in the text, as well as the thousands of others who allowed us to learn from their experiments and progress.

An outstanding office staff has likewise brought together the many details needed to complete this book. Special thanks to Shirley Shively and Jayne Bak for their herculean diligence in correspondence and interviews; to Dorcas McKown, Gwen Weaver, Karan Banando, Steve Engel, and Val O'Barr for their talented work on the graphics; to Dan Simpson, Greg Asimakoupoulos, Loren Brubaker, Bob Harris, Estela Salazar, Kelly Beasley, Karen Miller, Michelle Nicosia, and Pat McGlade for helping codify, organize, or transcribe material that became the starting text for this book; and to Claude Florent, Debby Evans, Bryan Feller, and the hardworking team at the Charles E. Fuller Institute for producing the seminars at which much of this content was presented as it developed.

Many thanks also to all who read the manuscript at various stages and offered both encouragement and valuable critique: Charles Arn, Lamar Austin, Michelle Bird, Bob Brady, Richard Bush, Brian L. Chronister, H. Robert Cowles, Mike Cunningham, Mark Edwards, David Ferguson, Marcia Gautier, Grace George, Jack L. Giles, James Hobby, David Hricik, Joey Johnson, Jeff Kent, Bob Logan, Janet Logan, Jay Mack, Scott Marshall, Rick Nash, Steve Ogne, Gary Schmidt, Hal Seed, Terry A. Smith, and John Soper.

Introduction:
A Personal Perspective

What counts is where the wind of the Spirit is blowing
and whether I catch that in my sail.

In 1978, after sixteen years of pastoral ministry, I became director of the Charles E. Fuller Institute of Evangelism and Church
Growth. This new responsibility thrust me into the role of a consultant, and over time churches[1] and districts from more than a hundred different denominations called on me to evaluate their needs
and make recommendations to maximize their potential.

These clients ranged from what I call the typical church in North
America (with a worship attendance of seventy-five)[2] to a number
of the continent's largest churches. Included among the clients
were old churches, new churches, urban churches, and churches in
transition.

Reluctance to Publicize

I was constantly challenged to find answers to problems but I
sometimes found that I didn't even possess the vocabulary to ask
the right questions. By 1986 after doing on-site consultations with
hundreds of churches across the country, I codified a self-diagnos-
ing tool that could express what a North American church looked
like. Based on these observations, I wrote the outline for a book.

But I sensed the Holy Spirit's indicating that I should wait. Also,
on a very human level, I was afraid to publish these observations

15

for fear that people might take them seriously. I had observed the consequences of following authors who wrote more than they knew and I decided that my associates and I should conduct further evaluations before releasing the findings.

From 1986 to 1988, as the ideas came into focus, I field-tested them secretly, case by case, in a variety of church settings. Each time, my clients would say, "That makes sense and seems to work."

In October of 1988 I organized the first seminar, a by-invitation-only event for four large churches to come together to carefully examine concepts previously announced as Meta-Church thinking. I explained the kinds of ministry emphases my mentors and I saw on the horizon and, at the conclusion of that three-day seminar, asked the participating churches whether they thought the principles were ready for more general exposure. They agreed that what we had identified was both accurate and unsettling.

Every three months throughout 1988 and 1989, I allowed a few more churches into the system. By that point I felt that I could head the Federal Drug Administration because my colleagues and I had been so very careful in how we had tested the various ideas and had watched so very cautiously for adverse side effects.

I had observed many people putting their careers on the line and believing passionately in these "new" perspectives. I concluded, "If anyone really commits to implementing these ideas and they aren't right, they will do serious damage to their ministries." So I kept the lid on the book idea and said, "It will not be let out until my associates and I are convinced that the concepts help more than hinder."

By 1991 and after five years of field testing, we had elicited enough feedback to identify the potential problems. The publisher processed the manuscript and released the book. We wondered: If the church of the future is different from the kind of church most people are experiencing today, then how do we get from here to there? That's what *Prepare Your Church for the Future*, released in October 1991 and now in its eighth printing, is all about.

As of this writing, my colleagues and I have tutored more than four hundred churches, each with a worship attendance of approximately seven hundred to three thousand, who have brought teams to similar two- or three-day events designed to plan their futures.

Other less-intensive forms of training have exposed more than ten thousand additional church leaders to these concepts.

Both Crash Course and Sequel

Prepare Your Church for the Future was a conversation to pastors and professional staff with certain lay leaders looking over their shoulder and then forming plans together in the boardroom and at other leadership huddles. The book you now hold is designed to facilitate the staff-to-supervisor group relationships, or the supervisor of groups-to-group-leader relationship. In short, it empowers leaders for the future to prepare for the coming church revolution.

In other words, this book represents (1) what a primary vision caster, usually a senior pastor, says to staff, (2) what a staff pastor says to lay coaches of small groups, and (3) what a coach could say to a cell leader.

Therefore, don't read this book alone. Think it through having your apprentice and those you supervise in mind. Note the sections

> I offer this book not with the intention of somehow inventing a future, but rather of discovering and responding to the future to which God is calling his people.

where you need to say to them, "Read this, let's talk." Use the discussion questions at the end of each chapter. Talk about the ideas with your spouse, close friends—and anyone else who has a passion for what tomorrow's church will be.

The Coming Church Revolution, as a sequel to *Prepare Your Church for the Future*, is both an advanced course and a stand-alone crash course. Thus it is designed to be helpful, whether it represents your first reading on the subject or your fiftieth—and indeed the literature involving Meta-Church ideas is forming an ever-widening stream.[3]

At the same time, I offer this book on the same basis as *Prepare Your Church for the Future*—not with the intention of somehow inventing a future, but rather of discovering and responding to the future to which God is calling his people.

Spiritual Preparation

When I became a church consultant in 1978, I took some formal study in the discipline and learned from my mentors that as I matured, I would go through cycles. I, as others before me, would stumble onto certain points of enlightenment in which I would begin to see similarities and patterns in how God prepares the way ahead. A milestone on my journey was one that dealt with my own body and mind. I recall, as if it were yesterday, flying back from New Orleans in the early 1980s. All of a sudden my whole body relaxed. I prayed, "Dear Lord, am I losing it, or is this okay?"

Then I realized that I had been carrying tension in my body for several years, bearing burdens and anxieties that I hadn't even been aware of. As I mulled over, prayed about, and tried to determine what was going on, the most compelling thought that came to mind was this realization: Over the years I had not gone to one single church where God had not preceded me. He wasn't arriving with me; he was already there. It was as if God had said, "Carl George, look around! Everywhere you go, I've been there long ago! Trust me; I'm always with my children." After all, hadn't I prayed for such divine appointments over the years? Prayer does prepare the way! I went home knowing that I was a church-growth consultant not only by title but also in dependence on God. A new era had opened in my life!

About that same time, I'd been reading C. S. Lewis's *Narnia* chronicles about the lion Aslan, who is the figure of God, and the breath of Aslan, which is the symbol of the Holy Spirit. Lewis speaks of Aslan's transporting the children to their next assignment by blowing his breath from the side of a cliff. The children tumbled into it and were gently carried, slowly tumbling and floating, until they touched down at the shore of the new land where their new adventure would begin. I had that same feeling of how delightful and how weightless someone must feel when carried about by the breath of God. I knew I'd be carried where I needed to go and that on arriving I'd be adequate for the task, replete with the necessary energy, rest, and wisdom. Why? Because God wanted to help someone, and I was merely the designated agent for facilitating the help of God. What a privilege!

My first realization, then, was one of process: God will always be with me if I am willing to be open to his Spirit. The second flowed from that: If I am following his call, I'll be a blessing to those he sends me to. God was not interested in helping only that church. He was also interested in helping me help that church. When I saw something and understood it, it was not a fortuitous incident. It was God's indicating, "Look at this. You need to see this specific snapshot. It's important." Those apparently chance conversations that I overheard in a hallway or in the back row of a church sanctuary were God's superintending the discovery process.

Further, all my formal education and training, while undeniably helpful, did not account for whatever success resulted from my consulting. Almost all the help I gave a church was the result of serendipitous occurrences—joyful surprises. For example, at an airport newsstand, I'd pick up a magazine that caught my eye, or on the plane I'd be struck by a thought from my Scripture reading for that day. An hour later at a board meeting the insight I'd just received was what the people needed. Or I'd go through my library as I packed and throw a couple of books in my briefcase. I'd open one of those books in my room that night and have the energy to read maybe one chapter. The next day, that was the very chapter that spoke to the church's need.

This timing was God at work! The joy I experienced as I flew home from New Orleans was a consequence of coming to understand that I was dealing with the body of Jesus Christ. God is more concerned for the health of his body than any human is. He is constantly making us "competent as ministers of a new covenant" (2 Corinthians 3:6; cf., Jeremiah 31:33). Whatever we lack his Spirit supplies if we have a teachable spirit. All the preparation I could do intellectually, though necessary, was inconsequential compared with the serendipity that God gives to his children. Isn't that the same model we see in Scripture? Virtually every neat thing that has happened in ministry occurred because God set it up.

Take, for example, the great conversion story of the Philippian jailer (Acts 16:16–34). Yes, the apostle Paul and his companion

Silas were amazing evangelists. But if *you* had a suicidal person fall on his knees in front of you and beg, "Tell me what must I do to be saved," you could be an evangelist too. All you have to do is answer the question! Paul looked so good because God was with him. I dare say that in the light of a conviction that genuine, Paul could have stammered through the gospel message and the man would still have grasped it!

I'm not discounting scholarship, preparation, or speaking skill. I'm saying that my confidence is not there; it's in the guidance of the Holy Spirit. The tools that have been developed for critical learning are very helpful in understanding today's church. Yet, in the presence of all those tools, it is the Holy Spirit who makes our work possible and of eternal significance. At issue is not how big a load I can carry or how steep a hill I can climb. What counts is where the wind of the Spirit is blowing and whether I catch that in my sail.

In short, if this book is of benefit to you, it will be because it helps you find out what God is blessing and then guides you to participate with him in that work.

The Attitude of a Leader

As you read this book, and see examples of how God is building his church, you may find yourself praying, "God, would you do that in the church I serve?" "Could that kind of leadership development and multiplication occur in our church, given our particular circumstances?" Chances are that God is far more willing to bless you than you are prepared to receive his blessing.

Here's a way to check your attitude. If you—whether you're a

> If this book is of benefit to you, it will be because
> it helps you find out what God is blessing
> and then guides you to participate with him in that work.

pastor or a lay leader—are properly sharing the ministry with others, then the prospect of more people and more ministry is a source of joy to you. If you're not properly sharing the ministry with others, then more people will feel like more work to you.

If you're eager to experience God's refreshing as he reaches an ever-enlarging harvest through the leaders you help raise up, then read on. Together let's not go on with business as usual as long as there is anybody who goes to bed at night crying himself or herself to sleep because of not knowing God's love.

Along with the prophet Jeremiah, this passion is the fire within my bones (Jeremiah 20:9). As I said toward the conclusion of my book, *How to Break Growth Barriers*, "As long as there is one person outside the fold, we cannot rest easy."[4]

PART 1

Grasping the Big Picture

1

Meta 101

Our purpose is not to invent a future but rather to discover the future to which God is calling his people.

The key to understanding this book is the ability to understand the difference between a caterpillar and a butterfly. Imagine a drab-colored caterpillar as it spins a cocoon around itself at the biologically appropriate time. Then, through the mystery of the chrysalis (or cocoon) experience, it becomes transformed. It emerges as something new: a beautifully winged creature. A leaf-eating grub has become a multihued, nectar-drinking butterfly.

The church today is experiencing that same kind of transformation. We have been crawling. God intends, I believe, that we should soar. A change is underway, and we're in the mystery of the chrysalis stage (see figure 1)—not so much a time of inactivity as of transition. The church now emerging is no more like the church we have known than the butterfly is like the caterpillar.

What changes in our thinking are going to be necessary to prepare us for that future? What reordering of our priorities and our church structure is required for us to be able to take flight, to be a part of God's great plan of redemption in the years to come? In order for us to deal with the changes that are coming, we must learn to think and act much differently than we do at present. A study of churches across the globe gives us a glimpse of the things that are to come and teaches us some of the next steps that can be taken to prepare us for the future. Our purpose is not to invent a future but rather to discover the future to which God is calling his people.

Church of the Future

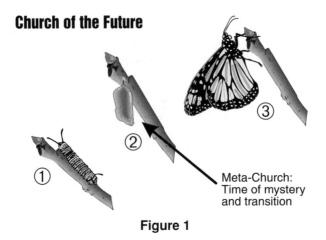

Meta-Church:
Time of mystery
and transition

Figure 1

Introducing the Meta-Church

This book will use a special term to alert church leaders to the changes and altered priorities that are underway. The term is *Meta-Church*. *Meta* is a Greek prefix. Most people will recognize it in words like *metamorphosis*, which refers to the change in form that the caterpillar goes through on the way to becoming a butterfly. Students of the Bible may know the Greek word *metanoia*, which describes the change in one's mind or thinking associated with repentance and conversion. Our minds and wills must "turn about" so that we no longer hold stubbornly to our former ways, which blocked us from being fully obedient to God.

Thus the idea of Meta-Church means a church in transition, a church that is turning, a church that is becoming. The full extent of where Meta-Church thinking will take us is not entirely clear. But as we study fast-growing (and therefore, in most cases, large) churches around the globe, we're finding a new paradigm emerging. They have blended evangelism and pastoral care with leadership development in such a way that they win people to Christ as they care for them; and as they develop new leaders, they are constantly able to expand to accommodate whatever harvest of souls the Lord of the harvest, the Father of our Lord Jesus Christ, is calling into the body of Jesus here on earth (Matthew 9:37–38; Luke 10:2; John 4:35; Acts 2:39–47; 2 Corinthians 10:13).

> The idea of Meta-Church means a church
> in transition, a church that is turning,
> a church that is becoming.

As many trend-tracking books have pointed out, a number of significant changes are occurring in societies worldwide. The most fundamental of these alterations is that, in an alarming number of cases, the biological family is not functioning well: People are increasingly unable to find the support, acceptance, belonging, positive role modeling, and sense of normalcy they need at home.

In response, Meta-Church thinking emphasizes a "re-envisioning" of how the family of God relates to one another. Consequently, it also calls for a significant shift in how ministry is perceived: The clergy's critical event involves the formation of leaders who can provide care, rather than the clergy's own hands-on, primary-care ministry; hence, the title and subtitle of this book—*The Coming Church Revolution: Empowering Leaders for the Future.*

Finally, the term *Meta-Church* also represents an accompanying change in organizational priorities and structures. It offers an alternative path to the future without the same theoretical limits that cause existing North American churches to stop growing because their quality of care has been diluted by size or other factors.

Why use the term *Meta-Church*?

- It alerts people to what God has begun to do.
- It describes the new way in which the family of God will relate to one another in the future.
- It emphasizes the importance of gifted volunteers (the laity).

What cautions must accompany the term *Meta-Church*?

- Our focus is to be on relationships and principles, not programs.
- Our focus is to learn to see what the Holy Spirit is doing.

The engine propelling a Meta-Church and leading to an exponential growth multiplication is the Holy Spirit's working through lay-led home-discipleship centers. These are affinity based, spiritual-gift dependent, lay-shepherded, supervised, evangelistic, and self-reproducing. Virtually all ministry is decentralized to these groups. Such a system frees clergy to focus energies on training lay leadership.

The Meta-Church, with a nurture cell of approximately ten people as its spiritual and emotional center, never has to abandon its most basic method: developing leaders who are capable of growing cells. It can accommodate every church size from 50 to 500,000. Churches can maintain quality, meaningful caregiving no matter how many of these spiritual kinship groups comprise the whole church.

> The Meta-Church can accommodate
> every church size from 50 to 500,000.

From Butterfly to X Ray

Another way to understand the Meta-Church is to compare a photograph with an X ray. A photo, say of your arm, indicates something about your size, skin color, muscle tone, and even "hairiness." But an X ray of that same arm shows something entirely different: It reveals the underlying bones, muscles, ligaments, and blood vessels that give your arm its strength and vitality. An X ray, then, is a diagnostic tool that enables someone to peer through the surface of things. It doesn't tell you how to treat what you see; that's a different matter. You still must apply judgment to decide what to do with what you learn.

Similarly, the Meta-Church paradigm helps you see more clearly what you are able to do, while giving you great latitude in deciding on courses of action. Why? The Meta-Church is a perspective, not a series of programs per se. Over time, it may have programmatic dimensions, but you won't introduce program first in the same way you would launch a Stephen Minister program, a Sunday-school program, or an Evangelism Explosion program.

The Meta-Church, therefore, is not the same as a small-group system (a definition of "small" will be given in chapter 4). It's much more. It's a way of understanding when cell-size ministry is *not* present, and where the probable blockages are.

The Meta-Church, properly understood, is not one of many competing models for how to do church. Rather, its use is like that of an X-ray machine: It offers a way to look at what you've got so you can figure out what's missing. As such, Meta-Church thinking applies equally well to liturgical and nonliturgical churches, traditional and formal churches, seeker churches, open churches, third-wave churches, and whatever else is to come (more on that idea in chapter 9).

You can X-ray a human being, whether that person is male or female, has white skin or brown, is nine months old or ninety-nine years old. Similarly, you can X-ray a piece of airline luggage whether it's large or small, whether it contains clothes, curlers, or compact discs. You can use Meta-Church tools, then, with any type or size of church because they describe arrangements for care,

> The Meta-Church, therefore,
> is not the same as a small-group system.

leadership connections, the setting of a vision, and the balancing between celebration and caring. These dynamics are present, in varying effectiveness, in every type of church.

So the benefit of Meta-Church thinking is not that it gives you a photograph—"Hmm. In this picture I see people using curriculum from Scripture Press!" Rather, it probes much deeper. It analyzes what's at the bones and ligaments of a church. It asks what needs to happen to enable a church to multiply its ministry (1) by commissioning lay people to be ministers, and (2) by redirecting the church's leadership to become producers of lay ministers.[1]

As a consequence, the Meta-Church is a highly flexible system for description, encompassing a theory of organizational development that's rooted soundly both in the Bible and in the social sciences.

A Meta-Church is . . .

- a new social architecture designed to maximize clergy-laity partnership in ministry.

- a church where the primary source of care is its network of groups, not its ordained ministers.

- a church organized around a system of lay-pastoral skills.

- a church intent on developing its staff and volunteer leaders into a network of evangelistic care units.

- a church prepared to handle large numerical growth without losing the personal touch and care of the individual.

- a church that's spreading the pastoral care load to reflect a partnership in which clergy and laity share the ministry.

- a church capable of ongoing self-diagnosis and corrective action as leaders regularly review both the total ministry and the proper functioning of each part.

New Insights on Cause and Effect

Until you've learned to conceive of a church system as an organism, using the same thoroughness as that of a medical specialist's diagramming the human body or a botanist the ecosystem of plants, you won't know how what you do affects the rest of the system. When you look at a leaf-covered shrub or bush, what do you see?—only the surface, because you lack X-ray vision. Similarly, if you try to understand the church you serve, and your powers of observation are limited to observing people in various meetings, you'll understand only the "surface" of the church. You'll probably not be able to see the underlying "branches," which signify your church as a society of groups related through linked leaders.

When you look at a bush, you know how the leaves are being held in place: Past experience teaches you that there must be stems present. If you apply this same concept to groups of people, who or what would be the equivalent of the stems?—the leaders, particularly volunteer leaders whose strength of personality influences others to follow them. Why is this idea important?—because it helps us know where to set our priorities.

Back in the early days of the children's Sunday-school movement, for example, everyone understood that the teacher was the starting point of a successful class. A lesson and a meeting room may have been predesignated, but the impetus originated with the teacher who went out visiting, recruiting boys and girls to become involved.

At a later stage, in many churches, Sunday-school attendance became large enough, and the system routinized enough that the existing Sunday-school members could be sent off to a classroom to await their teacher. The notion of leader was almost an afterthought. Whenever this later stage occurs, however, a church has usually lost the heart of what Sunday school is all about.[2] Sunday school can then degenerate into "sausage processing": stuff them in, close the door, and hope for the best.

In most cases, such a class loses its ability to grow. No longer is the teacher leading a unit of growth; he or she is now simply a way of managing a problem that membership growth has produced. What is the role of the teacher? Is the teacher more an entertainer or a recruiter?

Without Meta-Church thinking, we're in danger of dealing only with surface issues. A surface view leads us to observe how many classrooms or how much attendance is present, and, therefore, what teachers need in order to be plugged into the system. The true underlying issue, however, is how many proactive, visionary teachers you have who are calling on those existing and would-be members and bringing them together for growth in Christ.

We need to learn to see things internally—not only the surface effects but also the "underneath" effects. In order to know how to produce a worship service, we need to ask, "What goes on behind the scenes?" Similarly, in order to know how to produce nurture groups, we need to know what goes on underneath: What do the staff and other lay "coaches" do?

The word *Meta-Church* doesn't describe a church form so much as it announces the fact that "doing church" in our current way is an inadequate vehicle for all that Christ has called his body to do and be. We must change our thinking, our imagination of what God is trying to do. We must attune our hearts and methods to how he will go about doing it.

Why Meta-Church?

1. Our society's most fundamental care network, formerly built on the extended family, is crumbling.
2. People are dropping out of churches because they're not being assimilated into the life (or relationships) of the church.
3. Care needs are massive, both within a church and also in a church's "service area."
4. As a church grows, its staff must increasingly revise ministry to focus on volunteer-leader support.
5. Churches tend to become less evangelistic the larger they grow because transfer members throng them.
6. Church leaders need a systems perspective on their church as a whole, both its "external" and "internal" components.

Where Can You Find a Meta-Church?

In one sense *no* church is a Meta-Church; in another sense *every* church is. To label a church as a Meta-Church is to discern the intentions of its leaders, but to analyze a church with Meta-Church tools is to examine the degree to which this church is, in fact, practicing lay empowerment in ministry. So, instead of saying, "First Church is now a Meta-Church," it's more appropriate to say, "When analyzed using Meta-Church tools, the following strengths are apparent at First Church . . ."

> In one sense *no* church is a Meta-Church;
> in another sense *every* church is.

Meta-Church perspectives, for example, help explain many of the consistently fast-growing (and therefore largest) churches in the history of Christendom. Every church on earth with greater than twenty thousand in attendance uses some variation of a technology we analyze as Meta-Church. For example, here are some observations based on a composite of on-site observations by me, John Vaughan, Ralph Neighbour, and others[3]:

- The world's largest church—*more than a dozen times larger than any other in the history of Christendom*—is cell based. It happens to belong to the Assemblies of God family of churches, but the two largest Presbyterian, the two largest Methodist, and the largest Baptist church in the world are, likewise, cell-driven churches.
- Australia: A church in Brisbane has about four thousand members in three hundred cells. In Sydney, a cell movement begun in the mid-1970s now blankets the entire western side of that city.
- Portugal: This country, where Protestants comprise only 1 percent of the population, is the birthplace of a cell church that now encompasses some thirty thousand people.
- Chile: The largest church on the continent of South America, located in Santiago, is cell based and convenes at least fifty thousand people for corporate worship each week.
- Ivory Coast: A church in Abidjan, planted in 1975, now has thirty thousand members and more than two thousand cell groups.
- Malaysia: A church in Singapore has burgeoned from an attendance of two hundred in 1968 to well over five thousand at present, with more than four hundred cell groups.

Does Meta-Church Mean Megachurch?

Am I implying that a Meta-Church must also be a megachurch or super church? No. The Meta-Church concept represents a comprehensive approach to social architecture. It can begin at any attendance level.

In a recent seminar that I led in Knoxville, Tennessee, two pastors shared nearly identical stories of joys and successes in lay-led, cell-group ministry. One had four groups in a church of eighty; the other had thirty-two groups in a church of eight hundred.

True, until recently this technology tended to be the secret of super-huge churches in the Third World, or of past generations in England and North America, where the Wesleyan class-meeting movement established Methodism as a durable denomination. But no longer. Leadership development, as applied through lay-pastored cell groups, works in all sizes of churches with good results. The case studies in this book represent a wide range of attendance levels. Whatever their denomination or tradition, churches are discovering that the best way to get bigger is to become smaller through cell units: Sunday-school classes, ministry teams, task forces, nurture groups, recovery groups, support groups, and others.

In fact, various experts[4] have suggested that Meta-Church technology works primarily for large churches. I targeted my initial Meta-Church training to churches with an attendance above seven hundred because they were at a point, organizationally, where they were going to make some changes anyway—they had to simplify their board and the committee structure; they had to hire staff on a different basis than they had previously; they needed to figure out how to be systematic in their pastoral care. My logic went like this: "If they have to make some shifts, maybe they'll be open to an alternative path to the future, such as the Meta-Church observations suggest. Then, if the ideas work for them, they'll be in a position to turn around and help smaller churches. In addition, if a church had reached seven hundred or more people, its resources would enable it to capitalize on its opportunities very fruitfully with resulting growth gains."

So churches of seven hundred or more became a very natural focus group for Meta-Church intervention. At the same time, however, my files were filling with letters from pastors in small churches, who were likewise having a good success with Meta-Church thinking. Then, when *Prepare Your Church for the Future* was published, and when the Charles E. Fuller Institute[5] began offering "Meta" seminars and a "Meta" monthly audio-cassette club, both of which were open to smaller churches, the steady trickle of letters from smaller churches turned into a torrent.

Thus to those who suggest that the Meta-Church is a theory primarily for huge churches, I offer an alternative explanation: As a church becomes larger in size, it cannot continue growing if it becomes more complicated or more impersonal. In other words, show me a pastor-centered large church, and we'll find a very tired staff of clergy. Show me a lay-empowered, simply organized large church, where the clergy are not completely exhausted because they're doing too much, and I will show you a church that will not stop growing because it will be able to take good care of people as God calls them to new life through it.

Why This Emphasis on Counting Souls?

Many clergy become apprehensive when someone begins measuring their attendance, growth, number of new leaders, and so forth. They fear becoming sidetracked, or even trapped, in a numbers game. They feel that integrity in ministry requires that they give attention to persons without regard to whether they will contribute to the numerical growth of the church. According to this thinking, if we preoccupy ourselves with numbers and counting, we somehow cheapen our ministry or lose concern for Joe Schmo or Mary Smith or John Doe. A concern for statistics, they say, will prevent us from dealing selflessly and sensitively with the real, spiritual needs of people. Instead, we may become preoccupied with looking good in the eyes of our peers.

In response, let me first affirm the truth in those misgivings. It is indeed possible to abuse statistics and to use them as a basis for self-comparison in an unhealthy way. Human beings are so capable of sinful behavior that virtually any feature of any system of evaluation can be misused. Then along with pride can come false guilt or

> It is indeed possible to abuse statistics
> and to use them as a basis
> for self-comparison in an unhealthy way.

inappropriate shame. Further, there's a danger, in comparing one church to another, of becoming inappropriately critical of one's

Large North American Churches That Are Finding Help from Meta-Church Perspectives

In the United States:
(All churches have worship attendances of 3,000+ adults and children.)

1. Willow Creek Community Church; S. Barrington, Ill.
2. Mt. Paran Church of God; Atlanta, Ga.
3. New Hope Community Church; Portland, Ore.
4. Church of the Open Door; Crystal, Minn.
5. Eastside Foursquare Church; Kirkland, Wash.
6. First United Methodist Church; Houston, Tex.
7. College Avenue Baptist Church; San Diego, Calif.
8. Victory Outreach Church; West Covina, Calif.
9. Calvary Community Church; Westlake Village, Calif.
10. East 91st Street Christian Church; Indianapolis, Ind.
11. Briarwood Presbyterian Church; Birmingham, Ala.
12. First Baptist Church; Modesto, Calif.
13. Brentwood Baptist Church; Houston, Tex.
14. Prince of Peace Lutheran; Burnsville, Minn.

In Canada:
(All churches have worship attendances of 1,000+ adults and children.)

1. Northview Community Church; Matsqui, B.C.
2. First Alliance Church; Calgary, Alta.
3. The Wesleyan Church; Moncton, N.B.
4. Beulah Alliance Church; Edmonton, Alta.
5. Sherwood Park Alliance Church; Sherwood Park, Alta.
6. Grant Memorial Baptist; Winnipeg, Man.
7. First Assembly of God; Calgary, Alta.
8. Forest Grove Community Church; Saskatoon, Sask.
9. Centre Street Evangelical Church; Calgary, Alta.
10. Trinity Baptist Church; Kelowna, B.C.

Note: Thousands of *smaller* churches across the United States and Canada are applying Meta-Church observations to their ministries, and are reporting excellent results. Many other highly visible churches, such as Saddleback Valley Community Church, Mission Viejo, Calif., or Skyline Wesleyan Church, San Diego, Calif., strongly emphasize leadership development through small groups. These churches have not drawn their inspiration from the Meta-Church paradigm, but their methods and principles can be easily and helpfully described by Meta-Church systems.

comrades in ministry. Yes, sometimes the business of counting, as with King David (1 Chronicles 21), can be offensive to God.

The use of numbers, however, enormously simplifies our lives. Probably no one feels I'm being impersonal if I say, "seventeen of us met last night" rather than "Mike, Janet, Katherine, David, Ken, Carol, Marianna, Bryan, Clay, Bess, Raleigh, Jean, Wendell, Celia, Melanie, Michel, and Milton met last night." Conversation becomes very labored when you can't do some occasional summing. In addition, the Old Testament contains the Book of Numbers along with a host of tallies. The Gospels indicate, for example, that Jesus miraculously fed five thousand people. None of the accounts offer a listing of specific names. The same is true with the numerous references in the Book of Acts that indicate how many people were saved or added to the church. Likewise the great throng of people in heaven, described in Revelation, doesn't include a name-by-name list. The real question is this: What are the legitimate, proper, and spiritual uses of numbers? I believe that numbers should be considered people with the tears dried off.

Distinct Bias toward Conversion Growth

If you grow a church on quality, unless you bar the door, sooner or later it will become larger, even if it plants daughter churches. God wants to bring more people into his fellowship than a small church can handle; in most cases the church will grow as it reaps the harvest. If a church's leadership does what it ought to be doing, soon enough there will be both more churches and more larger churches.

In most cases, however, once a church passes four hundred, it tends to become a receptor church, with a high percentage of its newcomers being drawn from other smaller churches in the community. In other words, between 75 percent and 90 percent of the new members in the typical church of four hundred or more are transfers, not converts. There exists a widespread notion that North America's medium- and large-size churches are evangelistic centers. This view is, in most cases, regrettably only a myth. Instead, these churches are by and large centers for reprocessing believers, new and old alike, that throng to them from smaller churches.[6]

This situation leads to one of the largest spiritual dilemmas of our time: The bigger a church becomes, the less evangelistically responsible it needs to be in order to grow. As a church grows, it

> Numbers should be considered people
> with the tears dried off.

inherits the other churches' evangelism efforts. Regrettably, very few churches larger than four hundred do their own soul winning or primary spiritual formation. Rather, they simply reap the benefits of other churches' perceived failures.

Meta-Church thinking says transfer growth is no incentive to grow larger churches. Rather, those feeder-receptor circumstances are one of the penalties of going beyond four hundred. God has called his church to help people come into the presence of God and to find salvation through Jesus Christ (Mark 16:15; Luke 19:10; 24:45–47; Acts 1:8; 2:47; Ephesians 3:10–11; 1 Peter 2:9), and those truths are at the heart of a Meta-Church (see figure 2).

The people we're trying to touch are people who have an enormous need for God and for his love. They have an equally great need for inclusion within the fellowship of believers. We can do a much better job of planning for them if we're willing, from time to time, to take a look at the tallies and ask ourselves, "What is the meaning of these numbers?" A proper use of numbers can refocus our attention to our Lord Jesus' Great Commandment (Matthew 22:36–40) and Great Commission (Matthew 28:19–20) and keep us from drifting away from the heart of our mission.

The Meta-Church, therefore, is willing to use numbers to ask this question of every area of ministry: What are the numbers that, if given attention to, will fire us to pray with greater fervor, see with greater clarity, and touch people at a deeper level in their lives? Let's not apologize for using numbers, such as the ratio between transfer members and new converts whenever they aid us in responding to God's call.

Growth Focus

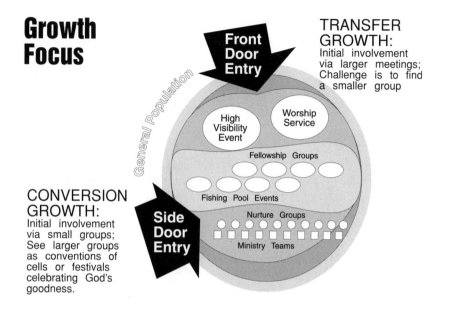

Front Door Entry

TRANSFER GROWTH:
Initial involvement via larger meetings; Challenge is to find a smaller group

General Population

High Visibility Event

Worship Service

Fellowship Groups

Fishing Pool Events

CONVERSION GROWTH:
Initial involvement via small groups; See larger groups as conventions of cells or festivals celebrating God's goodness.

Side Door Entry

Nurture Groups

Ministry Teams

Figure 2

Questions for Discussion and Application

1. What idea in this chapter rings truest to your own convictions? Which creates the greatest discomfort? Why?

2. According to this chapter, what is a Meta-Church? What are its biblical underpinnings?

3. In what ways is the church you are serving already informed by Meta-Church ideals? How could Meta-Church thinking further benefit your church?

with them? What defines a person's leadership is the people who follow him or her. If you don't have people following you, you're not the kind of leader being examined here—even if you have a vision, a title, or an impressive set of credentials! A leader inspires commitment in people to turn a vision into a concrete reality. To accomplish things alone requires only that someone be a hard worker; to reproduce a vision through other people, who adopt it as their vision as well as demonstrate it in their behavior, requires a leader.

Why make this leader-nonleader distinction? *The Coming Church Revolution* suggests a set of priorities that are different from what most churches are now pursuing. The Meta-Church paradigm proposes that the limiting resource on your church's part of the harvest is, in all probability, the lack of trained leaders. Thus the senior management of a church needs to decentralize leadership training so that the most basic and plentiful unit in your church— the small group of approximately ten people—becomes a forum for

> To accomplish things alone requires only that someone be a hard worker; to reproduce a vision through other people requires a leader.

developing new leaders.[1] Meta-Church observation informs a strategy of leadership development, through apprentice development, for any church size.

Fire Fighters and Fire Inspectors in Your Church

In frontier days, when a small fire got out of hand, most people's first response was to look for a bucket of water to throw on it. As a follow-up measure, if the area seemed to be fire-prone, those same people might place an empty pail or bag of sand nearby. After a few more fires, the residents might organize a volunteer fire department, and then eventually a professional fire department complete with alarm system. That way, as soon as the alarm sounded, the fire trucks could roll.

As time went on, and some huge fires overwhelmed the capabilities of the fire fighters, someone would work out a "bell" system, by which other stations could be summoned to fight the blaze. Also as technology advanced, someone would invent and install fire sprinklers and other on-site ways to contain the fire. Zoning boards would create codes requiring that even before a building is finished, it must contain a fire-suppression system.

Finally, somebody would suggest: "Maybe we can predict why these fires begin, and therefore prevent them from starting." So they would train volunteers to serve as fire inspectors. They would

> In order to provide enough preventative care
> at the grassroots level, a church must systemically
> utilize its most valuable and plentiful resource:
> the potential leaders among its lay people.

make on-site visits to friends' homes and businesses and say, "This rubbish is a fire hazard. Please clean it up!"

The predictable result of this scenario is that fewer fires flare up. The best fire-fighting system is the one in which you never see a fire truck roll because you've caught the hazard before the first sign of smoke. Most everyone would prefer a hazard-reduction system to a massive fire-fighting effort.

If that same fire-prevention analogy is applied to pastoral care, then fewer calls to "central" will need a staff person's attention. In order to provide enough preventative care at the grassroots level, a church must systemically utilize its most valuable and plentiful resource: the potential leaders among its lay people.

How to Find Apprentice Leadership

The model we increasingly find in healthy and growing churches is that the entry into leadership will, in most cases, be through the apprentice gateway. This concept of leadership development is capable of being both decentralized and constantly repeated. Its most fundamental formula is found in 2 Timothy 2:2 and elsewhere: One leader trains others, who in turn train others, who in turn train others.

The choke point evident in church after church is the response, "We'd love to extend the evangelism or care of our church, but we simply don't have enough leaders." The apprentice model in which every leader is cultivating at least one other leader is the most effective approach we know for overcoming that objection. Whether you direct choirs, teach Sunday school, lead a care group, do counseling, prepare the church bulletin, or organize trustee work projects, if you cultivate an apprentice, you will help instill a new culture in your church and open a door by which God can maximize the lay leadership potential among the gifted people he has already brought your way.

Who is responsible for bringing new leaders into your church? God may have already planted them in your midst, and now he wants to involve you in the discovery process—whether you're a paid pastor or a volunteer leader—in training people as your apprentices.

How then do you find apprentices? In other words, where do you look when you're trying to train and recruit new leadership? Let me suggest five simple steps for surfacing under-utilized talent.

First, there must be present a compelling vision that says "we need more leaders." The care needs in our communities, as well as in our churches, are massive. Heartache, loneliness, lack of hope, longings for meaningful friendships—these and other opportunities for demonstrating the love of Christ abound and are no farther away than our doorstep. The heart of compassion that the Spirit of Christ puts within each of his disciples is able to meet that need, especially if helped along by a cadre of volunteer leaders. If your church is to have ministry on that scale, chances are you need more leaders.

Second, you will want a clearly identified process by which apprentice leaders can be commissioned into ministry. In other words, are the lay leaders of your church aware of how to progress through the experiences necessary for them to move from apprentice to full-fledged volunteer leader?

Third, be aware of the early identifying symptoms of an apprentice. What criteria are you looking for, and who is likely to be a successful apprentice? Typically it's those who show interest outside the regular meeting time—people, for example, who study the Bible and hold times of prayer between the group's meetings, or people who stay after the meetings or come early because they have pressing questions or because they want to be around you.

Fourth, offer supervision, coaching, and encouragement to your rising leaders. See to it that every leader receives the training and the feedback he or she needs (this concept, known as manageable span of care, will be discussed in chapter 3).

Fifth and finally, you can go forward only as fast as you can travel on your knees. You may know the right person, but it may not be God's timing. You may have a potential candidate in mind, and God may indeed be calling that person at this time to be an apprentice—but to another group or ministry in your church. Pray until you've sensed God's mind. Remember that God is more interested that people be cared for than you are. Find out his plan, and then go forward, knowing that not even the gates of hell can withstand it.

More Than Studying Truth

Some people may question whether this emphasis on developing leaders will rob a church's emphasis on teaching and Bible doctrine. If we ever have to choose between how much Bible is understood or how much Bible is obeyed, my prejudice is in favor of obeyed truth. Also, an apprentice leader, facing the task of leading a group, will be keenly motivated to study the Word of God and will seek to understand it prior to his or her having to teach it. (This idea of adult learning will be discussed in chapter 5.)

> If we ever have to choose between how much Bible is understood or how much Bible is obeyed, my prejudice is in favor of obeyed truth.

A group of researchers did a Bible literacy survey of various denominations and discovered that the Southern Baptists had some of the highest Bible literacy scores of any denomination in the nation. How does one account for that statistic? I believe it partly stems from the fact that so many Southern Baptists, because of their extensive Sunday-school network, have had to take turns serving as teachers. A few years as teacher puts you in a position of high motivation to learn, with a resulting high-retention rate.

More Than Delegating

When church leaders first grasp the idea of what it looks like to share ministry with volunteer leaders in the church, they sometimes begin using the word *delegation* as the key for multiplying ministry.

The notion of delegation has been popularized in recent business literature. The idea involves one person, who has a certain responsibility and authority, realizing that he or she cannot do the job alone. So, looking down the hierarchy, this leader or manager says, "Here, you be responsible for this" and "You be responsible for that." The work, parceled out, is now in the care of others. This delegation process enables several people to be engaged in the work that previously was expected of one person, thereby enabling a larger task to be accomplished.

In empowering lay ministers, the concept of delegation is an inadequate one. The goal is not to "save time" for the clergy or other church professionals. The goal is not to create a mentality in which people's motivation is that of "helping" the pastor with his workload. Rather, the idea of apprentice development is this: "I am sharing the privilege of doing ministry with you, because you, with supervision and training, can be just as capable a minister, if not more so, than I am." Such an attitude communicates to apprentices that their presence is honored and contains a self-standing dignity.

> In empowering lay ministers, the concept
> of delegation is an inadequate one. Your goal
> is not to "save time" for the clergy.

It affirms the truth of Ephesians 4:12 that the proper and legitimate priesthood of all believers is "for the work of the ministry" (KJV). (See also the list of fifty-nine New Testament "one another" commands in *Prepare Your Church for the Future*, pages 129–31.)

Fellowship Evangelical Free Church

8000 Middlebrook Pike
Knoxville, TN 37909
Phone: (615)470-9800
Fax: 615-675-1247
Denomination: Evangelical Free Church

Senior Pastor: Doug Banister
Contact: Mike Edwards
Attendance: 800
Total Cell Groups: 25

Developing New Leaders with "Turbo" Speed

Virtually every church that experiences rapid growth reports a consequent problem: lack of enough lay leaders. This situation becomes especially acute for a new church, where the lack of trained, mature leaders can severely hamper efforts at discipleship and care.

A case in point is Fellowship Evangelical Free Church, Knoxville, Tennessee, which was launched in 1987. From the beginning, the staff was committed to involving the congregation in small group experiences. During the first year, when attendance was below one hundred, worship planners built small groups into the Sunday-morning schedule; immediately after the service, the people would break into groups for sharing and caring. During the next year, as attendance climbed from one hundred to three hundred, the staff designed other forums, such as Sunday evenings, for making small groups available.

"As new people kept coming in," says staff pastor Mike Edwards, "we needed to launch as many groups as possible, as fast as possible. The great need for leaders became one of our most important concerns."

Senior pastor Doug Banister had heard of the idea of creating a "turbo" group, where a number of potential lay leaders could be trained together. Soon twelve adults agreed to participate in the three-month turbo experiment, after which they could be released to form their own groups. The turbo format included modeling an actual small group, training in group dynamics and leader skills, and offering individual opportunities to practice leading.

"Modeling through turbo groups was a great vehicle to use in instilling a knowledge and vision for small group ministry," says Edwards. "It also offers an effective vehicle for identifying the strengths of potential leaders, and it helps us avoid putting someone into a leadership position inappropriately or prematurely."

Eight of that first turbo group's participants went on to start a new group. A second turbo group provided similar results.

The church, eight hundred on a typical Sunday by the end of 1993, continues to need new leaders, and the turbo idea has become one of three options. Says Edwards, "We believe the best solution for developing new small-group leaders is a combination of, first, slow-but-sound apprentice leader development; second, faster-track turbo groups for those who want to learn while seeing the concepts modeled; and third, quick, short-term leader training workshops for those with prior experience and confidence in leading groups."

More Than Modeling

In the training of an apprentice, sometimes ministry skills are transferred through a process of modeling. It is important to realize that shared ministry, and empowered volunteer leaders, does *not* mean that the professional staff withdraws from ministry. Rather, if at any time paid pastors or ministers are doing ministry and they fail to use the occasion as a modeling opportunity so that some apprentice is gaining the benefit from watching that process, then they are squandering a valuable church resource: the skilled practice of a professional ministry.

Sometimes, in churches just beginning to establish small groups and lay-leadership development, the staff best trained in this area will lead a small group as a model. A suspicion, borne from years of consulting practice, usually prompts me to go to the professional minister leading that small group to ask, "You're leading this small group as a modeling exercise?" "Yes." "Tell me, then, who are the apprentices that will be graduated from this experience and commissioned to ministry?" If the paid cleric says, "Well, I'm just hoping that someone will catch the idea" or "Here is my one apprentice," then I insist that they are in actuality doing volunteer work. The minimum requirement for a professional who is leading a small group is to raise up two apprentices. This accelerates the leadership-formation process.

The best justification for the use of a professional [D] in a small group situation is where the entire group is comprised of apprentices [Xa's], all of whom will be commissioned to ministry at some point, as a part of the ongoing life of that particular group experience. The idea also works with a lay supervisor of groups [L] launching the group. We call this process a Turbo Launch (see figure 3).

Thus you're intentionally modeling to people who will use your modeling to become leaders in their own right. If someone is going to accept a professional position on a church staff, the job description (or equivalent) should recognize that hands-on ministry will be done only in the context of modeling for others. It's the multiplying of lay ministers, not the hiring of more church staff, that holds the key to the advance and expansion of the church in the next generation.

Cell Launch Protocols

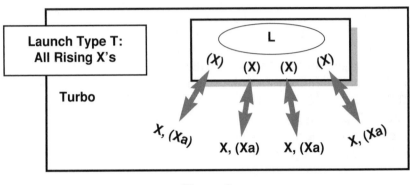

Figure 3

More Than a Promoter of Small Groups

Some people may think the goal of *The Coming Church Revolution: Empowering Leaders for the Future* is to promote small groups. It's not. True, small groups have played a crucial role in my own life—Sunday-school classes, home Bible studies, couples' fellowship groups, men's prayer groups, and the like. Yes, in the books I write, and the seminars I lead, I inevitably talk about small groups. But small groups are not the solution to what the church needs most desperately. Rather, churches rise and fall on the availability of trained, talented, and Spirit-gifted leadership. And the best possible context anyone has ever discovered for developing leadership occurs because of a small group.

The small group is the primary vehicle for legitimizing a lay minister. "This person is our group leader." That statement differentiates your lay pastors, shepherds, (or whatever you call them) enough from their peers that one-on-one conferences between group leader and group member carry the mantle of an official appointment between meetings. The fact that the small-group leader is coached, receives additional skill training, and is championed from the pulpit further affirms the blessing of the clergy on this person.

An astounding 98 percent of church leaders surveyed by the Charles E. Fuller Institute during 1993 indicated that developing volunteer leaders is a crucial aspect in the ministry of every local church. Yet, ironically, most churches still suffer from the lack of a leadership team that will partner with the professional leadership.

> Churches rise and fall on the availability of trained, talented, and Spirit-gifted leadership.

How to Help Someone Want to Be a Leader

My experience is that you, as someone looking for an apprentice, cannot make people desire to develop and use their leadership abilities. Rather, you persuade and motivate by your contagious enthusiasm and enjoyment. The very attractiveness of your pleasure in the experience of leading causes other people to begin to develop a hunger for it. In short, the desire for apprenticeship is a caught, rather than a taught, feature of leadership.

As such, apprentice development is a relationship-based process (to be discussed further in chapter 4). Do not, therefore, underestimate the enjoyment and companionship factor in apprentice training. Remember that the most important ingredient of the early tutelage Christ gave his twelve disciples was the framework of his invitation to them to be "with him" (Mark 3:14).

What, then, is required for someone to recruit an apprentice? You need to nurture a desire within some other person to be with you, to spend time with you, to do things with you, to hold animated discussions with you, and to share mutual interests with you that go beyond the anticipation of task.

Yes, there are some individuals who are much like Martha in the New Testament (Luke 10:38–42), who find their greatest joy in tasks and who manage their lives around the principle of staying busy. But only a few are preoccupied with tasks to that extent. Most would like some sense of camaraderie, some sense of the thrill of involvement. One thing that can be said for the twelve disciples is that life with Jesus was anything but boring!

Not everyone is an extroverted, bubbly sort of personality who seeks out continual high adventure. But anyone who is a leader (as defined by the ability to produce a following) will be able to find one or more apprentices who, when they see this leader coming, are excited enough to say, "This is going to be good!" and to demonstrate it with a lift in their spirits.

Leaders communicate that the thing they are involved with contributes to the most important objectives in the world, is eminently worthwhile, and provides a sense of energy and light. When a leader is aflame with a new or compelling idea, apprentices will find themselves attracted to what's going on; that's the nature of leadership.

The Results of Decentralized Apprenticeships

What happens when an apprentice culture has been established in a church? For churches driven by clergy care, the prospect of more people means more work. But for a minister-maker kind of church, more people are an opportunity. Volunteer energy is the most valuable resource in any church, whether it comes in the form of new converts, or whether it is transfer growth.

Will setting up an apprentice network establish your highest church priority as evangelism? No. New converts will be a consequence of your highest priority. If you focus on putting people who are already committed to Christ into leadership positions for recruiting and organizing care systems, then they will attend to the

> Volunteer energy is the most valuable resource
> in any church.

evangelism. Their efforts will multiply many times over what staff-run programs could have done by themselves.

Once you get these apprentice concepts clearly in mind, and have spread the leadership training and development task across the entire leadership cadre of your church, then the entire church will function as a leadership-production system. God will be in a position to entrust you with souls, new converts, new members, and

First Presbyterian Church

1850 East Avenue R
Palmdale, CA 93350
Phone: (805) 273-4424
Denomination: PCUSA

Senior Pastor: Jim Barstow
Contact: Todd DuBord
Attendance: 330
Total Cell Groups: 40

What Happens When You Intentionally Train Your Leaders

It was a "good news-bad news" time for Jim Barstow, senior pastor of First Presbyterian Church in Palmdale, California. On the positive side, the church, founded in 1919, had begun to experience numerical growth. People were being cared for in small groups, and the finances had improved so that the church could hire additional pastoral staff.

Then the downside set in. The church, whose worship attendance averaged about eighty when Barstow became pastor, grew to a point where the staff was no longer able to effectively care for the needs of the congregation. "People wanting to set up a counseling appointment with one of the staff pastors were having to wait two to three weeks," says Barstow. As a result, attendance began to decline.

From seminars, books, and ministry colleagues, Barstow latched onto the idea of equipping his parishioners to serve as lay shepherds. "We are part of a mainline, traditional denomination where change is not looked upon favorably," says Barstow, age thirty-seven. "Yet we are seeing new life come from the old—we have made great strides in empowering lay shepherds."

"Over the years, I've become increasingly convinced that the role of the pastor is not to *do* the ministry, but to equip the lay people to do ministry," says Barstow. So, in an effort to better train and equip their care-group leaders and those who coach care-group leaders, the staff began to offer monthly training, solely for the leaders. They call it, VHS Shepherd's Meeting, to indicate the vision-casting, huddling, and skill training that occurs in this meeting.

"Based on the new perspectives gained from the training, many of our groups have opened themselves to newcomers," says Barstow. "We're developing and planting the desire for relationships to be built in small groups so that more people can be cared for and encouraged to plug themselves into ministry."

In Barstow's eight years at the church to date, the number of small groups has increased from four to forty. "Now we, on the pastoral staff, spend our time sharing vision and equipping leaders, and our people are getting the care they need," he says. "I'll tell anyone: It works, even in an old-time Presbyterian church!"

undiscovered talent as never before. Why? Because he knows they're going to be treated exquisitely well.

Advantages of Emphasizing the "Apprentice" Role

The apprentice role . . .
1. Follows the model of Jesus with his disciples.
2. Creates less individualism and more of a team effort.
3. Reduces the probability of cell leader burnout.
4. Distributes, or decentralizes, the task of leadership development.
5. Guarantees an ever-present supply of future leaders.
6. Teaches leaders how to share ministry and avoid a "dependency syndrome."
7. Offers a forum where people are affirmed into the courage to experiment.
8. Accomplishes skill training through the modeling process.
9. Enables churches to offer quality care because new groups can be formed.
10. Cultivates less an attitude of "Pastor put me up to this" and more of "God did this!"

Questions for Discussion and Application

1. Why does this chapter place so much emphasis on the training of new leaders?

2. In the church you serve, what is the present process for recruiting and training new leaders?

3. What can you do next to recruit and release new leaders in the ministries you currently put the most time into?

3

Workable Spans
of Care

The bottom-line message of this chapter: If you don't
limit your leaders' scope of responsibility, even highly
skilled people will burn out from fatigue.

Most consultants, when called in to help a church, ask the church
to collect, in advance, certain statistics and trend analyses on itself.
These questions track everything from visitor follow-up to worship
attendance to the number of caring units.

In an exceptionally well-organized church I once met with, one
number was significantly out of line from the norm. The average
attendance in the home Bible studies was seventeen, and several of
them were running thirty-five or more people weekly. I'm able to
predict, based on both research and experience, that participants in
groups this large become neglected. Also the leaders of such groups
usually feel overwhelmed.

When I pointed out that these attendance levels far exceeded the
healthy range for effective groups, the church staff didn't seem too
concerned. "Well, we've got several 'size 35' cells," they said.

"Do you have any problems in your cell ministry?" I asked.

"Yes, but a different kind," they said. "We can't recruit enough
leaders for our other groups."

"Do you have any idea why?" I asked.

"No, we never had that problem before. It's come up only in the last couple of years."

"According to your statistics," I pointed out, "these last two years are the same time period that you allowed the cell sizes to become so big."

That story represents an all-too-common occurrence. Most volunteer leaders, if properly encouraged and supported, will willingly take on a group of about ten people. In many cases they'll not only provide excellent care, but will also find great joy and fulfillment in doing so.

When that same person looks at the challenge of caring for thirty-five people, however, the answer is usually a hasty, "No thanks. That's too big a job for me."

Had those "size 35" groups been training apprentice cell workers and birthing new cells in order to keep the average cell sizes down to less than a dozen, the church wouldn't have experienced the same problem in its recruitment searches. Incidentally, I suspect that the people in this church who were successfully leading the

> A cell-group leader needs a manageable span
> of care in order to be effective.

groups of thirty-five were more like charisma-gifted leaders of large groups than like facilitators of small groups. I'll define these roles later in this chapter and in chapters 11–13.

In short, how does one make a cell leader's job manageable? Keep the scope small. Don't ask people to do too much.

Any mother will tell you that caring for twins is a great deal different than caring for one newborn. If a young mother gives birth to triplets, she needs all kinds of special assistance (and a medal) in order to be able to sustain that kind of load. A new parent, like a cell-group leader, needs a manageable span of care in order to be effective.

Jethro Revisited

Most churches and parachurch groups, when working through issues of organizational development, sooner or later study Jethro's

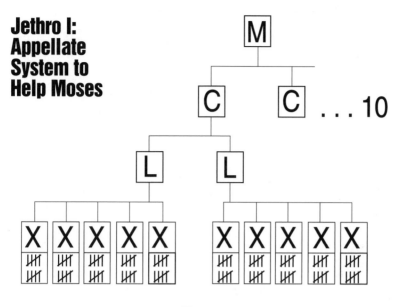

Jethro I: Appellate System to Help Moses

Figure 4

advice to his son-in-law, Moses. My book, *Prepare Your Church for the Future*, describes how Jethro's perspective (Exodus 18) has been pivotal in my own spiritual pilgrimage and understanding of today's church.[1]

Here's a summary of that passage, which I refer to as Jethro I (visually summarized in figure 4):

1. Moses, in trying to dispense justice to his people, grows weary. The queue of needy people is unending.
2. The Israelites, in turn, aren't receiving the help they need. They are impatient and frustrated.
3. Jethro observes a day in court as his son-in-law, Moses, apparently tries to handle the entire load himself.
4. Jethro proposes an alternative: a "kick-up" appellate court system with "lay judges" who each handle ten families. More difficult cases move up to their supervisors. The only cases that reach Moses are the most difficult ones.

5. The first result is that people go home satisfied! Their needs are met quickly and effectively, because the span of care never exceeds a ratio of 1:10. Sometimes it's 1:5 and occasionally 1:2.
6. The other result is that Moses doesn't burn out from fatigue.

Jethro had said, in effect, "You have some repetitiveness here, and we could codify your ministry in a way that lay judges can cover most of it." Those judges, once trained, handled all the repeat problems by precedent. Moses took the remaining hard problems to God for a ruling.

Jethro II

Many churches today are applying Jethro's principles to the issue of pastoral care needs. Notice, according to Exodus 18, that Jethro didn't offer his advice as a command from God. Instead he said, in essence, "If this seems good to you, and if the Lord your God approves it, then proceed" (see Exodus 18:23).

Pastors and church leaders today would do well to adopt that same perspective. As we listen to Jethro, a management consultant who got a plan approved by Moses and God at an earlier time in history, we might evaluate it on the same basis: "If this makes sense to you, and if after you pray and the Lord says to proceed, then I recommend it to you because empirically and practically it works." For example, a pastor I know installed seventy volunteer care leaders in the church he serves. I asked him what happened as a consequence. He replied, "My phone stopped ringing." I asked him what he did with the time that he had previously spent doing all this informal counseling by telephone. "I use it to prepare sermons for the church and to train my leaders," he said.

Notice that the reduction in the number of phone calls did not occur because people were being neglected. Rather, people were finding answers to their needs much sooner than before. The parish became so well cared for that the need load virtually dried up by the time it reached the level of the senior pastor.

That's one of the goals of a Meta-Church and of any effective organizational system: to assure the highest level of care at the lowest level in the structure. And the more effective the system is, the more the ministry is shared between paid staff and volunteer leaders.

> That's one of the goals of a Meta-Church:
> to assure the highest level of care
> at the lowest level in the structure.

Applications for Today

The primary application of Jethro II is that it allows part-time lay volunteers to do a significant, quality, ministry job without fatigue's burning them out in the process.

How many volunteer leaders can a staff member look out for, and then get back to, in a reasonable length of time? Here's what happens when we take the principles of Jethro I and apply them to a church setting. The results, called Jethro II (see figure 5), can be summarized by using Roman numerals. This coding system, though anachronistic, does add clarity.

I = individuals in a group
X = leader of a group of ten
L = leader responsible for five groups of ten people
   (5 x 10 = 50)
C = leader responsible for one group of one hundred people
   (1 x 100 = 100)
D = leader responsible for the equivalent of fifty groups
   (10 x 5 x 10 = 500)

One other addition is that we use a lowercase "a" to indicate when someone is an apprentice:

Xa = An apprentice (or rising) X
La = An apprentice (or rising) L—usually an "acting L"[2]
Ca = An apprentice (or rising) C
Da = An apprentice (or rising) D

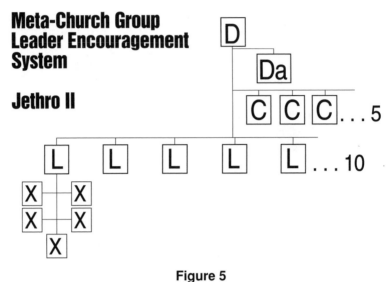

Figure 5

In comparing the two charts representing Jethro I and Jethro II, you'll notice some differences. What's the rationale?

First, we emphasize Ds (captains of five hundred) instead of Ms (captains of one thousand), in Jethro II. This is the result of our going to Korea and asking Dr. Cho, pastor of a church with more than fifty thousand cell groups, "How many cells can one of your full-time pastors handle?" His general experience, which has been confirmed in numerous other contexts, is that they can handle approximately fifty; for about every fifty cells they need one full-time paid staff member. (By the way, while Cho's church has a huge staff, the office space is comparatively small. That's because staff members aren't paid to sit around. Instead, they spend their time in the neighborhoods with the cell leaders.)

Second, in Jethro II, Cs (captains of one hundred) do not supervise Ls (captains of fifty).

This is for two reasons: (1) doing so makes the connection to the D more direct for the L, and (2) in the Jethro II model, Ls and Cs frequently represent two very different personality types. As individuals who can convene a group of 25–175 or so, Cs typically effervesce with pizzazz, sparkle, ego strength, and attention-holding capacity. Their strengths come out under the spotlight,

Willow Creek Community Church

67 East Algonquin Road
S. Barrington, IL 60010
Phone: (708) 765-0070
FAX: (708) 765-5046
Denomination: Nondenominational

Senior Pastor: Bill Hybels
Contact: Willow Creek Association
    at the above address
Attendance: 15,000
Total Cell Groups: 725

The Quality Gets Better and the Church Gets Bigger!

If any church shows the potential for growing to beyond-huge proportions, it's Willow Creek Community Church, located in a northwestern suburb of Chicago, Illinois, and led by founding pastor Bill Hybels. Given its 1993 average worship attendance of some 15,000 children and adults, Willow Creek is currently North America's best attended church on a week-by-week basis. With 130 acres of buildable land and 400,000 square feet already under its roofs, the church has no reason to be limited by inadequate facilities.

Facilities, however, are not its key to ongoing growth. "Our goal is to make average, ordinary lay people extra-ordinarily successful in shepherding the six to ten people entrusted to their care," says Jim Dethmer, a teaching pastor who gave the small-group ministry impetus from 1990 to 1993. "I, Senior Pastor Bill Hybels, and every other staff member exist to serve and make these volunteer leaders successful." According to Bill Donahue, who currently oversees many of the church's small-group ministries, "The most strategic person in the life-change process of the church is the small-group leader."

"This philosophy of ministry," explains Dethmer, "enables a church of 15,000 to provide better care than most churches of one hundred." How? By promoting measurable, low-ratio spans of care. In many smaller churches, the pastor attempts to meet the needs of a hundred or so people. At Willow Creek, the standard is different: Everybody's cared for by somebody, and nobody cares for more than ten people. As Bill Donahue says, "We believe it violates a person's ability to give care if he or she has more than ten people to shepherd."

As a consequence, no matter how many people the entire church body becomes, each small group remains about four to ten people in size. Each group leader receives coaching by someone responsible for only about five leaders. And each coach, in turn, receives guidance from a pastor who works with ten or fewer coaches. "Size does not need to mitigate against quality," says Hybels. "It is our desire that everyone here will become part of a small group and that the small group is their church."

With quality of care as a primary goal, Willow Creek Community Church continues to reach an ever-enlarging harvest of unchurched people for Christ.

often more as song-and-dance soloists than as team players. As such, they're better at communication than at managing and coaching others.

By contrast, Ls tend not to be stars. They're lovers and nurturers who take delight in making others succeed. They're problem solvers, consultants, and managers. As you can imagine, our finding is that relatively few people have the ability to excel both with the soft shoe of a C and with the detail orientation and perseverance of an L. Consequently, Cs tend to be of little help in supervising Ls. But side by side, they make a great team in a church!

Even so, most Ds have a bit of C in them, for example when they preach, as well as a bit of L, for example when they manage others. Generally pastors, who are selected because of their presentational skills, tend to have more C qualities than L qualities. A pastor's ability to fill the role of the D lies primarily in his or her recognizing that Cs, Ls, and Xs are needed, and then in casting a vision to raise up those leaders. Hence the title of this book, *The Coming Church Revolution: Empowering Leaders for the Future.*

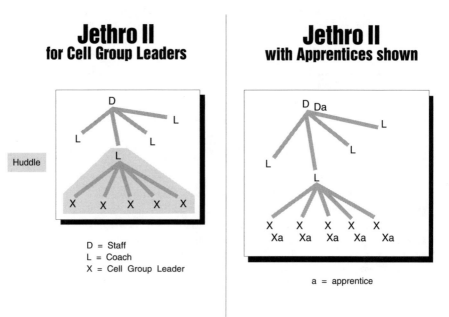

Jethro II
for Cell Group Leaders

D = Staff
L = Coach
X = Cell Group Leader

Jethro II
with Apprentices shown

a = apprentice

Figure 6

Third, in Jethro II, apprentices are an essential part of the system (see figure 6). In Jethro I they may or may not have been present. We don't know. Perhaps they were not necessary for an appointed, judicial-appellate system. We do know, however, as was observed in chapter 2, that the limiting resource for most churches' part of the harvest is usually the lack of trained leaders. The model we increasingly find in healthy, growing churches is one of apprentice that leads to leadership. Further, the apprentice model of every leader's cultivating at least one other leader is the most effective approach we know of for overcoming this oft-heard dilemma: "We'd love to extend the evangelism or care of our church, but we simply don't have enough leaders."

The most important function of the L is to help the X develop an Xa, or an apprentice leader, so that the entire leadership development task can be decentralized. Since the whole system depends on trained leaders' being available, the number of groups cannot grow if you are not multiplying the number of Xs.

If a church's leadership is able to grasp those principles, they will become wonderfully effective in promoting a cell system. Growth in a parish that fails to grasp these basic principles will be accidental and serendipitous but not necessarily predictable and consistently fruitful.

The bottom-line message of this chapter is that manageable spans of care enable leaders to provide effective care. Stated negatively, if you don't limit your leaders' scope of responsibility, even highly skilled people will burn out from fatigue. This principle applies to both clergy and volunteers; burnout is no respecter of persons.

Questions for Discussion and Application

1. What is the typical span of care in the groups you lead (or participate in)? Is it a workable and appropriate span of care, in your opinion? Why?

2. Why, according to this chapter, is span of care such an important issue? How does span of care affect church health and growth?

3. What are the next steps you will take in handling the span of care in the groups you lead or supervise?

4

Relationships
More Than Programs

Relationship-based leadership is not something we
assign after we've gathered people. Rather, relationship-
based leadership is the something that gathers the people
and sees to it that they receive care.

The Meta-Church creates a structure where mutual care becomes
as helpful as primary care. As such, the cell begins to take up the
slack created by an all-too-often disintegrating extended family. It
helps rebuild the broken family structure. It elevates relationships
over curriculums, methods, and programs.

Most church leaders, if they possess any kind of formal education, have not been taught to see ministry architecturally; rather
they view ministry curricularly. They think in terms of content, not
process. Formal education also encourages people to become fixed
on methods. Perfectionism (which is commented on in the next
chapter) declares an orthodoxy of method: There is one right way
to do everything. Relationship-based ministry places priority on
another set of values. Rather than fitting people into an organization, it helps people find an affinity basis. In the church of the
future, pastors will focus on developing people who are capable of
relational ministry. Cell leaders will focus on relationships more
than meetings, and every small group—whatever its task or objec-

tive—will deeply value nurture and one-to-another, peer-based caring.

A "New" Set of Priorities

Gone are the days when the church bell rang, the people came, the parson gave his homily, everyone went home, the week structured itself around pastoral acts (weddings, funerals, visiting the sick or homebound, praying at community events, and so forth), and the kingdom of God went forward. In relationship-based ministry, the assignment of clergy is to develop a growing community of faith by facilitating relationships. Obviously ministry will always involve a certain number of tasks, but tomorrow's leaders will be characterized by a relationship-driven emphasis.

Relationship-Based Ministry

- Helps people move from dependency toward development.
- Empowers people to use their spiritual gifts in community.
- Concerns itself more with changed lives than with methods or curriculum.
- Groups people by affinity-based relationships more than by alphabetization of last name, ZIP code of residence, or age.
- Motivates by example, more than by shame, guilt, or "oughts."

If a church's "product" were something that could be glued together, boxed up, and loaded on a shipping dock, then ministry could focus on doing and delegating. Relationship building, however, doesn't lend itself to an impersonal process. It calls for leading, modeling, and releasing. It involves tactile, contagious enthusiasm as well as the deployment of spiritual gifts. Even when a leader is training someone in a task, the apprentice needs to learn the spirit of relationship building just as much as the specifics of the tasks involved.

The bottom line is that church staff and volunteer leaders need to re-perceive the nature of their assignments. The watchword of the future is not to "delegate," in the sense of handing work off to someone else, but to "share the ministry."

Care needs in today's churches are so great that a pastor's personal energy, availability, and talents are but meager resources by comparison. How, then, can we see more people loved, cared for, embraced, and encouraged? By leveraging one person's ministry through the lives of willing others; by investing in others who will respond, follow, and seek to replicate what God, through his Spirit

> The watchword of the future is not to "delegate,"
> in the sense of handing work off to someone else,
> but to "share the ministry."

and Word, is blessing through the mentor. In relationship-based ministry, the people who touch others are those who have been personally touched.

How Curriculum Can Support Relationship Building

Unfortunately, at this time in history, churches are not the best place to learn relational skills. The structure of most churches is wrapped around teaching models that elevate information over relationships. Today's churches contain many great teachers who are skilled in presenting teaching about relationships; however, the best place to learn about relationships is in a relationship. And in most current teaching models, relationships are more a nice-to-have bonus than a must-have foundation.

Some of the most important principles to unlearn, then, are the assumptions on which many curriculums are built. Regrettably, some of today's programming doesn't acknowledge the profound shift in North-American society toward a hunger for personalization and intentional relationships. People today are increasingly asking to come together around common goals, wishes, or dreams

College Avenue Baptist Church

4747 College Avenue
San Diego, CA 92115
Phone: (619) 582-7222
FAX: (619) 582-5346
Denomination: Baptist
  General Conference

Senior Pastor: Jerry Sheveland
Contact: Greg Bourgond, Associate Pastor
Attendance: 2800
Total Cell Groups: 134

Shifting Ministry from Program-Based to Relationship-Based

"We evaluate our pastors now, not on how many ministries they can get up and running, but how many lives are being changed through these ministries," says Greg Bourgond, an associate pastor at College Avenue Baptist Church, San Diego, California. "Our goal is to be a church of groups, not a church with groups among its many programs."

"The mission of College Avenue Baptist Church is to make disciples—committed followers of Jesus Christ," says Senior Pastor Jerry Sheveland. "We believe that the central strategy for making that happen is large-group celebration and small-group nurture. So we're committed to the reproduction of small groups."

College Avenue, a century-old church, has a strong heritage of excellent programming. As the pastoral staff builds on that foundation, they're creating a structure in which every leader is mentored, coached, and encouraged on a regular basis. The staff doesn't create a ministry and then find leaders and people to fill it. Rather, they focus on developing leaders and helping those people build and multiply a ministry.

Virtually every new group or class, for example, must involve an apprentice leader, so that there is ongoing leadership training on the widest possible scale. Every group is also connected to the staff, usually through a volunteer coordinator, who assesses and advises a handful of groups.

"This superstructure is just like a skeleton inside a body," says Bourgond. "You don't see it, but you're certainly aware of the fact that without the skeleton you become a gelatin mass."

Another oft-used analogy around the church involves the idea of an amoeba. "An amoeba has structure, but nevertheless it can form-fit around anything it meets and ultimately consume that object," says Bourgond. "That's how we see our groups, especially what we call Shepherding Groups. They're slowly working their way into every nook and cranny of our church, embracing those molecule Christians who are not involved in care-based, small-group relationships."

This gradual transition is being well received by both newcomers and old-timers alike. "You just can't argue with changed lives," says Sheveland. "What better evidence of discipleship could anyone hope for?"

in order to find a sense of support, normalcy, belonging, and acceptance. Often they're looking for a sense of family to substitute for places where their own biological family has not functioned well. They may want a group that will serve, in their healing process, as a surrogate or modified extended family. While some curriculums

> The best place to learn about relationships
> is in a relationship.

today do offer helpful answers to the groundswell of people who are saying, "Please help me find my way," good content is only a small part of the solution.

The vast majority of church leaders, both volunteer and paid, cannot effectively use these curriculums until they've emptied their heads of old ways and reprogrammed their actions. One of the most stubborn thought forms is the desire for a "cookbook" methodology that offers steps 1, 2, 3, 4, and 5. I work hard to minimize this kind of formula, because I want people to accept responsibility for their own learning (an idea we'll discuss in the next chapter). Whenever someone follows an instruction list, and arrives at the last step without the desired fruit, he or she often says, "The teaching was flawed." I'd much rather say, "Here are twenty steps that some people think can get you there. Use these at your own peril. But the bottom line is, if you don't have the results, you don't keep the job."

This kind of thinking supports the leadership definition of chapter 2: "We don't furnish you with people, we give you a license. Go find people, recruit them, teach them, and lead them to become disciples of Jesus Christ." Is it appropriate to say, "Here are some steps we've found to be helpful in that process"? Yes, as long as you also indicate the following: "If you follow these steps and they don't work, then find some steps of your own!" That's what leaders do. Leaders make change. Leaders are accountable for results.

Most long-time churchgoers assume that if we put people in programs long enough, they will mature. If we expose them to enough curriculum, they will make progress. I don't find that to be the case. As a matter of fact, I'm a little frightened of some of the things I find in North-American churches. I'm afraid that people have been almost taught to be "knowers of the Word" without being "doers of

Sherwood Park Alliance Church

1011 Cloverbar Road
Sherwood Park, AB T8A 4V7
Phone: (403) 467-8404
FAX: (403) 467-1454
Denomination: Christian & Missionary Alliance

Senior Pastor: Delbert McKenzie
Contact: Mike Shellenberg
Attendance: 1350
Total Cell Groups: 55

Women Find Great Fulfillment in Small Groups

"A lot of the load for people care, which used to come to me, now no longer does," says Del McKenzie, senior pastor of Sherwood Park Alliance Church near Edmonton, Alberta. "The reason is that we're transitioning or repurposing the entire church into relationship-based care units. One highlight of that new approach is the women's cells."

Women's ministries at Sherwood Park previously revolved around large-group meetings. These programs still exist, but they are now supported by nurture cells. In fact, the existence of smaller units is one of the key reasons why the bigger meetings have gained a sense of renewal and vitality. For example, women's ministries at Sherwood Park trace their roots to a prayer fellowship designed to support overseas missionaries. This large-group women's ministry provided much of the impetus for the church's missionary committee and its annual missionary conference. In recent years, however, both programs began lagging in participation and momentum. Then a cell dimension was added to the women's ministries.

The results? At the 1993 missionary convention, the ten women's cells came together for a special large meeting, which was far better attended than recent years' large meetings that had no underlying cell infrastructure. Just as important, several of the women's small groups have "adopted" a missionary that they personally met. (About fifteen other mixed-sex cell groups in the church followed the lead of the women's groups and likewise began building a personal, small-group-based relationship with an overseas missionary.)

The leaders of the women's groups also receive ongoing nurture and training at a special meeting called VHS, for Vision, Huddling, and Skill training. "This all-church leadership-community meeting gives them a vision of where the church is going," says staff pastor Mike Shellenberg. "It's possible to be in cell groups without ever understanding how the cells come together to build the entire church."

Why have women been so attracted to the affinity-based small groups for women? Marion Dicke, Director of Women's Ministries, suggests four reasons. "Women are basically relational, and small groups work quite well for building relationships. Second, whether by divine design or by role assignment, women tend to be nurturers and caregivers, a quality that fits the model well. Third, many women are leaders, but they don't know it. They do well as small-group leaders and apprentice leaders and they appreciate the training of the VHS meeting. Finally, women seem to have a lot of natural contacts in the community and schools, many of whom aren't connected with a church. So it's a natural process to bring friends along to a small group."

"We've become strongly convinced that the most important people for newcomers to meet when they come in the church door is a lay pastor, not a staff member," says Mike Shellenberg. "They'll get to know us in time, but to be really cared for, they need to develop a relationship with a lay pastor. That dynamic is especially true when women build relationships with other women."

the Word" (see James 1:22–25). There's too much "feeding" going on in churches and not enough "training" and "exercise"!

Implications for Cells

Most "program" approaches to church lack the categories necessary for building an organization through relationships. Programs tend to be content or information focused. The more dynamic model of relationship-based ministry enables a leader to understand who people are and how to help them move away from dependency and toward development. The tendency is to apply a programmatic thinking inherited from the public schools and say, "Okay, let's allocate ten people to that teacher and ten people to that person. We'll give a list of twenty-five here, let's put twenty-five people there, and we'll ask our computer to group people by ZIP-codes."

It's not long before the program takes preeminence over the relational needs of those it's trying to help. It soon begins to disrespect who people are and what their needs are. When a church doesn't respect the affinity and personal-chemistry issues involved, it ends up with a system that many people elect not to take part in.

By contrast, relationship-based ministry releases people to look around for those in pain and, as Paul Tournier says, "Feel around the rim of their lives as one feels delicately around the cracked and precious piece of china until one finds the crack. And there is the work to be done to repair that life." Thus, in the church of the future a leader won't be known for his or her ability to handle a quarterly or written study guide so much as for a skill in relating to people in such a way that they allow access into their lives. When someone trusts someone else enough to tell where the area of hurt is located, then true ministry can begin.

This idea is a far cry from the teacher who waits for assigned people to fill the chairs or who uses scolding tactics on those who were absent. If people don't find the help they want, they drop out of the system, and no amount of truant-officer work will make them return.

If teachers hope to see people seriously committed to obeying and applying the Scripture in their lives, they need to be aware that they influence not one but two behavior settings. The first is the hour or so between the official beginning and ending of the class.

Most people can tolerate a curricularized portion of that, although a relationship-centered approach to teaching makes sure that a portion of the meeting time is spent in relationship building. People must have the opportunity to interact with each other, and in the process draw out a fuller appreciation for how they are accepted and loved and learned from, as well as how valuable they are to each other. The second setting involves the dozens of hours between meetings. That which happens from minute sixty to the next meeting's minute one is *more* important than anything that happens from minutes one to fifty-nine.

What Is a Cell?

This chapter, and this entire book, continually speaks of small groups (or cells) as the primary building block of the church of the future. What exactly is meant by *small* and what is meant by *group?*

This book takes an approach similar to that of a social psychologist. While taking into account the excellent body of literature on the subject of small groups, both secular[1] and church oriented,[2] the Meta-Church looks for functional results. It asks what kind of social unit best contributes to intimacy, accountability, mutual support, pastoral care one to another, discovery and usage of spiritual gifts, hands-on prayer, service to people and society, and attraction of newcomers. The most effective size seems to be about ten people, although small-group functions can be present with as few as three people and as many as thirty-five or more.

A cell is a place where people have enough social reference points to find themselves sustained emotionally and spiritually. It's a context for meeting needs for intimacy and trust. As such, the Meta-Church defines *cell* in a way that goes beyond the traditional notions of "class." A cell is the premier vehicle for leadership development: The managed leader is (1) being supervised, (2) developing an apprentice leader, (3) facilitating one-another ministry, and (4) taking responsibility for evangelism.

> A cell is a place where people have enough
> social reference points to find themselves
> sustained emotionally and spiritually.

When asked about cell groups in their church, many leaders will say, "Yes, we have small groups." In my experience, most statements like that typically miss 80 percent of the groups in a church. When most people think of cells, they're usually defining them as a Bible study held in someone's home under the umbrella of the small-groups department (or ministry or program) in their church. If those same people carefully think through the rest of church life, they usually end up multiplying their tally of small groups five- or tenfold! Cells include Sunday-school classes, ministry teams, outreach teams, worship-production teams, sports teams, recovery groups, and more. When seen in this way, the typical church has dozens of regular gatherings that may not be formally recognized as small groups, though they easily have the potential to function as groups in providing emotional care; gift-based, one-another ministry; teaching; and so forth. (Chapter 17 will comment further on the issue of "pure" cells versus other kinds of cells.)

So one of the first tasks in the Meta-Church transition is to redefine every ongoing church event by saying, "Generically, any time sixteen or fewer people meet together, you have a small-group meeting. And if so, what kinds of opportunities are present at those meetings? How do the lives of the people in that group bear on one another? How are they impacted by the work of other groups? What role does the staff have in guiding, superintending, resourcing, coaching, mentoring, and modeling the leadership tasks of those groups so as to ensure a very high quality of compassion, care, and truth in those various groups.

When this kind of conversation takes place among church leaders, it reshapes a host of paradigms, because it tends to unleash far more potential in a church than does the more typical path of program-based thinking.

Chief Qualities of Effective Leaders

The chief quality of an effective small-group leader, and, in fact, the heartbeat of cell ministry is not a programmatic organization or curriculum, but a highly relational organism that stems from a person-to-person kind of ministry (see figure 7). Relation-

Paradigm Potentials

Conventional Growth Management	Meta Growth Management
by 100s	by 10s
Touch 1,000s	Touch 10,000s
Programmatic based	**Relationship based**

Figure 7

ship-based leadership is not something we assign after we've gathered people. Rather, relationship-based leadership is the something that gathers the people and sees to it that they receive care.

I remember when I first began to get a grasp on what it meant to release people to this kind of ministry. I had read works like Frank Tillapaugh's *Unleashing the Church*[3] and had visited different churches around the country, such as the in-town location of Perimeter Church in Atlanta. In all instances, I saw them basically saying, "We're here to give you permission to do what God is calling you to. We aren't here for you to lay your vision on us like a

> The heartbeat of cell ministry is not a programmatic organization or curriculum, but a highly relational organism that stems from a person-to-person kind of ministry.

work order. Instead, our work is to empower you by saying, 'Go for what God is leading you to do.'" That way of approaching things is different from that of most churches!

By releasing people to do their thing for God, you're actually releasing God because it's he who gives the gifts for ministry. You're challenging people to say, "Lord, show us what you would have done here. Let us be your eyes and hands here." What an exciting adventure that becomes!

Push or Pull?

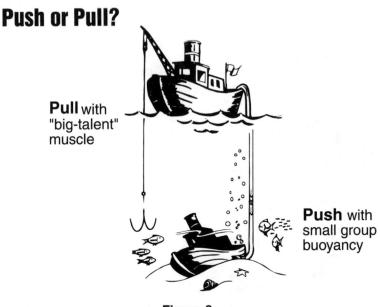

Pull with
"big-talent"
muscle

Push with
small group
buoyancy

Figure 8

Implications for Celebrations

How does relationship-based ministry infiltrate and influence churchwide worship celebrations? Consider a sunken boat that needs to be raised. Is it easier to *pull* it up with a powerful winch, or to fill it with air and thereby *push* it up? Obviously, the latter. By comparison, is it easier to use stellar speakers and other entice-ments to pull people to a church service, or to discover another motivation—the relationships inherent in a cell system—that will push them to the corporate worship service? As the landscape dot-ted with ministry-fatigued clergy indicates, pulling is the road to burnout. There must be a better way that can wield a push effect.

The pull model usually focuses on program; the push on rela-tionships. In the church of the future, the nature of leadership and the assignment of the leader will be relationship based, not primar-ily task based. (See chapter 9 for more on the idea of celebrations as conventions of cells.)

Relationships in the Meta-Church

Meta-Church theory, in forcasting a major reformation in the way we handle roles in the church, calls more for roles than programs. It looks for relationships more than curriculum. A relationship-sensitive church will contain many elements of the following (which are described in the shorthand of Meta-Church jargon introduced in chapter 3):

- Cell leaders [Xs] who get people to a cell meeting and make sure the cell functions healthily.
- Staff [Ds] and coaches [Ls] who ensure a live-wire worship celebration, so that when the cell group comes to the worship, its people will say, "This was really worthwhile, this was wonderful, thank you. See you next week."
- All levels of leaders who each give special attention to developing an apprentice and who see to it that the leaders they supervise continue to develop an apprentice, all within a manageable span-of-care range.
- Staff [Ds] and coaches [Ls] who put priority on offering supervision outside the cell, so the supervisor and group leaders [L and X] can get together in a huddle, and so that the senior pastor can encourage, praise, and affirm to the cell leaders, "You are doing exactly what we want done. Continue, with our backing in every way we know how, to lay hands on your people in prayer, to invite them to a deeper walk with Christ, to reach out to newcomers, and to create a healthy base for peer counseling."
- Some "fishing pools" constructed to help fill the open chairs in various cells (explained further in chapters 11 and 12).
- Some additional ministry opportunities for the strong, growing Christians that God produces, enabling people to retain their loyalties to the cell group while at the same time entering another context for team service.
- Some recovery ministry, support ministry, therapy groups, or one-on-one counseling referrals available, as people open new chapters in their life stories of becoming whole.

Bigger is simpler, though not necessarily better. But "better" that is simple gets bigger. I don't write this book to urge readers to have large churches. I urge you to take good care of people. I predict that if you do, God will bring you a steady harvest of new people to take care of.

The challenge for the future is to build relationship-based, leadership-development structures, taking feedback from everyone involved, all the while bragging on them, celebrating their successes, helping them resolve their problems, applauding them, and making heroes of them. In so doing, the ministry of the body of Christ will multiply far beyond what any program or series of programs could accomplish.

Questions for Discussion and Application

1. How does this chapter define relationship-based ministry? Why is it important to church health and growth?

2. Give three examples of relationship-based ministries in the church you serve. Give three examples of program-driven ministries.

3. How could the main group(s) in which you're involved become more relationship based? What can you do to bring about that change?

5

Problem Solving
as an Adult Motivator

Adult motivation for learning rises dramatically in the
presence of a problem.

Imagine a first-time paratrooper, with parachute strapped on,
seated in a military airplane at three thousand feet. The side door is
open and the plane is slowing to a speed suitable for jumping. The
parachute's ripcord, affixed by a static line to the plane, dances
from the vibration of the propellers as the officer in charge shouts
out a countdown: "Five, four, three, two. . . ." In all likelihood, that
paratrooper is quite open to coaching at this point! A teachableness
is in the air, so to speak.

In the same way, from the time someone in your church is named
to a role, such as being an apprentice Bible-study leader, until that
person becomes the actual leader, there's a period of special anxiety. The person is particularly susceptible to instruction—a "learning moment."

Most adults, by habit, economize their energy and exert themselves most when solving immediate problems. We find that adult
motivation for learning rises dramatically in the presence of a problem. Thus, if adults face an obstacle or quandary, they give energy
to learning. In the absence of that kind of challenge, they may be

willing to be entertained, but in most cases they will feel they've learned enough already. Problem identification, then, is usually the first step toward adult learning. If you can't begin with a consensus in regard to a problem, you won't find much motivation toward a solution. These observations, if true, have serious implications for how to develop and train leaders in a church. This chapter offers an apologetic for the social psychology of learning and leadership formation.

Assignments before Information

Most children can be persuaded to hold still and soak in all kinds of comprehensive training. In some cases their motivation is the teacher's promise that someday an assignment will come for which they'll need what they've learned. The widespread assumption, in working with children, is that a teacher should assume ignorance on the child's part and more complete knowledge on the teacher's part. Learning, therefore, becomes the process of making marks on a blank, moldable piece of clay, or pouring from the teacher's full pitcher into the pupil's empty one. This is perhaps an extreme statement because the best educational theory today emphasizes learning readiness and looks upon a child from a developmental perspective.

Yet there are still many instances where education boils down to this attitude: "Sometimes it's nice to supplement my teaching with activities that whet your curiosity or build your excitement about learning. But the bottom line is that I know the subject (and I have the power), you ought to listen (and you don't have any power), so please be quiet while I teach, or you'll go to the hallway." Or, a more dignified way to say the same thing would be, "Please work with me so that I can impart knowledge to you, which you will, no doubt, find helpful sometime in the future."

Years of grade school, high school, college, and Sunday school, all based on this same pedagogical model, have socialized most adults to accept this form of teaching as beneficial, natural, and right. To most Western adults, any suggested alternative may seem counterintuitive. Could it be that adults can be better trained through another process? Experience shows that adults learn best if you can get them first to commit to an assignment. Then furnish problem-solving training as needed. The key issue is not the content of how to prepare leaders but the sequence.

You are following a sequence of assignment-before-training whenever you ask, "Will you take on such-and-such a job?" or "Will you be responsible for such-and-such results?" For example, you might say something like this: "Jayne and Brad, will you form a group of about ten people to meet regularly for prayer, mutual care, and Bible reading? As part of facilitating the group, will you encourage them to join us in worship at the main church, and will you meet with the pastoral staff for ongoing coaching? You won't

> Experience shows that adults learn best
> if you can get them first to commit to an assignment.

be alone, because the first two people you'd recruit would assist you, one as an apprentice and another as the host. Would you prayerfully consider accepting this assignment?"

You then delay the problem-solving training until the new leader (or leaders) says, "I'm doing pretty well except I don't know what to do when Bob starts dominating the conversation." When a leader voices those words, or anything similar, a learning readiness has developed. The person who is supervising this leader can then respond, "Yes, that's a problem. Would you like to talk about it?" Thus begins the coaching process. Over time a competent supervisor will walk this leader through almost every skill needed. The supervisor can do so by one-on-one coaching: "Can I phone you tonight, and we'll talk about it?" Or the problem can be addressed during in-service training: "I'll put this topic down for our in-service training class next week, and we'll get back with you. Thanks for raising it." Either way, the supervisor is now working with a motivated leader, addressing the kind of things this particular leader wants to hear.

In developing appropriate assignments, know that simply attending a class is not a leadership assignment. Rather, a leadership assignment is "Here's what's got to be done. If you need to take a class to fulfill that assignment, then we'll help you enroll." In the Bible, the assignment-before-training sequence happens all the time. Abraham says to his servant, "Fetch a wife for my son." The servant says, "What am I going to do? I guess I'd better pray like crazy." And ultimately God gives a wonderful answer (see Genesis 24). Sometimes God gives the assignment: "Go, join yourself to that chariot" (see Acts 8:26, 29) or "Go to that man's house and do not give him static because he's not Jewish" (see Acts 10:17–23).

Similarly, church leaders will want to set up benchmarks, timelines, and other means of supervision so that no worker feels abandoned or uncared for. Perhaps some people in your church know more about groups and leadership than you do. As such, you might be presumptive to think you can teach them. But if they are willing to accept an assignment based on what they already know—or think they know—they would probably be willing to report to you or another supervisor for feedback. In this way the training comes after the adult has already tested his or her knowledge and skills against an assignment.

The assignment-before-information idea is similar to the Navy's system of swimming instruction: Put everyone in a boat, row to deep water ten meters off shore, and throw everybody in. If the recruits need help getting to shore, you offer to enroll them in a beginning swimming class. Next week you repeat the same process twenty meters off shore. Soon each person will learn to reach shore without help.

In summary, the traditional model of adult learning, even if sensitive to the learner's needs, may be summarized as "teach, assign, do." The preferred leadership development sequence is "assign, do, teach" (see figure 9). If an adult accepts an assignment and begins working on it, at that point you can offer training ("What would you like to learn about how to do your responsibility better?"). That person will be, in most cases, a highly motivated learner. You will have begun the process of contract and prescription for more effective adult learning.

Training Sequence

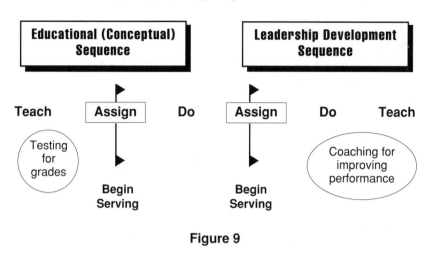

Figure 9

Contracting for Learning

What does it mean, in a church context, to contract adult learning? You ask people to tell you what they need to learn. After they identify where they want help, you agree to provide it for them. This method of adult learning usually results in a very mature skill-training program.

I've conducted workshops with adult learners, such as small-group leaders, across the continent. As I begin, I ask for the areas in which they'd like to improve. Whether I'm in Florida or British Columbia, the resulting list inevitably looks similar. Why not, then, codify these topics into a curriculum, publish it on Mt. Sinai, and deliver it into everyone's eager lap? Because the recipients would, in most cases, show little interest. Why? I haven't allowed them to prescribe the order of the topics according to *their* current levels of pain. In general, learners are motivated if they decide what to study next; they're bored if they feel you're trying to impose something on them, even if it's the very same topic or curriculum they would have chosen! This approach to learning is not merely something I've documented by experience over the years. Many others, both trained educators and church leaders, have suggested similar conclusions.

Four Guiding Principles of Adult Learning

1. Adults generally have a deep need for self-directed learning, even if that need varies among adults.
2. Adults increasingly appreciate learning that takes place through experience.
3. The learning readiness of adults arises primarily from the need to accomplish tasks and solve problems that real life creates.
4. Adults see learning as a process through which they can raise their competence in order to reach full potential in their lives. They want to apply tomorrow what they learn today.

Malcolm Knowles, educational theorist[1]

Training on a Need-to-Know Basis

What is a need-to-know approach? It asks of every Sunday-school class, training institute, or other equipping vehicle in your church, "Why would someone need to know what's presented here?" Answer: If people see the information or skill as something they must "solve" to get where they want to go, then it qualifies for a need-to-know basis.

Sometimes I wish we could treat Bible knowledge that way. Yes, I stand with those who are concerned about the rise in biblical illiteracy throughout today's churches. I also feel that we do too much entertaining and too little "hard" Bible study with some of our people. And I am aware that the Holy Spirit is present to help people learn the truths of the Bible (John 14:26, 16:7–15), with or without the help of human teachers.

But what would happen if Bible teaching were available primarily to those who are willing to use whatever they learn in their ongoing service to God? Consider this scenario. I have a missionary friend who reported that he was returning to the field for his third term. "What I need to do is teach an advanced course to those national pastors I've already trained," he said, "but I can't because there are still too many people who need the basic course."

"Are your students in the basic course taught well enough that they could teach that basic material when you've finished?" I asked.

He said, "Yes."

"Then announce that you'll teach the advanced course for anyone who will teach a section of the basic courses."

He went back to the field and wrote me, saying, "I'm finally doing what I've always wanted to do. I'm now teaching the advanced course to teachers of the basic course, which means a lot more people are being taught than previously." This teacher did something that makes perfect sense but wasn't an obvious option because he had never seen it modeled before.

Suppose, by analogy, Bible training in your church becomes available only on a need-to-know basis. That is, no one is allowed to have exposure to Bible teaching (other than on one's own) who hasn't obeyed what he or she already knows. This week's lesson is on tithing, for example. Next week everyone comes back expecting another topic. Instead you ask, "What did you learn last week?" "Are you obeying it yet?" "Have you taught it to anyone else yet?" "No? Then the lesson this week is again on tithing. Let's continue."[2]

"Well I want something else," you hear.

"If you're not obeying what you know, why talk about something else?"

"Well, I just want to know the Bible."

"I'm sorry, that's not one of the goals of this church. Our staff was hired to make ministers, 'to equip the saints for the work of ministry' (Ephesians 4:12 RSV). Their job is to do wholesaling, so to speak—the developing of leaders."

Coaches on a sports team talk like that. "We're here to teach you how to run, receive passes, and tackle quarterbacks. If you're not going to play, this team is not for you." So do bosses in the business world. "Don't take the seminar in time management unless you intend to develop a greater productivity." Why can't churches? Is the advance of the gospel hindered by the fact that too many

Christians today already know far more truth than they could apply in a lifetime?

Realistically, in the vast majority of churches, the church staff could not implement this idea without wholesale rioting. But they could adopt a new mindset. They could become more behaviorally driven in terms of giving people ministry assignments, and then focusing their energy on helping the parish succeed in those assignments. By doing so, most ministry would fit into a problem-solving sequence where motivated adults understand what they will gain and where staff tailor the training to fit the role or assignment that the adult learner has accepted. In short, churches will develop more and better leaders if they put greater focus on training than on informational instruction. To cultivate the leadership gifts in an adult, don't start with lectures on leadership.

To be blunt, the typical church approach to training lay ministers is nothing more than a cut-down copy of college and graduate-school course work (chapter 19 develops this point further). As a result, we lecture people to death. We have become word centered, not action centered.

Instead, ask the leader-in-training, "For what leadership responsibility may we hold you accountable?" If this person can't think of

> Churches will develop more and better leaders
> if they put greater focus on training
> than on informational instruction.

anything, then offer an assignment. Wait until he or she asks, "Where do I get the people? How do I track down the resources I need?" Then offer training.

Adult learners are more capable of figuring out how to do something they *want* to do, than they are at figuring out the reasons why they *ought* to do something. If a teacher can expand a person's mind to invoke a response of "Yes, that's a great idea!" then that individual will begin looking for ways to do things *he* or *she* thinks ought to be done. The "how" that a teacher presents will never be as creative or adaptable as the "how" the learner figures out, based on a desire to do something.

How Much Pretraining Is Advisable?

Those who plan training and leadership development in churches tend to overdo orientation training and underdo supervision. Why? Their own educational upbringing has made them comfortable with orientation training but relatively unfamiliar with the notion of supervision. By contrast, most churches would be more effective if they shifted from being orientation heavy to being supervision heavy.

How much pretraining does a typical adult need before being able to lead a group of ten people? I'm extremely reluctant to state a tally of hours because I don't want to be misunderstood as trying to promote a particular curriculum or program. Meta-Church thinking, as described in chapter one, tries to be descriptive, not prescriptive.

Let me precede my answer with "It depends." A Christian who two years ago joined a church-sponsored 12-Step group, who is consistently experiencing personal victory over his or her besetting sins and addictions, and who has actively served as an apprentice leader for the last six months, will probably need little training. Likewise, a veteran Bible-study leader, who has given birth to half a dozen

> Most churches would be more effective if they shifted from being orientation heavy to being supervision heavy.

groups, but whose employment forced a transfer to another city, may need exposure to the heritage, personality, and programs of the new church but little training in how to lead an effective group.

In short, any growing Christian who has enough moxie and savvy about life to pull together ten people, including an apprentice, and to keep a group healthy will be able to put together lots of the pieces on a common-sense basis with only a small amount of instruction.

But the norm is more the other extreme. In fact, some churches carry their orientation training to levels that are literally absurd. In one church in Texas, for example, a future volunteer leader must spend up to 435 hours in formal classroom instruction before being certified as a lay minister. Then this person's entry-level assignment is limited to three choices: (1) be a parking lot attendant; (2) be a greeter-usher; (3) help with seasonal pageantry. Regrettably, many qualified people are excluded from leadership. I knew of one person at that church who spent two years being trained and then the week after "graduating" received a job transfer to another city!

What is a more realistic alternative? In those instances where a church staff is committed to ongoing supervision of their volunteer leaders, experimentation has shown that new leaders, such as lay pastors of small groups, can serve effectively with as little as six hours of orientation or six months of apprenticeship.

In short, the amount of training a person needs before beginning service is a function of how skillfully that lay minister is to be supervised. The poorer the supervision, the richer the orientation has to be. The thicker the supervision, the thinner the orientation has to be. Adult learning that is rooted in behavior change opts increasingly in favor of supervision and on-the-job training rather than on orientation.

These principles work, by the way, in many disciplines, from the cure of souls (the church) to the treatment of bodies (the medical community). In the late 1960s, for example, the Center for Disease Control in Atlanta conducted an assessment of worldwide medical education. Researchers asked, "Is there a way to train a more clinically skilled doctor with less time and money?" The best medical minds in the world got together and came up with what they called the docent system for medical education. The word *docent* means someone who learns while teaching others.

Discussions about the docent system influenced a whole generation of medical educators, because it very cleverly brought together several critical elements of adult education. The kind of training institute that the task force envisioned is both a medical clinic and a medical college. Its objective would be to turn out fully proficient general practitioners through a professional track that combined college and graduate school in six years' time. Students were to be organized in teams under the guidance of a skilled practitioner. A first-year student would serve on a team with a third-year student, a fifth-year student, and a teaching doctor.

During the morning they would all make rounds through the examining and treatment rooms. At noon there was a break for food. By then their heads would be spinning from everything they had observed and wondered about that morning. Their notepads would be full of descriptions of symptoms, new medical terms, and perplexing cases. The afternoon would be spent in the learning center with a computer-indexing system and a series of audio-visual self-instruction modules. According to a motivational sequence basically elicited from the student's own life and response pattern, the student would spend the time searching in the library. In the evening, they attended a lecture on one of the many general principles that they'd been learning about.

So the docent center would offer direct contact with reality, with a mentor group that would be treating real patients, with a medical encyclopedia that would go as far as any encyclopedia could ever go, and with a progressive system for covering all of the bases before the end of six years. A second-year student would follow a fourth- and a sixth-year student, and another teaching doctor. Each step along the way, knowledge would be tied directly to a patient case of the kind that the student would see in the future. This experience represents a motivated-learning sequence because the student is not asked to learn things because of a desire to become a medical doctor but as a response to exposure to raw human need. These little chunks of exposure give a chance for corresponding bursts of education.

The docent system has several merits. First, it promotes motivated learning because of contact with real people and real problems. Second, tri-level learning goes on: You learn from other learners, and after your first two years, you are responsible to teach others. You are both exposed to teaching skills and challenged to develop your own learning skills. Finally, the training is both on the job (learning while doing) and also in service (learning through coaching).

If this docent system were applied to a Meta-Church context, the coach [L] would facilitate the cell leaders' [Xs] learning from each other as they huddle. These cell leaders, in turn, are training apprentices [Xas]. Each person in this schema learns both on the job and also in service.

Accepting Responsibility for Results

A few years ago, I counseled a pastor of a large church that had dropped, in about nine years, from sixteen hundred people to eight hundred people. The pastor asked, "What should I do?"

I replied, "I don't have a clue."

He said, "But you're a church consultant; you're supposed to be able to tell me what to do."

I replied, "What is the problem you're trying to solve?"

"We need to turn the attendance around and raise the offerings. Otherwise we'll be broke and on the street in nine months."

I acknowledged his statement with a nod.

He said, "Well, what's involved?"

I said, "It means the willingness to put the inspiring of your people, getting them into action, and recruiting newcomers into the service ahead of your golf game. It means not telling your board that the musicians tried hard, but they alienated half the parish anyway. Rather, either fire them up or fire them—and make the service so attractive that the building throngs with people who are excited about meeting God! In short, take responsibility for meeting the goals you just set."

He understood that I was asking him to commit to results. He understood that if the advice that I or anyone else gave him proved inadequate, he would still be responsible for those results.

He said, "Well, if I could just get my people behind this."

I said, "Doesn't a leader, by definition, get the people behind him? Saying 'if' is not going to cut it. Can you burn so brightly that your people will follow that light? Is that how you want to spend your next year?"

He took a couple of weeks off, came back, and resigned. I think he did the honorable thing.

True leadership commits to results. Leaders pour their energy, excitement, prayer, blood, and sweat into solving the obstacles between them and the vision God has given for that church.

Maturity More Than Perfection

I was greatly helped in my youth by holiness preachers. In my pursuit of personal holiness, however, I somehow embraced the idea that to have any hope of the blessing of God, I had to be absolutely errorless. I came to demand constant perfection in myself, even though I kept bumping into Scripture passages that show how God used recovering liars, murderers, cheats, and run-arounds to do his work. Moses, for example, was highly impatient. David abused power, committed adultery, and murdered an innocent man. The apostle Paul, an intellectual zealot of his day, delighted to see people locked up and tortured. Yet God did mighty deeds through these kinds of people when they walked closely to him!

By contrast, whenever I would fall away from what I thought was right, good, and pure in God's eyes, I would start feeling so sorry for myself, and so much into playing the role of victim, that I would become immobilized in my walk with God. I didn't understand how to get cleaned up as I went along.

Then, in my church consulting, when I began to study pastoral ineffectiveness, I found a similar whimpering and whining on the part of many pastors. They too had accepted the same spin on perfectionism that I'd adopted.

Eventually, I realized that I had confused flawlessness with maturity. Consequently, I came to a new understanding of a dynamic kind of holiness, almost a progressive maturity that says, "Hey, it's the batting average that counts. The reason you don't have more home runs is because you don't have enough strike-outs." People who don't swing the bat hard enough to strike out also don't swing hard enough to hit a home run.

> True leadership commits to results.

I've found that a sense of wholeness is more important than a sense of being flawless. As I interviewed veteran Wesleyan and Methodist pastors, for instance, I discovered that the defeated ones were, like me in my earlier years, fixated on achieving perfection, and the ones who had made a triumph out of their ministries had learned that when they fell, they were not to sit in the mud forever remorseful. Rather, they're to sincerely confess and genuinely repent of their sins, get back up, and keep going.

What are the implications for developing lay leaders for ministry? Warn people away from the things that lead to sin and harm. Otherwise, give them coaching through positive affirmation.

> Anybody can tell when something is perfect.
> The harder test, requiring more maturity,
> is to discern when it's good enough.

I went into one church that conducted postmortems after every event. They required their staff to write out all the things that had gone wrong so they could be corrected next time. When I opened an event evaluation folder, it would say: "Here is the event; here's what we did; and here's what went wrong." Not surprisingly, the staff were all depressed. I said, "I want to respecify your event productions. Describe what you did, list ten things that worked exceedingly well, and list three things you want to do differently or better next time. Then close the folder."

The difference in attitude toward their own work changed enormously. They had been driven by perfectionism to confess things that weren't even sins. Doing things right is a far less important factor than doing the right things. Anything worth doing is worth doing imperfectly.

Anybody can tell when something is perfect. The harder test, requiring more maturity, is to discern when it's good enough.

Most church-based instruction is so focused on perfection that we completely lose sight of what is important: the motivation to learn. Those being taught could devote a lifetime of energy pointing fingers at the professors who don't do this right, who don't test adequately, or who don't represent an appropriate value system, as if it is they who are ultimately responsible for our lives. The bottom line is that every Christian is responsible before God to be a learner—that's what the word *disciple* means. Making excuses and playing the helpless victim generally do little to enhance learning.

In addition, we're not in class. There is no test at the end of this chapter! From God's perspective, the proof of learning is life based: How are you at making disciples of Jesus Christ? How are you at loving God and your neighbor? What kind of faith relationship do you have with Jesus Christ? (Matthew 28:19–20; Luke 9:23–25; John 6:29, 47; 15:1–17)

That which saves you is not how right you get the content of a lecture, but the grace that enables you to accept responsibility for responding to God's call. In most cases, an ability to regurgitate facts will not make you successful in that process. Rather, it's your ability to rally the troops around ideas that offer opportunity to successively improve what they're doing in the crucible of actual contact with human beings.

Today's church needs not only teaching that is brilliant, but also teachers with brilliant ability to manage attitudes toward learning. What counts is not what the teacher knows or says, but the teacher's success in teasing out and creating a learning climate. The essence of the artful teacher is the knack for building a hunger, a teachable spirit, and a contrived moment when people apply knowledge in a way that changes their behavior—whether they eventually achieve perfection or not!

How Do *You* Learn Best?

When I describe adult learners as problem solvers, would you include yourself in their lot? For instance, presumably you are reading this book because you have a need (or list of needs) that you'd like to solve. Perhaps one of those perplexities is the one described in the title and subtitle of this book, "How do I bring on the coming church revolution by empowering leaders for the future?" That question can be answered, in part, by adopting what may be a new perspective on how adults learn. A good starting point is to think through what causes *you* to give energy to learning. Here's an illustration from my life, which may have parallels to yours:

C. Peter Wagner has authored more than thirty books on the subjects of church growth, prayer, and missions. One of his earlier titles was *Your Church Can Grow* (1976), a work that sold more than 100,000 copies in its first ten years of publication. When I ran across the book—the first I'd ever read on that subject or by that author—I was the mission pastor for a new congregation in

Gainesville, Florida. We were growing, but with a great deal of pain and effort, and I was always looking for ideas to help us build our leadership community.

I bought the book, and after I had worked through it for several days, I began to pace the floor at home, read passages aloud, and ask my wife, Grace, what they meant. When she finally ran out of patience, she said, "I don't know what he means; just call him and ask."

When I eventually quit ranting and picked up the phone, I successfully reached Dr. Wagner at his home. It was a Saturday morning, and he had just come in from feeding the chickens in his backyard in Altadena, California. He said he had about ten minutes to talk. In that time, he didn't answer a single one of my questions. Rather, each time I asked him something, he asked me a question back. As I thought through his probing, I began to learn why I couldn't find answers to my own questions! Most people know more than they understand. And a master teacher like Wagner helps us verbalize the questions that open windows of understanding on what we already know.

> Most people know more than they understand.
> And a master teacher helps us verbalize the questions
> that open windows of understanding
> on what we already know.

My quest for insight led our family to spend that summer's vacation in Ft. Lauderdale, where Wagner taught an extension course. From the first hour of the class, I started asking questions. By the end of the first week, a pattern developed in which I constantly hammered questions at him. I was so hungry!

On the first day of the second week, he stopped at my second question and said to his guest presenter, John Wimber, "Didn't I tell you at breakfast that George would ask that question when we got to this place?" Yet at the end of that week, Wagner took me aside and said, "Will you come to work for us?" Although I said no (for the time), the damage was done. I had been encouraged to develop my questioning capabilities.

A year later, I was still pastoring and still asking questions. Now, however, Grace was too! One September evening she said, "If you were using your God-given gifts to serve the kingdom, what would you be doing?" When a pastor's wife asks that question, something serious is afoot!

Without a thought I blurted out, "I would be a church analyst. I would be a church-growth consultant."

She said, "That's right. That's what you ought to be doing." Then she asked, "Now, what's the next step?"

I replied, "I don't know. And since I don't have a clue as to how to get started, I guess we get down on our knees and say, 'God, we heard you and we don't know what the next step is. If you'll show us, we'll take it.'"

She agreed.

We knelt and prayed, "Lord, here we are; we've surrendered. The ball is back in your court now."

That was 10 P.M. on Sunday night. We both went to bed and had a peaceful sleep.

The next day, fourteen hours later on the clock, Peter Wagner called from California. "What's God doing in your life these days?" he asked.

"How interesting that you'd be the one to ask," I said, "because last night God called me to be a church-growth consultant—and I don't have the foggiest idea what that means."

He said, "You've just been nominated to chair the Department of Church Growth here at the Fuller Evangelistic Association."

My jaw dropped to the floor. I couldn't turn it down flat, based on my prayer the night before. I agreed to pray about it.

"By the way," he said, "I'll be in Gainesville this Friday; maybe we could talk in person."

So, in the providence of God, Wagner traveled three thousand miles to my town, and we had opportunity to talk and pray in person.[3]

At each critical step in the story above, I sought information and training because of a difficulty or pain that I needed to overcome.

Without that motivation, had someone put Wagner's book in my lap, I might not have read it. Had someone given me the tuition to take Wagner's course, I might not have attended. And had someone asked me to move to California, I probably would not have been interested. In short, I needed a problem I couldn't solve before I would be stimulated to receive teaching from others. My motivation, as that of most adults, rises dramatically in the presence of a problem. If you want adults to learn, present them with problems they feel are significant.

> Learners refine sets of questions that will, in turn, yield better and better answers. That's the quest of any church as a learning organization.

Questions for Discussion and Application

1. What is the main concept presented in this chapter? How does it square with the way Jesus trained and prepared his Apostles? What advantage could that concept be to your church?

2. In what ways does the church you serve already practice the teach-assign-do sequence? In what ways have you personally experienced that sequence?

3. How can you give the ideas of this chapter a wider application in the church you serve?

6

Evangelistic Care Units

Linkages cause a group to become the binding social
context in which the Holy Spirit is greatly freed to do a
convicting work, and then to knit the newcomer's heart
into the social fabric of the church as a whole.

I had the privilege, when ministering in South Africa in 1993, of
having breakfast with David Yonggi Cho, founding pastor of the
largest local congregation in the history of Christendom. (In 1992
he changed his name from Paul to David, as part of a gesture of
friendship to help reunify certain Christian groups in Korea.[1])

Dr. Cho is widely misunderstood in North America among Christians whose worldview is more influenced by early American deism
than by first-century supernaturalism. Dr. Cho's teachings, in
almost every instance, represent the blending of a Lutheran concept
of grace, a Wesleyan passion for discipleship, and a classic Pentecostal interpretation of Scripture. His worldview may provoke discomfort among some Christian leaders, but it is constantly
informed by his looking to Scripture as his final authority[2] and by
waiting on God in prayer (as described later in this chapter).

After we chatted a bit, I asked him, "Dr. Cho, what do you see as
the future of evangelism?"

He replied, "You know, we don't do evangelism in Korea the
way you do it in the West. Our church involves 700,000 people, and

we're asking God for 1,000,000. We'll probably have 100,000 new members and converts this year.

"How will God accomplish this? We have 50,000 cell groups, and each group will love two people to Christ within the next year. They select someone who's not a Christian, whom they can pray for, love, and serve. They bring meals, help sweep out the person's store—whatever it takes to show they really care for them.

"When the person asks, 'Why are you treating me so well?' our people answer, 'Jesus told us that we're supposed to do good to all men, and we want you to know that we love you, and so does Jesus.' After three or four months of such love, the hardest soul softens up and surrenders to Christ." Cho is not talking about two "decision cards" per group. Rather, his people win a person to the group, to the Lord, and then to the specific tenets of the faith.

New people, without objecting to what is happening, are caught within the pastoral-care network of these groups. Linkages cause a group to become the binding social context in which the Holy Spirit is greatly freed to do a convicting work, and then to knit the newcomer's heart into the social fabric of the church as a whole. In short, Cho and others have discovered how to blend evangelism,

> A Meta-Church is a church intent on developing its staff and volunteer leaders into a network of evangelistic care units.

assimilation, pastoral care, and leadership development within their small groups in such a way that they are constantly able to accommodate whatever growth God is calling into the church.

Do church leaders truly grasp what can happen when cell-group leaders, along with their apprentice leaders, are released in a climate where cell-based relationships are the foundational, most critical unit of a church? It means they are harnessing the most powerful evangelistic tool conceivable—the body of Christ.

As chapter 1 pointed out, a Meta-Church is a church intent on developing its staff and volunteer leaders into a network of evangelistic care units. A Meta-Church's organization around a system of lay-pastoral development enables it to handle large numerical growth without losing the personal touch and care of the individual.

Iceberg

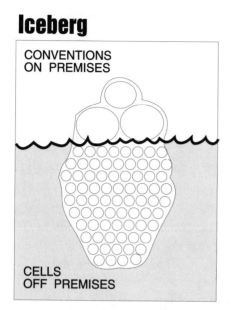

CONVENTIONS
ON PREMISES

CELLS
OFF PREMISES

CHO MATH

1979	100,000	
1989	600,000	20%
	8+2=10	25%
	10+2=12	20%

Figure 10

Can This Kind of Evangelism Work in the West?

The essence of what Cho says, both in his seminars and in his books,[3] is this: "I have a system and it's very simple." According to Cho, you ask a small lay-pastored group to lead two people to Christ each year and incorporate them into their group. If the group has eight and they add two to it, the net total is ten—or a growth rate of 25 percent. If the group has ten and they add two more, the net total is twelve—or a growth rate of 20 percent. Average those two rates and you come out with what Cho's church has sustained from 1979 to 1989 (the period for which we have verified data; see figure 10).

I submit the following as ten key factors that undergird what is frequently referred to as the "Cho phenomenon." If they are accurate, then I see no reason why God would not grant the same rate of growth anywhere else in the world where people are responsive—including *your* city, town, or village!

- Naïveté. Cho started out being naive as to the "proper" way to build a church. As a result, he did not intuitively gravitate toward standard, accepted practices. Instead he looked to God for guidance, with few prior biases as to how things ought to be done.

- Listening Prayer. Cho spends between one and five hours a day in prayer, and requires similar standards of the clergy on the church staff. As I described in a previous book, *How to Break Growth Barriers*,[4] there is a pivotal difference between talking at God and listening. I believe Cho has learned how to listen.

- Staff support for lay-pastor behavior. Each of the staff pastors are responsible for about five hundred people in about fifty cells. During most of their working hours, these clergy won't be found in the church building, planning the program, or laying out the calendar. They're usually out in the community where the action is, coaching volunteer leaders and modeling ministry for these lay leaders.

- Lay-led cells. Cho offers a place for men and women, old and young, upper class and blue collar, growing new believer and veteran saint, to use their spiritual gifts and energies to facilitate lay pastoring. In his case, some 85 percent of the church's cell leaders are women. They work under Cho's authority and carry a symbol of that delegated authority (so as not to be perceived as violating certain Scriptures[5]).

- Cell-driven celebration. How can Cho get people to come to a 3:00 Sunday-afternoon service? Why would people in the main sanctuary be willing to sit in a balcony behind a pillar and watch via a TV monitor? The answer is not found in dynamic preaching or impressive music, so much as it is found in the persistence of cell leaders. Large gatherings are not pulled to Cho or the music ministry so much as they're pushed by their cell leaders (a concept explained in chapter 4). If your cell-group leader says, "We're going to worship at 3:00," you worship at 3:00 because corporate worship, for you, is a convention of cell groups.

- Discipline for not winning souls. I once said to Cho, "Suppose somebody doesn't win two souls to Christ in a year?" "Not do that?" he said, virtually coming out of his seat. "We put them under church discipline!" I asked, "What does that look like?" He said, "I say to them, you have disobeyed the Lord Jesus and your pastor. You must either fast and pray or repent of this evil until you get your heart right with God, and you have the blessing of those two converts." To facilitate such prayer, the church owns a prayer encampment, called Prayer Mountain, to which their people go to get their lives straightened out with God. Spiritual procreation is the main issue for this church. It can be encouraged in any church without the leadership's being legalistic, spiritually abusive, manipulative, or inappropriately controlling.

- Relationship making as a priority. Lay leaders are taught to schedule relationship making into their daily lives. They do not value going to celebration and worship at the church nearly as much as they value spending time serving people. Yes, you ought to celebrate; yes, you ought to attend your cell meeting, but you are in a unique time in your life to serve your neighbors. The failure to do so leads to spiritual deadness.

- Side-door entry. Cell meetings are a frequent side door to the church, with prayer and social ministry provided within the cells. What about people who visit a church service with no prior contact? Do they fall through the cracks? In the Yoido church most people don't come unaccompanied. You come because someone won you to the cell group and now is bringing you to worship as a step toward formal church membership. The church does little to encourage a "consumerist" mentality.

- Sacrificial and proportional giving. The cells, as well as the central church, teach sacrificial and proportional giving of one's finances. Young children, homemakers, and everyone else in the church is given a financial envelope. Sometimes offerings are received at the cell-group meeting; they are promptly receipted in order to maintain a high standard of accountability.

- Few expectations by unchurched people. In a country deeply shaped by Confucianism and Buddhism, new converts have few demands as to what should happen in church. Working with so many relatively unchurched people, church leaders have the freedom to negotiate any form of discipleship that they choose.[6]

Why couldn't any church, anywhere, reach out to unchurched people through a similar organizational structure for harnessing efforts and providing spiritual direction? What prevents you from beginning to introduce new standards that will result in the next one hundred people who come to Christ in the context of your congregation's becoming the finest Christians you will ever have the privilege of leading? Would you dare to ask God to grant you a harvest that comes primarily from conversion growth?

Ten Churches That Report
60 Percent (or More) Conversion Growth[7]

The following sampling represents churches that have been trained in Meta-Church organization and that answered "60 percent" (or higher) to this question: "For your church's fifty (or so) most recent new members or new regular attenders, what percent are new converts—i.e., are *not* transfer growth or biological growth?"

Bible Assembly of God, Henry Perez, Sr. Pastor, attendance*: 500 (10125 California Ave., South Gate, CA 90280-6007, phone 213-569-2477, FAX 213-569-7128)

Community Christian Church (Indep.), David Ferguson, Sr. Pastor, attendance: 650 (1163 E. Ogden Ave., Suite 705-105, Naperville, IL 60563-1687, phone 708-983-5444, FAX 708-983-2524)

Ginger Creek Community Church (Indep.), John Henderson, Sr. Pastor, attendance: 600 (777 Roosevelt Rd., Suite 200, Glen

Ellyn, IL 60137-5913, phone 708-858-5999, FAX 708-858-6049)

Grace Community Fellowship (Nondenom.), Sandy Mason, Sr. Pastor, attendance: 2400 (9505 Dearreco Rd., Timonium, MD 21093, phone 410-561-8424, FAX 410-561-1192)

Inland Hills Church (Indep.), David Stoecklein, Sr. Pastor, attendance: 700 (13721 Roswell Ave., Unit D-F, Chino Hills, CA 91710-5463, phone 909-393-1577, FAX 909-627-2891)

New Hope Community Church (Indep.), Dale Galloway, Sr. Pastor, attendance: 5500 (11731 SE Stevens Rd., Portland, OR 97266-7597, phone 503-659-5683, FAX 503-774-1133)

New Song Community Church (Conserv. Baptist), Hal Seed, Sr. Pastor, attendance: 250 (4065 Oceanside Blvd., Suite T, Oceanside, CA 92056, phone 619-940-1500, FAX 619-940-8144)

Sarasota Baptist Church (S. Baptist), Dave Clippard, Sr. Pastor, attendance: 600 (7091 Proctor Rd., Sarasota, FL 34241-9259, phone 813-922-1449, FAX 813-922-9421)

Sunset Presbyterian Church (PCUSA), Ron Kincaid, Sr. Pastor, attendance: 1300 (9100 SW Wilshire St., Portland, OR 97225, phone 503-292-9293, FAX 503-292-4356)

Victory Outreach (Assemblies of God), Sonny Arguinzoni, Sr. Pastor, attendance: 3000 (454 Coberta Ave., La Puente, CA 91791, phone 818-961-4910, FAX 818-961-7710)

* Average weekend worship attendance, adults and children.

I challenge you to pray, "Oh God, what is it you will be pleased to do in my community in terms of drawing people to yourself? For my part, I will see to it that leaders are trained such that new people and old will be well cared for in groups of no larger than ten." If that is your prayer, then you may see a transformation in your ministry and in the lives of your people that exceeds any dream you have been able to put together up to this point. You won't necessar-

The Wesleyan Church

945 St. George Boulevard
Moncton, NB E1E 2P9
Phone: (506) 857-2293
FAX: (506) 857-9016
Denomination: Wesleyan

Senior Pastor: L. D. Buckingham
Contact: Ed Bagwell
Attendance: 1400
Total Cell Groups: 45

Pastor Now Sleeps Well at Night

"I used to wake up in the night," says L. D. Buckingham, senior pastor since 1969 of The Wesleyan Church, Moncton, New Brunswick. "I'd be in a sweat thinking about different people who needed to be ministered to."

"But in 1990," he continues, "we implemented a lay-pastor ministry so that people could be assimilated into fellowship groups and cared for by friends there. It's encouraging and burden lifting to know of all the lives that are receiving ministry. I don't have to worry whether their needs are being addressed."

Since launching the lay-pastor ministry, The Wesleyan Church has grown in worship attendance by about 125 newcomers per year. Sixty percent are new converts, according to Pastor Buckingham. Such responsiveness is unprecedented for that entire Maritime Province.

"It's impossible for paid pastors to minister to our total constituency of 3000 people on a daily basis," says fellowship group leader Brun Fillmore. "In a very large church, unless you can create a family feeling, people have a tendency to leave."

What's the church's solution? "The lay pastors typically make about eight hundred total personal phone calls or visits each week," says Fillmore. "We use our lay-pastor groups to reach out to all who walk through the church doors, whether they're first timers or they've been here for a long period of time."

The groups do more than provide quality care, however. Pastor Buckingham continually prods them with his passion for evangelism. He frequently meets with the lay pastors on Sunday afternoons and asks various ones to recount stories about people in their groups who have accepted Christ. They also give testimony about those who rededicate their lives to Christ while attending a fellowship group.

"At times we even look at the video of the Sunday service," says Fillmore. "Whenever shots of the congregation reveal new faces, we ask, 'Has anybody met these people?'"

Earl and Judy Kervin co-lead a singles fellowship group. Earl reports, "We're attracting people who had not been to a church in ten or fifteen years. They say, 'You know, this is meeting my needs so I want to come out Sunday morning too.'"

"The mission of the church is to seek and save the lost," says Judy Kervin. "I never thought of myself as being able to participate in anything that wonderful."

Ed Bagwell, one of the staff pastors, feels the same. "Our lay-pastor ministry is not some new program. It's a biblical method of reaching people for Christ and caring for those who are saved. It's all happening because our people are answering the call of God by either leading a group or assisting a group."

ily become a super-pastor or super-saint. Rather, you will be taking the gift of the Holy Spirit that is given to every single believer in your church and saying to those people, "God has given approximately one out of every ten of you a gift of leadership such that you can nurture the spiritual lives of newcomers."

This way of viewing the body of Christ, known as the Meta-Church construct, works equally well in the Australian outback as it does in the inner city of Seoul, Korea, because its fundamental principles are transcultural. It does not depend on the eventual size of the church either. It takes care of people, ten at a time, and thus any multiple of ten can become a Meta-Church if lay-led peer groups do the cultivation and the evangelization.

Only in North America

My first book on the Meta-Church, *Prepare Your Church for the Future*, forecasted a certain evolution of organization. If the word *meta* indicates what's coming next, then when we talk about Meta-Church thinking, we're saying that the way we did business in the past appears to be breaking down. If we forecast the next stages of church growth, the future will look more and more like artificial extended families called cells. All cells will contain some degree of nurture. Some cells, due to the amount of brokenness in society, will need special proficiencies for dealing with recovery, support, and various mental-health issues.

Few people disagree with this observation. Their biggest hesitancy, I believe, comes from not being in touch with credible role models.

For that reason, this book is peppered with some forty case studies of churches who are applying, with very positive results, organizational technology that can be described in Meta-Church terms. These churches range from denominational to independent, from young to old, from center city to rural, from New Brunswick to Texas, from Ohio to California. They also range from small to super-huge. (Some of the churches we first met when they had an attendance of fifty had grown to several times that size by publication date.)

Victory Outreach

454 Coberta Avenue
La Puente, CA 91746
Phone: (818) 961-4910
FAX: (818) 961-7710
Denomination: Assemblies of God

Senior Pastor: Sonny Arguinzoni
Contact: Charlie Moreno
Attendance: 3500
Total Cell Groups: 100

Cell Leaders Play Pivotal Role in Evangelism

"Every home Bible fellowship in our church is a lighthouse," says Raul Mata, a volunteer leader at Victory Outreach, a Pentecostal-style church in the Los Angeles suburb of La Puente. "A lot of new people come into the church through the home Bible fellowships. If the group leader has a vision to go out and evangelize—because he's the one who's going to motivate the people—then the people will follow. It starts with the group leader."

"I help train the group leaders to go into the community to share the gospel," says Mata. "Typically the members meet as a group for an hour of prayer. Then they go out by twos. Also, maybe once every other month they'll use a school or community center to show a film or feature music in order to draw people in."

Victory Outreach, as a church-planting ministry under the apostolic leadership of Sonny Arguinzoni, is continually launching satellite churches. Small groups play an integral role in that expansion and also in caring for the needs of church people. "Section leaders such as Raul Mata help keep prayer and evangelism going in our small groups," says Charlie Moreno, an associate pastor. "They each oversee several home Bible fellowships and they make sure the group leaders receive ongoing training."

"Our small groups are constantly involved in meeting the needs of the church, assimilating our people, and doing evangelism," explains Moreno. Other times, especially during the summers, we do a lot of outreach: door-to-door, street meetings, and drama, as well as 'hot spot' evangelism to areas of heavy drugs or crime. Different small groups cover different areas of the city. Then, at other times, one of the pastors may call the whole church together to do evangelism."

The net result of all this energy is an evangelistic momentum that enables the parent church and its many offspring to keep surging forward, with the various lay leaders as the key point people in that advance. "The responsibility of the section leader is to develop new leaders," says Mata. "I hold discipleship classes monthly that are geared to developing and raising up the men and women who have a heart for home Bible fellowship ministry. Then we take them through the church's School of Ministry for further training."

"We have different components in our ministry that are designed to develop future pastors and church planters," summarizes Moreno. "We use our satellite ministries as training grounds. The different group leaders are a pivotal part in that process."

Taken together, these forty snapshots convincingly demonstrate that the church of the future is close at hand. For these churches, "the future isn't what it used to be."

Questions for Discussion and Application

1. Of all the people that affiliated with your church during the last six months, what percent would be new converts? transfer growth (i.e., people who are already Christians)? biological birth (births or adoptions among people who are already members)? How do those percentages compare to the previous five years? What changes in these tallies would you like to see in the future?

2. Identify three major trends of how people come to Christ through the ministry of your church. What is the most common first point of contact? How are they assimilated? What role do small groups play in evangelism and discipleship?

3. According to the information in this chapter, what is the foundation for evangelism in the Korean church led by Dr. Cho? Which elements of that strategy are transferable to North America?

PART 2

Making Leadership Development Work

7

The Meta-Globe
as a Diagnostic Tool

The goal of the Meta-Globe is to depict the core reasons
why certain churches experience phenomenal growth, to
identify how that "ideal" differs from present reality in a
given local church, and then to decide what steps might
be taken to move toward that ideal.

At any given time, clouds cover many segments of the earth's
surface. Thus, under normal conditions, it's impossible for astro-
nauts or satellite cameras to see the "big picture" of what the surface of our planet actually looks like. Over a period of time, one of
America's aerospace corporations took thousands of satellite pho-
tos of different sections of the earth. Then technicians culled out
the ones that were obscured by clouds, and pieced together the
remaining ones to show an "ideal" surface view of a cloudless
planet.

Meta-Church organization enables church leaders to do the same
kinds of things with a church: pictorially envision an ideal model of
what a church might look like if every part of the "body" were
functioning with health and maturity. One objective of Meta-
Church diagrams and charts is to depict the core reasons why certain churches experience phenomenal growth, identify how that
ideal differs from present reality in a given local church, and then
to decide what steps might be taken to move toward that ideal.

Advantages to Using Visuals

1. Memorable: It offers an easily remembered ordering of all parts of an organization.
2. Focused: Labeled parts and interfaces allow for fixing attention and reflection on group and inter-group functions and their cultivation.
3. Diagnostic: It helps with rapid determination of adequate versus inadequate function areas (or present versus absent functions).

The Meta-Globe as an X-ray Machine

In the opening chapter of this book, I suggested that the Meta-Church is an X ray designed to show where, in any local church, different functions either occur or, perhaps more importantly, are missing. In many cases, Meta-Church perspectives help locate gaps that need to be filled. If these problems aren't fixed, things won't work well in the future for that church, just like an injured knee joint, until remedied, won't allow freedom of mobility.

I emphasized that the Meta-Church is first a perceptual tool more than a prescriptive or programmatic model. Programs and plans, no doubt, need to come, but only as you decide what to do about what you've learned. The essential first step involves learning to see with a new perspective. The same principles apply for the graphically depicted Meta-Church, which we call the *Meta-Globe*. The

> If these problems aren't fixed, things won't work well in the future for that church, just like an injured knee joint, until remedied, won't allow freedom of mobility.

Meta-Globe, therefore, doesn't offer a formula for action any more than an X ray tells a physician how to set a broken arm. An X ray shows us how things are, not what must be done.

If you have enough knowledge of what things look like when they're working well, then you might look at the X ray and say,

"This looks like a fracture. We need to take the following steps to treat this problem to put things back into alignment." Then, after you've worked at it a bit, you can take another X ray and conclude, "Yes, this is how we want it to be."

How does this analogy apply to a church? Your purpose is to learn to visually represent your church's meetings and groups so that you'll know the leadership training and supervision needs of every place in which care, discipleship, and evangelism are—or could be—regularly occurring. The Meta-Globe also tries to make sense out of various meeting sizes and to differentiate between the roles of staff, lay leadership, and consumers in the church system.

Shape Represents Group Type and Size

The Meta-Globe analogy, introduced in *Prepare Your Church for the Future*,[1] field-tested by planning teams from hundreds of churches and summarized in this chapter, offers a systems perspective on a church akin to the above-mentioned satellite views of planet earth.

In its simplest form, the Meta-Globe likens a church to a planet, as in figure 11.

Meta-Globe, Two Views

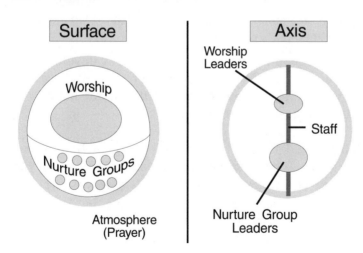

Figure 11

- The atmosphere, essential for human life, represents the prayer life and intercession that must blanket a church. A planet's atmosphere, which cannot be seen, reminds us of the constant movement of God's Holy Spirit ("The wind blows wherever it pleases . . ." John 3:8). The air we breathe is the unseen yet necessary part of reality. But also Satan is the "ruler of the kingdom of the air," (Ephesians 2:2) and we're told of "spiritual forces of evil in the heavenly realm" (Ephesians 6:12). The atmosphere of the Meta-Globe, therefore, symbolizes the role of prayer in the opposition of evil, and in the movements of the breath of God.

- Large continents represent large worship services (celebrations) involving around two hundred or more people. Somewhat arbitrarily we have assigned these to the Northern Hemisphere.

- Middle-size islands represent medium-sized seminars and groups of around 25 to 175 people (congregations), such as adult Bible fellowships or large adult Sunday-school classes. We place these in the equatorial zones.

- Small islands represent small groups (cells) of approximately ten people. These could be a small elder board, a small worship team, a small-group Bible study, a small service or task group, or a small 12-Step or support group. Most of these will go in the Southern Hemisphere.

- The axis represents church staff as they develop volunteer leaders through training, supervision, and coaching. The axis starts in the north polar area (Arctic Circle) and then travels through the heart of the sphere.

Using these definitions, and a few other guidelines provided in chapter 14, church leaders can use the Meta-Globe analogy to construct a map of their specific church. A *Meta-Map* is like a series of team snapshots for all the groups in a church, but with the added benefit of also making possible the visualizing of people-flow pathways and leadership links. For example, how can someone explain the dropout factor experienced in many churches? The Meta-Globe,

New Life Fellowship

40–03 National Street
Corona, NY 11368
Phone: (718) 424-0122
FAX: (718) 457-1133
Denomination: Independent,
   affiliated withChristian & Missionary Alliance

Senior Pastor: Pete Scazzero
Contact: Craig Fee, Director of cell ministries
Attendance: 750
Total Cell Groups: 65

Fortifying the Atmosphere of Prayer

"Without an atmosphere of prayer, this church can go nowhere," Pete Scazzero continually reminds the leadership of New Life Fellowship, Queens, New York. "There is a war to be won in setting the church free to do God's calling. If people aren't meeting God at our meetings, they are crummy meetings, no matter what else goes on there."

This pastor and his people trace a direct correlation between prayer and fruitfulness. "In one housing project we tried four different times to start a cell group," says Scazzero. "Each attempt failed and each leader burned out. Why? I'm convinced it's because we didn't have an adequate level of prayer coverage. You can't win a place until you've wept over it before God's throne."

New Life, which has used cell-church principles since its founding,[*] ministers in a community that the *New York Times* has called "the most international place on the face of the earth." The church is comprised of two different congregations, one Spanish-language and one English-language. Both are led by Scazzero.

Several cell groups in each of New Life's congregations are devoted solely to intercession. One is a deliverance team. Others pray over specific needs in the church and community. Still others play a role in the worship services, interceding with those who come to the altar during a portion of the service.

The privilege of prayer is not limited to these groups, however. The leaders in each of the fourteen zones (a regional or language group of three to five cells) gather together regularly. At least one of those meetings a month is given to prayer.

A similar opportunity is given to the entire church constituency. Every few weeks there will be a Friday evening meeting that sees between 200 and 250 adults convene for an all-church half-night of prayer.

"Our heartbeat at New Life is to get people to God through worship and cells," says Pat Selvey, an intern and a prayer coordinator at the church. "Prayer is a huge part of our cell life—in fact, of everything we do."

[*] For the story of how the church was started, see *Prepare Your Church for the Future* by Carl George (Grand Rapids: Revell, 1991), 199–204.

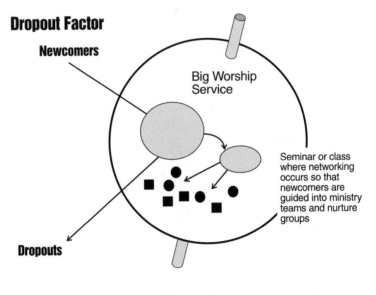

Dropout Factor

Newcomers

Big Worship
Service

Seminar or class
where networking
occurs so that
newcomers are
guided into ministry
teams and nurture
groups

Dropouts

Figure 12

as in figure 12, can show where assimilation does—and does not—
occur, and, therefore, how a church can close its "back door." These
graphics remind you that intimacy rarely develops in a large-group
setting, such as at a celebration. Rather, the smaller the setting, the
more likely friendship and personal nurture will be cultivated.

Or, how could someone analyze and set goals for the youth ministries of a church? Figure 13 gets you started by identifying all the
meetings in which youth are involved. Now you know, for example,
where and how much leadership is needed.

Colors Signify Group Function

In addition to representing a group according to its size (celebration, congregation, cell), the Meta-Globe uses colors to signify a
group's function. These colors come from the artist's pallet:

- Purple indicates governance. This is not a title ("we are a governance group") so much as a function ("our job is to make

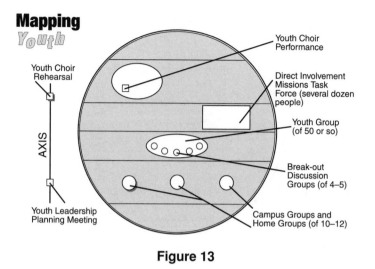

Figure 13

decisions, set policy and develop consensus for actions, appoint group leaders, or approve a budget").

Probable examples: Church staff, church board, elders, Christian-education committee, and others.

- Red indicates everything that relates to plenary celebration and worship arts, whether large or small. If a group uses the sanctuary, it will in most cases be red and go in the Red Zone. Teams that produce such services are also red.

    Probable examples: Large worship services, city-wide praise rallies, plenary worship sessions at denominational gatherings, etc., as well as smaller worship teams, usher teams, sound-technician teams, Scripture-readers' guild, among others.

- Orange indicates those groups that do not necessarily *directly* contribute to the numerical growth of that particular local church. These groups may be of any size.

    Probable examples: Overseas missions, cross-cultural missions not targeted to the enlargement of membership, new church developments, and those groups that have no fishing-pool (newcomer admission) effect, such as certain in-house

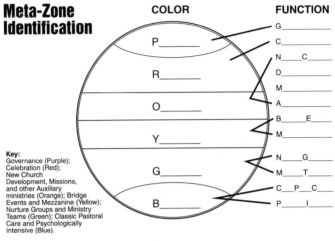

Figure 14

adult Bible courses, bookstores, cassette ministries, radio/tele-vision ministries, church-sponsored schools, as well as others.

- Yellow indicates congregation-size groups that serve as bridges for attracting outsiders and "mezzanine" groups that encourage acquaintance, referring to other groups, and fellow-ship. These medium-size groups represent anything that brings people together in groups larger than a cell *and* that contains an intentional acquaintance-making dimension.

    Probable examples: High-visibility outreach seminar, pro-gram of backyard BBQ suppers, golf tournament, children's school performance for parents, large Sunday-school classes, a scouting troop, and a "reunion" of cell groups that all started from the same parent group.

- Green indicates nurture groups and ministry teams.

    Probable examples: These may range from small Bible studies to small Sunday-school classes, from a small meals-on-wheels task force to a baseball team.

- Blue indicates all ministry that is psychologically intensive, from intercessory prayer to counseling, or that is traditionally

Multiple Entry Points

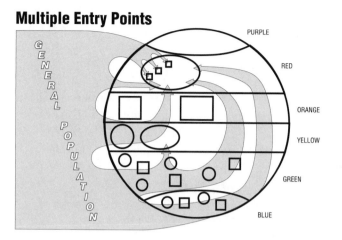

Figure 15

done by clergy and paraclergy under the rubric of "classical pastoral care."

Probable examples: Support groups, recovery groups, 12-Step groups, telecare[2] teams, Stephen Minister teams, crisis response teams, deacon groups (if they provide pastoral care), lay counseling ministries, and prayer teams.

Figure 14 allows you to review these colors and functions.

By the use of colors you can understand your church in many fresh ways. For example, color-zone-based depictions of the Meta-Globe can help a church recognize its "entry points," such as in figure 15. Which ministries would be the most strategic to strengthen or repurpose in order to attract more newcomers to the church? The Meta-Globe can greatly clarify and simplify the decision-making process.

Understanding the Rest of This Book

For the remainder of this book, the Meta-Globe will be used for two primary purposes. For the remainder of this section—part 2 chapters 8–13—we'll examine the process of leadership development, zone by zone. How do you empower lay leaders in the context of the teams that produce large meetings and worship services (Red Zone)? Why does that process differ from developing teams that plan high-visibility outreaches (Yellow Zone bridge events)? What special needs do the leaders of nurture cell groups have (Green Zone), and how do those circumstances compare to the training process for leaders of recovery or support groups (Blue Zone)?

The next six chapters, then, will address leadership development, according to the various types of ministries in a church.

> Another use of the Meta-Globe: setting goals
> from where you are "now," to what you believe
> God is calling your church to become.

Part 3, beginning with chapter 14, will offer another use of the Meta-Globe: setting goals from where you are "now" to what you believe God is calling your church to become. As such you'll develop a greater ability at mapping the specific groups in the church you serve. You'll use these insights to help your church transition wisely. You'll prepare your church for the future, for the coming church revolution, by developing a specific game plan for empowering (volunteer) leaders.

Questions for Discussion and Application

1. According to the above material, what is the purpose of the Meta-Globe? How could it prove beneficial in describing your church?

2. If you've ever dreamed about the ideal church, what did you come up with? How did you pictorially depict your thoughts?

3. From memory, try sketching a Meta-Globe. Can you identify where celebration-size groups are located? congregation-size groups? What are the colors and what does each signify?

8

Strategic Uses of Staff Roles: Purple Zone

> In the Meta-Church, the work and ministry of the professional staff is to create volunteer ministers who are capable of being leaders of groups or teams.

Meta-Church thinking suggests that your ultimate core business will be pastoral care and nurture of new converts. To be the church of God in your situation may require a prophetic thrust, a social-service thrust, or even a political thrust, but the great churches of the future will primarily be places where people meet God and the body of Christ, and then from that base, they will have the strength to organize themselves around good works.

In that regard, you might find it helpful to look at leadership development in terms of preparing multiple teams for leading worship. How many worship services will you hold? The answer depends on how many lost people are present in your region who, if converted, would need to worship. How many cell groups should your church have? Again, the answer depends on how many lost people are in your region who, if converted, would need to be cared for.

Thus your church will probably need as many cell groups as you can develop leaders for, and multiple worship services because, as time goes on, you'll fill your worship services from your cell groups.

> Your church will probably need as many cell groups
> as you can develop leaders for.

Structuring for Growth

If you follow general Meta-Church organizational thinking, you will develop five emphases in the general structure of the church of the future, especially as that church becomes large. Eventually the most sizable leadership group will be the staff who handle the cell infrastructure.

Meta-Church Staffing Emphases

Purple and Orange Zones

1. Board (generically described as a governing board, policy board, or executive board).
2. Primary vision casters (senior pastor, and perhaps also an executive minister) for managing staff.
3. Staff who handle administration (money, buildings, personnel, advertising, auxiliary enterprises such as Christian day schools, etc.).

Red Zone

4. Staff who produce worship through cell groups.

Yellow, Green, Blue Zones

5. Staff who handle cell infrastructure.

Clear, Measurable Goals for Staff

In the Meta-Church, the work and ministry of the professional staff is to create volunteer ministers who are capable of being leaders of groups or teams. If you are fueled by such a clear objective, it's fairly easy to set measurable performance goals for each staff pastor.

Here's the ultimate test for whether one staff member or all staff members are doing their job: At the end of each year they're with you, how many new volunteer leaders have they installed? What counts is not their personal productivity, but how many leaders they produce. Can they say, "Because Pastor Soper was here, there are two dozen more volunteer leaders now in service-convening groups or cells than there were a year ago"? Of course this assumes you've given them assignments that are consistent with leadership development. For examples, see the following chart.

Measurable Assignments
Consistent with Leadership Development

1. Not: How many communions did that pastor administer?
   Better: How many communions have been administered by the deacons (or eucharistic ministers)?
   Or: How many people did the pastor train to conduct a communion service (whether to shut-ins, etc.)?

2. Not: How big was the group the youth pastor led?
   Better: How many members of our college-age group are leading weekday high-school youth activities?

3. Not: How many phone calls did the pastor make?
   Better: How many teams of "telecare" volunteer phone callers did the pastor train and deploy?

4. Not: How many hours did the pastor of counseling put in?
   Better: How many lay counselors did he or she develop?

5. Not: How well does the minister of music's choir sing?
   Better: How many singing groups are there?
   Or: How many lay music directors have been developed?

6. Not: How many programs did the pastor of missions promote?
   Better: How many direct mission involvement teams, led by lay people, were sent to a cross-cultural mission field, here or abroad?

The key factors are competency and ability to make things happen through others. Graduate education and an ordination certificate can be helpful toward that end, but they in no way guarantee it! A person may even be an eloquent, powerful preacher—but regrettably that charisma may have no correlation with a willingness to be accountable for results or a skill in recruiting and coaching a corps of volunteers. Applause addiction often leads to someone's being a great communicator but a poor developer of leaders.

Increased Clergy Productivity

Clergy productivity is currently measured at somewhere between 70 and 150 people per clergy, according to general consensus among researchers. My use of the term *clergy* here is quite broad; it includes ministers, whether they are officially ordained or not. Many people serve on a church's professional staff without being ordained. For example, in many cases, youth workers, women's ministries coordinator, business administrators, and others carry the program load of the church as much as any ordained clergy does. Also, for purposes of this discussion, the people I'm describing invest at least twenty hours a week in the ministries of the church, and are in most cases on the church's payroll. But from Mormons (all local officers in the Mormon sect are unpaid volunteers) to

> Applause addiction often leads to someone's being
> a great communicator but a poor developer of leaders.

Third World churches, we see that alternative social organizations are available in which a church doesn't have to pay to have ministry done!

What happens as churches become larger? In the early stages you hire a volunteer coordinator on a part-time basis. That's when you're still treating volunteers on a one-on-one (one-at-a-time) basis. At a later stage, you'll develop a concept that all work is done by high-performance teams. At that time the teams become led by volunteers and are comprised of volunteers. This is a paradigm shift so enormous that it will take you into productivity gains of two and three times what you now achieve.

Trinity Lutheran Church

1101 Kimberly Way
Lisle, IL 60532-3175
Phone: (708) 964-1272
FAX: (708) 964-1468
Denomination: Lutheran Church,
  Missouri Synod

Senior Pastor: Art Beyer
Contact: Dan Grissom
Attendance: 950
Total Cell Groups: 39

Cell-Group Members Make Better Disciples

Art Beyer, senior pastor at Trinity Lutheran Church in Lisle, Illinois, has concluded that people who are plugged into groups make better disciples than those who aren't involved with a small group. "In our new members' class, for the first time in memory, more people were drawn in as a result of our cell groups than because they happened upon our worship services," Beyer says. "In the class, which we call Basics, we ask people to tell why they came to Trinity Lutheran," Beyer says. "Nowadays, the majority of the class explains that their involvement in the church began because of a connection with someone in a small group."

After comparing statistics, Beyer and his staff have concluded that discipleship at Trinity Lutheran pays little respect to whether someone was previously churched or unchurched, or even Lutheran or non-Lutheran. Rather, the more influential factor in a church member's long-term faithfulness is the connection with a small group. "On average," Beyer says, "our statistics show that if new people go into a small-cell group, they tend to attend three out of four Sunday worship services a month; if not, they attend only one out of four." Beyer's research of the church, which numbers 950 people on a typical Sunday, also indicates that by the third year, most of those who don't participate in a small group have completely left the church.

"Previously, our back door was wide open. We were bringing between 150 to 200 new members a year into the church, but couldn't gain ground," Beyer says. "That has significantly changed now. Our attendance, our stewardship, and our assimilation all have increased because we're able to retain these people through our cell-group ministry."

As a church continues to mature and reflect Meta-Church characteristics, clergy productivity will also rise to two or three times the present ratio—perhaps to 1:250 or as high as 1:400. That higher ratio is what we observe in the beyond-huge churches of the Third World. For example, in Cho's church of 700,000 (introduced in chapter 6), some three hundred ministers are currently on staff; only about fifty of them have preaching responsibilities. He has a complete seminary. Larger churches in North America are already functioning in many ways as their own denominations—First

> This is a paradigm shift so enormous
> that it will take you into productivity gains
> of two and three times what you now achieve.

United Methodist Church, Houston, has an archaeologist in residence; Eastside Foursquare, Kirkland, Washington, has a theologian in residence.

Those familiar with Jethro II (see figures 5 and 6) will perhaps ask why the clergy productivity ratio couldn't reach 1:500, as indicated by the Roman numeral D. The reason is this: Many people are in more than one group, and if a clergyperson is looking out for a staff of fifty cells, some of the people in those cells are also in other cells. Thus, the double participation causes an overlap.

If a church can afford a lower clergy-to-parishioner ratio, such as the present range of 1:70 to 1:150, why not continue as is? Present trends suggest that fewer and fewer churches will be able to afford that luxury. But more important is the God-ordained role of the paid clergy: Are the clergy to be primary caregivers or producers of ministers? My book, *How to Break Growth Barriers*, argues both biblically and functionally that current practices need to be reevaluated and realigned: what boards do, what staff does, and what laypeople do.[1]

Finally, why include business administrators in the above discussion? Business administrators are usually key-program staff people. I meet very few who aren't carrying supervision of volunteer ministry as part of their portfolio. They'll have a volunteer staff for book tables, for the parking lot, for security, and for technical sup-

Irving Bible Church

2700 West Finley Road
Irving, TX 75062
Phone: (214) 252-5539
FAX: (214) 252-2082
Denomination: Nondenominational

Senior Pastor: Andrew McQuitty
Contact: Andrew McQuitty
Attendance: 700
Total Cell Groups: 20

Transitioning to a New Definition of "Fully Committed Disciple"

Chuck Swindoll was a pastor there. So was Dallas Theological Seminary professor Stan Toussaint. Under leadership of that caliber, Irving Bible Church, in suburban Dallas, Texas, came to be known as a place for serious-minded students of the Word.

That venerable heritage began to pose a dilemma for the current senior pastor, Andy McQuitty. As the church drew a generation of people who were new or untrained in the Christian faith, he saw an increasing need for leadership development and relationship-based discipleship.

"Great teaching has historically been the cornerstone of this church's ministry," says McQuitty. "We don't want to lose that, but we want to package it in a way to help people become less sermon oriented and more application oriented."

McQuitty's preaching style is strongly expository, but it's also clearly life related. Says McQuitty, "I want people, as they leave the church building, to ask, not, 'Was the sermon exegetically accurate?' but 'What am I going to do with it?' or 'What does God's Word say that I need to change or become?'" As such, all the main points of McQuitty's messages imply action and application.

These shifts have augured some major implications for the church. For example, "We've focused our definition of what it means to be a fully committed disciple of Jesus Christ," says McQuitty. "Our old definition might have been that true disciples know the Greek meaning of certain Bible words and come to hear the preaching at least three times a week."

The standard today? "We still teach the intellectual foundations of our faith. But we heavily emphasize the lifestyle, behavioral, and relational aspects of discipleship. That paradigm involves being part of a community, usually through a small group."

The public services help publicize these small groups as part of McQuitty's goal to legitimize a culture of lay caregiving. One Sunday's service, for instance, might feature a commissioning prayer for a new crop of small-group leaders. Another week might include a sermon illustration of a church member who, individually or through a small group, is modeling what the day's Scripture text teaches.

"We're working hard to raise the banner of lay involvement," says McQuitty. "I find every opportunity I can to give illustrations of people in the church who are doing ministry, and who are doing it well. Lives are changing, and more and more people are becoming disciples. It's hard to argue against that kind of fruit!"

port. It's very common to find the business manager of a church carrying as much responsibility as the clergy in terms of directing the work of volunteers.

New Staff, Next Staff

Why hire an additional staff person? Your motive is not that of "helping" the senior pastor by serving as a sidekick. Rather it's to produce new lay leaders. The traditional triangle of leadership as it is represented in many North-American churches involves worship, fellowship, and education. Meta-Church would propose an alternative triangle: large-group celebration, small-group caring, and if necessary, medium-size-group bridges and mezzanines.

If the central task of the church becomes leadership development, then you're no longer looking for those who will do ministry, but those who will produce ministers. That means not people who sing, but those who train singers; no longer choir directors, but those who will commission choir directors to create multiple choirs.

> You're no longer looking for those who will do ministry, but those who will produce ministers.

You want to hire people who have a track record for coaching others, not those who specialize in doing hands-on ministry, except as a way of modeling for new leaders. They will probably come from the business community and from nonprofit organizations (YMCA directors, soccer-league presidents, etc.) because that's one of the best sources of high-achievement people.

Many of them will be raised up in-house. Don Cousins, a long-time staff member at Willow Creek Community Church (see case study on page 59), reports that 90 percent of their staff pastors are raised from within. This statistic describes their hiring pathway both before and now while the church is using Meta-Church technology. It appears, unfortunately, that people who can tolerate three years of full-time classroom theological education tend not to be very achievement oriented in terms of developing those who build community.

What about a "Minister of Small Groups"?

In the future you won't have a minister of small groups. You will perhaps have a minister who carried the portfolio for organizing the VHS[2] agenda, but practically every staff member is a minister of small groups or teams or task forces when their role is rightly understood. Most so-called ministers of small groups could more accurately be called "ministers of home Bible studies" or "ministers of twenty-two of the church's groups." Obviously titles like that, which are more accurate, could become rather cumbersome! My point is this: The ministers of small groups that I've interviewed typically oversee only a fourth or so of the groups in that church. The remaining three-fourths are usually capable of providing pastoral care and spiritual help, but after doing so they're not recognized for that.

For now, however, in churches with only one duly recognized minister of small groups, the senior minister's role is to hold that person accountable for training leaders, to encourage him or her, and to be sure that the message from the pulpit is consistent with the strategy of the small group. If the sermons regularly emphasize clergy performance and laypeople's dependence on clergy ministry, a small-group system will never fully fly.

As a church grows, will it need a different senior pastor?

Pastors of larger churches are usually made through what they've learned in the field, subsequent to their academic training. When a church grows, the pastoral leadership has three choices: Reposition to another location, stretch to learn new skills, or the

> If the sermons regularly illustrate clergy performance
> and laypeople's dependence on clergy ministry,
> a small group system will never fully fly.

more widely adopted option, limit the church's growth to the current comfort level.

Legitimizing Lay Care

The stories in the sermons identify who is the hero. If the clergy are the champions, the laity will feel that their ministry is unimportant or unappreciated. If, however, the stories and sermons illustrate peer ministry, mutual-care ministry, one-another ministry, lay-led ministry, and group-based ministry, the pastor won't even have to preach the need for it (see figure 16).[3] The illustrations alone significantly raise that awareness.

Popular Meta-Church Texts

"Therefore go and make disciples of all nations. . . . " Matt. 28:19–20

"Now to each one the manifestation of the Spirit is given for the common good." 1 Cor. 12:7

"We have different gifts, according to the grace given us." Rom. 12:6

"And the Lord added to their number daily those who were being saved." Acts 2:47

"Day after day, in the temple courts and from house to house, they never stopped teaching and proclaiming the good news. . . . " Acts 5:42

"The harvest is plentiful but the workers are few. . . ." Matt. 9:37

" . . . new wine must be poured into new wineskins." Luke 5:38

"The things you heard me say in the presence of many witnesses entrust to reliable men who will also be qualified to teach others." 2 Tim. 2:2

" . . . to prepare God's people for works of service, so that the body of Christ may be built up until we all reach unity . . . and become mature. . . . " Eph. 4:12–13

"Moses' father-in-law . . . said . . . 'What you are doing is not good. You and these people . . . will only wear yourselves out. The work is too heavy for you; you cannot handle it alone.'" Ex. 18:5, 17–18

Figure 16

What happens if volunteer leaders get into too many groups by choice or compulsion? I suggest that you needn't care, in most cases, how many groups they're involved in, but that you only allow them to lead one group. In short, they may lead one group and participate in as much else as they have time for. That way the priority is established. That arrangement offers a far greater likelihood that ten people will be certain to receive quality care.

> Volunteer leaders lead one group and participate
> in as much else as they have time for.

Structured Leadership Training

Those who have read *Prepare Your Church for the Future* or
have participated in a seminar with me or other Meta-Church afi-
cianados will be aware that VHS signifies more than a type of
video-cassette system. It represents the *Vision*, *Huddling*, and *Skill*-
building components that must be present if volunteer leadership is
to be effectively cultivated. The VHS concept will be presented in
greater detail in chapter 12 (Green Zone) and may be located as
part of the Meta-Globe Axis as in figure 17.

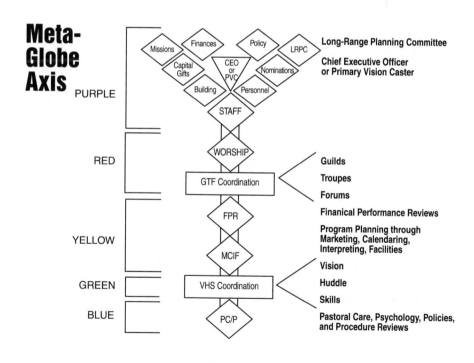

Figure 17

What if a church says, "We don't have a leadership community meeting frequently, so I guess we're not a Meta-Church"? Wrong. Are you deliberately and intentionally and explicitly providing for those functions for each of your leaders? If I interview your leaders, can they tell me what they're about? Do they know what Bible teaching you as a church endorse? Do they know who the heroes of your church are? Do they feel empowered to minister to people? Are they reporting to a supervisor? Are they bringing apprentices on board? Do they have a place where they can get additional skill training as they need it? Are those things going on?

If your answer is yes, then you've met all the tests because you are doing VHS functions. The programmatic mindset insists that you provide supervision in a group setting or, with more effort, on the fly. As with the aspirin analogy that I'll develop in chapter 17 (see figure 62), the vital ingredient—aspirin—is far more important than the outward form—rounded, capsulized, or time-released.

Engendering Greater Cell Involvement

How intensively will cells be developed? If a pastoral staff does nothing to encourage cell involvement—and, of course, doesn't forbid it—the typical response is that 20 percent to 30 percent of the adults will be involved in a small group. These groups might include Sunday-school classes, a women's prayer circle, a long-standing home Bible study, the missions committee, and the like. If the church has an extensive lay-superintended Sunday-school program, the percentage will be higher. (See figure 18.)

Next, if the church assigns a staff person to facilitate small groups, the involvement-level numbers will double. In most cases, a staff person will get twice the participation that a lay person will, simply because of the time and energy he or she has to put into it.

If the senior leadership of the church says, "We want all the staff to develop leadership for a small-group system," you can push the percentage up another 20 percent (see figure 19). These churches will still watch people walk through the front door saying, "Thanks, but no thanks" to small groups.

Finally, a point will come where your group enrollment will exceed your worship; that is, people will get more out of the group

Cell Ratios

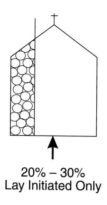 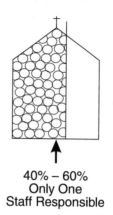

20% – 30%
Lay Initiated Only

40% – 60%
Only One
Staff Responsible

Church building = total attendance at worship celebration
Circles = percentage of cell groups

Figure 18

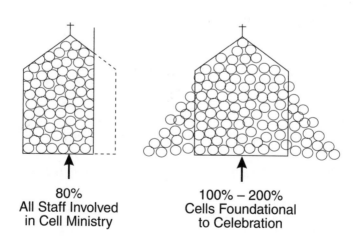

80%
All Staff Involved
in Cell Ministry

100% – 200%
Cells Foundational
to Celebration

Figure 19

experience than they will the corporate worship. When they have to choose between what they value the most, they value the camaraderie of the intimate fellowship of faith over the formalized plenary worship. Lest this idea seem doctrinally deviant, answer this question first. Is it wrong to prioritize committed discipleship, as defined by tithing, mutual ministry, outreach, and service over being a spectator at a larger service? People need both cell and celebration. But should the circumstances arise, can the people of your "future" church do just as well on worship every other week, as long as they are sustained continually in a community of faith?

A Final Word

If you don't walk with God, you can't take other people to where he is. Those are the dues you must pay. In addition, across your life's span, you will have periods of time where you cannot seem to get your act together, but if you're following after the Lord, you will experience periods of convergence where many things that God's been working in you will come together.[4] God may be teaching you many lessons, which will accumulate, wave upon wave, until you reach a point when you say, "It's blast-off time." Don't ever become so preoccupied with organization and management that you sacrifice those personal times with the Lord of the universe.

If you've been in ministry for many years, please do not think of yourself as too old to learn. Peter Drucker is fond of describing cellist Pablo Casals's death at age 94 at 2:00 in the afternoon, after spending four hours that morning practicing the scales. What kind of a man can fill a concert hall in his tenth decade? A man who spends four hours practicing scales. Scales? That's the most basic thing you can practice. If Pablo Casals needed to do that in order to be the world's greatest cellist, church leaders likewise would be wise to follow suit.

The basics or fundamentals to be mastered are these:

- Pray by *listening* to God as much as you *talk* to him.
- Learn to develop cell-group leaders. That is the most important single thing that you need to do as a leader of a church.

Grace Community Church

2511 Sentry Drive
Anchorage, AK 99507
Phone: (907) 344-7780
FAX: (907) 344-7187
Denomination: Grace Brethren
Churches

Senior Pastor: Brian L. Chronister
Contact: Brian L. Chronister
Attendance: 1300
Total Cell Groups: 30

Pastor "Gives Up" on Trying to Coach His Leaders

"In the beginning, I found it relatively easy to work with our cell group leaders," says Brian Chronister, senior pastor of Grace Community Church, Anchorage, Alaska, of the church he founded in 1989, and which was averaging 1300 in worship by the end of 1993. "We had only four leaders, and we met twice monthly for encouragement and instruction."

As the church continued to reach more people, Chronister kept thinking he could handle the leadership-training load. "Only when we passed the mark of having twenty adult groups, plus youth and children, did I acknowledge that the task had outgrown me," says Chronister.

Problem is, his leaders were already feeling the neglect. "I was the only coach for almost four years," says Chronister. "It's my observation that even the very best of my leaders who are gifted, experienced, well-trained, and self-sufficient began to wither under the pressure of delivering care to their people. It's vital to their well-being that someone they respect give them affirmation and encouragement. I was too slow about apprenticing myself, and were I to describe the strengths of the church, the list would not include that particular facet."

By early 1993 Pastor Chronister had commissioned several lay coaches [Ls], and they met once a month in homes, as small cells of cell leaders [Xs]. They also gathered together once a month for training and encouragement.

"The coaches, both men and women, emerged rather naturally from our pack of cell leaders," says Chronister. "But it has taken years for them to develop the capability to handle the task. They need wisdom, experience, and most importantly, credibility and stature as mature Christian leaders."

Chronister's vision for Grace Community Church is that of a cell-driven ministry. Because he finally "gave up" on being the coach for every cell leader, today there are more coaches, more leaders, and thus more cells than ever.

- Become good at casting vision. Learn how to describe the future in such clear terms that people salivate to get to it. Build a dream—whether you're twenty-four or sixty-four.
- Become quality driven. Anything else—whether your ego needs or your satisfaction with being better than average—is a dangerous foundation. If the church you serve is to grow larger, it must be because its quality is better. With each passing month, are your people more warmly in love with Christ? Do they practice one-another ministry? Do they have fewer "bugs" in their lives, fewer sins, less surrender to the flesh, more compassion, more strength, and more service than ever before?

A church isn't better because it's large; if it's better, though, it deserves to get larger, and you can assist in that transition.

Questions for Discussion and Application

1. What is the core idea presented in this chapter? Why is that so important?

2. Name three new insights you gained from this chapter. Name the idea in this chapter that makes you the most uncomfortable.

3. What can you do next to support the senior leadership in the church you serve?

9

Strategic Uses of Teams That
Lead Large Meetings: Red Zone

> When leadership development and worship ensembles are paired
> together, a church can provoke celebrative worship in ways
> beyond your wildest imagination.

In a Meta-Church at least five functions must be present:

1. Leadership development (Purple Zone)
2. Celebration (Red Zone)
3. Marketing strategy and bridging (Yellow Zone)
4. Psychological and spiritual wholeness (Blue Zone)
5. Cells (all zones, with Green Zone becoming the largest)

The celebration function, which includes number two and number five, will probably contain sermonizing, but it goes far beyond preaching. The festival-like qualities of true celebration are best released by ensembles of people with the appropriate gifts and skills (see figure 20).

Thus, a discussion of leadership development for the Red Zone (celebration and worship arts) will go far beyond talking about preaching or even music; we're talking about eliciting a spirit of praise within a convention of groups. The prompters and producers

Types of Ministry Teams

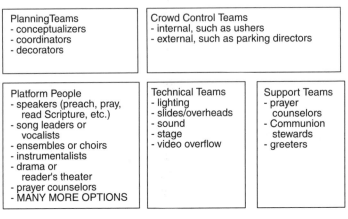

PlanningTeams - conceptualizers - coordinators - decorators	Crowd Control Teams - internal, such as ushers - external, such as parking directors	

Platform People
- speakers (preach, pray,
   read Scripture, etc.)
- song leaders or
   vocalists
- ensembles or choirs
- instrumentalists
- drama or
   reader's theater
- prayer counselors
- MANY MORE OPTIONS
	Technical Teams
	- lighting
	- slides/overheads
	- sound
	- stage
	- video overflow
		Support Teams
		- prayer
		   counselors
		- Communion
		   stewards
		- greeters

Figure 20

of worship are likewise small groups—people with the ability to create celebration-arts ensembles.

For many people, the idea of cell-driven celebrative worship is exactly opposite everything they've been taught. This paradigm is

> We're talking about eliciting a spirit of praise within a convention of groups. The prompters and producers of worship are likewise small groups—people with the ability to create celebration-arts ensembles.

conceptually difficult to grasp and requires that several key concepts be discussed first.

What Celebrative Worship Looks Like

God's people have always joined with one another to attribute greatness ("worthship") to God. The psalmist's cry, "Come, let us bow down in worship, let us kneel before the LORD our Maker" (Psalm 95:6), describes the tribes of ancient Israel when they assembled for various feasts and festivals, as well as the house churches of the New Testament era when they came together in praise. The creed and practice of churches for two subsequent millenniums have been: "Let us not give up meeting together" (Hebrews 10:25).

What is celebrative worship? A church, when it comes together, should so recognize the presence of the Lord Jesus Christ that it lives in joyful expectation of a loving God's descending in its midst. It expects the kind of blessing from heaven that gives it hope for the here and now.

What did the praises of the people of God sound like in Scripture? Worship is the victory shout by a triumphant army. Worship is the human emotion that says, "We have conquered through our God and against a god that seemed undefeatable." Worship is an exuberance that enables people to say from their hearts, "God is great! He has released us from our sins and made us triumphant through the Lord Jesus!" Worship is having a picture of God that's bigger than the way the tide of your circumstances is ebbing and flowing. Worship affirms that the eternal is still the benchmark against which you are operating. Worship acknowledges the larger canvas on which God is painting. God is a high-voltage God. He's willing to put power into a place that's willing to cheer, in word or in spirit or both.

What Makes a Large Worship Service Celebrative

The Meta-Church understands that these celebrations are not an end in themselves. Rather, they're a means to an end—a way of helping cells experience a festive dimension of worship that's rarely, if ever, possible in the solitude or reflection of one's prayer closet, or even in the intimacy of a small group.

For an event to be celebrative, to have sparkle, to be larger than life, to be exuberant, and to be a truly festive occasion, several factors must be present.

Vision

Vision offers meaning to life. Vision says, "What you are doing is significant. It is worthy of the sacrifice you are putting into your life and ministry."

Preachers over the years have recounted the story of an interviewer on the premises of a cathedral under construction, asking the various craftsmen the meaning of the task they were performing. "I'm breaking stone," explained the first workman. "I'm feeding my family," said the second, as he thought of the money coming to him for his labor. "I'm building this cathedral to the glory of God," said the third, "so that a thousand years from now the witness to our faith will still be apparent to generations on earth." Visionaries are able to transform a mindset of breaking stone into one with a millennial meaning.

Remember how excited the United States became when President John F. Kennedy declared, "We will place a man on the moon by the end of the decade." Recall how many billions of dollars Congress released, how many hundreds of thousands of people focused on that issue, and how excited everyone was when they saw an American flag planted on the moon's surface. By contrast, relive the empty feeling you felt when the space shuttle *Challenger* exploded, and school teacher Christa McAuliffe and her crewmates

> Participation in God's kingdom is the only activity
> that has ultimate and eternal meaning.

disappeared in a puff of smoke—all because of a simple malfunction. Our finest dreams as a nation tumbled to earth, dashing the hopes of many.

Nothing is more fragile than visions originating from technical prowess because we're constantly making them obsolete and removing their significance. The same can be said of political stature. The power of Moscow's Red Square, the shoot-to-kill guard patrols atop the Berlin Wall, the popularity or genocide edicts of a president or dictator—each pinnacle of human power can crumble, seemingly in a day.

The calling of God utterly dwarfs the momentary greatness brought about by revolutions of technology or political ideology. Participation in God's kingdom is the only activity that has ultimate and eternal meaning.

Every Christian is a partaker of that noble purpose. God wants to work his power through us. His desire is to use *us* in making this world a better place. He seeks to lead us into his joyous, everlasting

Vision and Artistic Communication in Worship

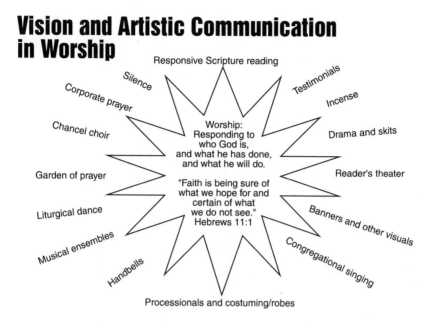

Figure 21

fellowship, characterized by a freedom and peace that passes all understanding. When corporate worship renews this vision in our minds, hearts, and spirits, we should be so inspired that we can barely get our feet onto the ground to take us home!

It is almost a malpractice for worship leaders to let any disciple of Christ walk away from a great celebration without a sense of connectedness with God and mankind, meaning, and fulfillment. True worship can make us thankful with every breath that God is on his throne, that Jesus Christ is his Son, that the Spirit is given, the Word is available, and the Christian church is here on earth as our nurturer (see figure 21).

Power

Celebrative worship also communicates the realization that God's power is at work.

Some believers experience God's power the way Gideon did— angels of the Lord show up, sacrifices disappear in a puff of smoke, dreams cause terror in the enemy camp, a few underdogs rout the toughest armies of that day. Gideon's service to God was one long, wild ride! How do you think Gideon felt when he overheard the conversation that named him as the person who would overcome the enemy Midianites (Judges 7:9–15)? I believe he and his men

> When worship is all it ought to be, God's children
> sense the meaningfulness of their own work
> and sense the size that God brings to a task.

held a quick worship session on the spot! He went back to camp with a sense of awe: "God, you know what I need."

Other believers experience God's power a little more "decently and in order." Their life is more analogous to Abraham's servant as he journeyed to find a bride for Abraham's son Isaac. The first young lady who came up to him offered him hospitality like he'd never known before. Abraham's servant, upon inquiry, discovered that she was a member of the very household in which he needed to be searching. His response? "I, being in the way, the LORD led me" and he worshiped (Genesis 24:27 KJV). No one, by human wisdom, treks across the desert, strolls into a town, and meets the very candidate for marriage for whom he's looking unless someone supernatural is at work.

In stories like this, God behaves a little more anonymously in how he handles life's affairs, seeming to enjoy the mysterious behind-the-scenes role of divine providence. His hand at work offers the assurance of another case of God's knowing what he's doing and letting us in on it. Whichever of these models is closer to your particular understanding of divine power at work, when worship is all it ought to be, God's children sense the meaningfulness of their own work and sense the size that God brings to a task.

Artistic Communication

One of the prophetic ministries God has raised up in this era is that of the artist who touches the heart and conscience of those assembled. In making sense out of life, the artist uses his or her intuitive abilities to cause people to respond deeply, "Aha, yes, I see!"

Size

When the number of people involved exceeds well over one hundred, worshipers cannot personally know everyone else present. As a result people realize, visually, that they're not alone; they comprise a great throng in the presence of God. They're encouraged to see so many other people who, they presume, are walking with God. They even impute to these people potential that they might not even see in themselves. As a consequence, an electricity of emotional excitement circulates around the room.

Cell Relationships

Finally, a sense of security, "comfort zone," comes from the knowledge that friends (or acquaintances) are present with us in corporate worship. No matter how large the gathering—whether it's a Billy Graham rally, a denominational convention, or a large church with seating for thousands—we can feel at home when those in our spiritual kinship networks are nearby (see figure 22). The cell-celebration mixture can cause any church to seem like the "biggest little church" or the "smallest big church" around.

Relationship before Celebration

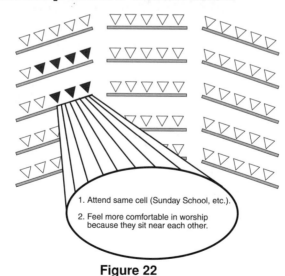

1. Attend same cell (Sunday School, etc.).

2. Feel more comfortable in worship because they sit near each other.

Figure 22

Worship Services as Conventions of Cells

A celebration of worship is like a Democratic or Republican National Convention where delegations from scores of states and territories are clustered throughout the large assembly area. The difference is that the delegations are "Joey LeGunn's young married's Sunday-school class" or "the group that meets at Samantha Dietz's house" or "the group that meets at Chillino's Pizza for brunch each week after the early worship service" (see figure 23).

A fundamental perception needs to change. The leaders of worship—both the pastoral staff as well as various leaders of worship teams—need to treat any celebration-size gathering as a convention of small groups, led by lay ministers, that have assembled for public worship and formal teaching. When these groups leave the worship room, they resume a life of faith and prayer together until they reappear at the next scheduled public teaching. Therefore, the key to assembling great crowds for preaching is not only the quality of preaching but also how committed to a common objective the small-group leaders are as they work with ten people at a time (see figure 24).

Worship as a Convention of Cells

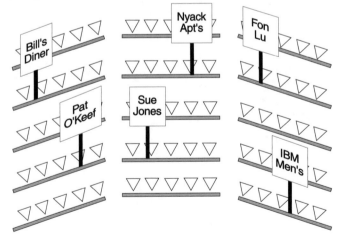

Figure 23

New Song Church

355 S. Lemon Avenue, Suite G
Walnut, CA 91789
Meeting site:
   Royal Oak Intermediate School,
   Covina, California
Phone: (909) 869-7750
FAX: (909) 468-9809
Denomination: Conservative Baptist

Senior Pastor: (none at present)
Contact: Janine Letherer
Attendance: 1200
Total Cell Groups: 121

Never a Shortage of Celebration Arts Leaders

If any church has reason to be totally out of breath, it's New Song Church, a "baby buster" church where the average age is twenty-six and where 75 percent of the people are single adults. The growth rate since 1986, from a handful of people to twelve hundred, invites predictions that the church probably suffers from a perennial shortage of leaders.

"Not!" reports Dieter Zander, the founding pastor who resigned in late 1993. In every area of the church, people receive nurture and care through small groups, and new volunteer leaders are being continually developed in the process.

Janine Letherer, for example, serves on staff as director of Celebration Arts. But at any of the three weekend services, she's one of about fifty different people who help prompt and produce the worship. Instead of filling the role of star performer, Letherer has developed a volunteer leadership team of about ten people (also called directors) who each head up a different area of the arts—music, drama, sound, setup, etc. Each of these people, in turn, oversee about five teams.

Where does all this trained talent come from? "We depend heavily on an apprentice system," says Letherer. "In all of our groups, we strongly emphasize the need for constant development of new leaders. At present about half our groups contain leaders in training, and that percentage continues to increase."

Does the rapid growth and the task-based emphasis cause a turnover of leadership, due to burnout or people's feeling uncared for? "We emphasize small group participation as the most important meeting of the week," says Letherer. "In all team meetings and rehearsals, leaders try to put an emphasis on nurture. The low span of care—typically one leader for every five group members—allows for the personal touch that everyone needs."

The various leaders, in turn, receive nurture and care from a leadership community meeting that takes place twice a month. In fact, volunteer leaders have become so empowered that they tend to solve major problems in their groups without needing to involve the pastoral staff. In one instance, a crisis arose while Letherer was out of town. The leadership team acted quickly and effectively to make all necessary adjustments. Says Letherer, "Even in a crisis situation, ministry takes place because of the strong leadership network that has been developed."

Both "On" and "Off" Premises

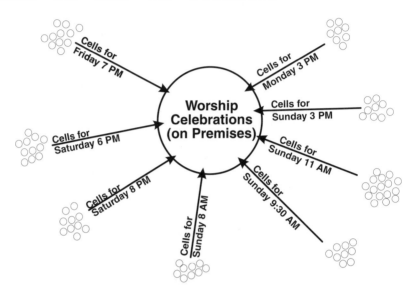

Figure 24

Once you perceive the church you serve as a collection of cells, you will begin to see cells everywhere. You'll see almost every program, gathering, or activity as a meeting. For each of these groups that contains less than a dozen or so people, you'll think of it as having cell characteristics, even if it doesn't acknowledge itself to be a cell. And you'll begin to understand that attendance at a plenary worship celebration can be predetermined by multiplying the number of cells willing to commit to the event by ten.

> The key to assembling great crowds for preaching
> is not only the quality of preaching but also how committed
> to a common objective the small-group leaders are.

Calvary Church

135 W. Robertson St.
Brandon, FL 33511
Phone: (813) 653-0422
FAX: (813) 653-1972
Denomination: Southern Baptist

Senior Pastor: Tim Wilson
Contact: Galen Scott
Attendance: 2000
Total Cell Groups: 160

Worship, Drama, Stage, and Artist Guilds Can Be a Tool of Discipleship

Galen Scott, pastor of worship at Calvary Church in Brandon, Florida, has found a successful way to train a group of people who are often overlooked in a church's discipleship plan: the artists and musicians who produce the worship services.

Scott, who comes from an entertainment background, decided that the church needed more than just a quality production team. He desired that the church's artists would evidence spiritual role modeling and growth as well. "I asked God to surround me with godly men and women who could become leaders in both production and discipleship," Scott remembers. "We've seen many people rise to that challenge. God had given our church the talent; we just needed a vision for how to cultivate it."

This Southern Baptist church, which started in 1988 with a small core group, has grown rapidly and steadily, exceeding the two thousand mark in average worship attendance during 1993. "Over time," recalls Scott, "we have expanded with God's help to more than fifty team leaders, who together comprise a multifaceted production team. All of them have been trained through the cell-group ministry in our church."

Once a month the production team department heads meet together at Scott's home for an informal training meeting, called Vision, Huddle, and Skills—or VHS for short. "The first segment of the meeting casts the vision, the second breaks into smaller departmental discussion groups, and the third brings everyone back together for a period of discipling," Scott says.

"That last segment is where I deal with areas of the Christian life," he continues. "First I deal with these leaders' relationship with Christ; second, marriage; third, children; fourth, financial giving; and fifth, I challenge my people to take a leadership role. I talk to them at every VHS meeting about the qualities of a leader."

Scott believes that the time invested in the VHS community instills a leadership vision in the production team department heads. They're challenged to be better, more Christlike leaders, and to reproduce themselves every month. "They share our vision of who we're aiming to reach, with what method, and what type of message," he says.

Worship Services as More than Preaching

There are many ways to categorize or discuss worship styles. No matter what labels and classification schema are used, however, the worship service in every growing, healthy church includes some form of proclamation of God's Word through Scripture.

One of the greatest oratorical preachers of this century was Dr. W. A. Criswell, longtime pastor of First Baptist Church, Dallas. His delivery kept listeners of all ages spellbound. His content represented some of the finest literary quality in the entire Southern Baptist Convention. His editors must have felt a bit like television's Maytag washing-machine repairman; there's little to do other than box it and send it out.

Several years ago, I spent some time with Dr. Criswell. We discussed the primacy of preaching and the shifting styles of worship that were noticeable across several denominations. He said, "Well, you must know that I am firmly in the camp of those who believe the preached Word is the superior way to handle the worship service."

"I understand," I replied, "but may I probe the extent of your preference for the preaching style?" He consented.

I said, "I would imagine that your sermons are comprehensively researched and completely outlined in advance of the worship service, even though they are extemporaneous in style."

He agreed. "Would it be fair," I continued, "to say that, given the amount of time you devote to sermon preparation and to praying over your sermon outline and the points that you are to make, you are confident you have found the mind of God for your audience for that day?"

Again, he concurred. "Then let's suppose a situation similar to that which several ministers have reported to me as something they've experienced. What would happen if, having prayed over five points of an outline, and knowing clearly in your mind what the mind of the Spirit is for the teaching burden of this sermon, you came into the service and unbeknownst to you, through ministry of the Spirit and prayer, the worship team had prepared a series of features for the service in which the opening vignette covered point one better than you had planned to in your sermon, leaving the audience in awe.

"Then the next feature of the service is a solo that illustrates point two in such a way that people are sitting there with tears in their eyes. Point three is addressed in the pastoral prayer, as led by another pastor on staff, even to the point of the prayer's retelling the very Scripture you are going to use in the sermon. Point four is covered adequately by the morning anthem beyond anything that you have ever had reason to believe.

"Now, as you rise to speak, the only 'unpreached' point of your sermon is the benedictory point. Are you willing to grant, on the basis of your knowing what the mind of the Spirit is, that the Spirit has in fact spoken and done so through other service elements, and that all you have to do is close the service? Or would you still find it necessary to preach the sermon and replow that ground?"

Dr. Criswell replied, "I know what the 'right' answer is, but I would still preach the sermon!"

I love Dr. Criswell's candor because he represents the sentiment of tens of thousands of pastors across this continent.

Let me be clear: I'm not preaching against preaching! I'm not even questioning the legitimacy of long sermons! And I don't think a time is coming, in the foreseeable future, when worship will exclude the preaching of God's Word. In fact, of the two distinctives that I observe in the worship services of growing churches, one involves the role of prophetic ministry and the importance of the pulpit. (The other is that the number of "Hamlet" churches is increasing ["The play is the thing wherein I'll catch the conscience of the king," wrote Shakespeare] with skillfully performed drama that can't help but connect with worshipers.)

Rather, I'm affirming that there are times when the Holy Spirit moves, such that God's message is communicated as effectively— or perhaps more effectively—by elements of the service other than preaching. Further, I'm suggesting that the Spirit may have a far more creative flare than most pastors and lay leaders are prepared to receive.

> There are times when the Holy Spirit moves, such that God's message is communicated as effectively—or perhaps more effectively—by elements of the service other than preaching.

The Church on the Way

14300 Sherman Way
Van Nuys, CA 91405-2454
Phone: (818) 779-8000
FAX: (818) 779-8008
Denomination: Foursquare

Senior Pastor: Jack Hayford
Contact: Pastor's Seminar Office
Attendance: 6500
Total Cell Groups: 365

Discovering the Relationship between Cell and Celebration

During an era of rapid growth for Church on the Way, a church with worship attendance of 6500 based in greater Los Angeles, senior pastor Jack Hayford made a significant discovery about the modular nature of cells. He learned by experimentation that worship celebrations can be sustained by cells, and that cells, in turn, can fuel the celebration.

"Back in 1971 I sensed an inner voice speaking to me saying, 'I've given my glory to dwell in this place,' meaning the small sanctuary where we held worship meetings," recalls Hayford. "The very next Sunday our church of 100 had 170 people in worship. Thus began a growth explosion that had no rational explanation. Soon people were standing in the back of the sanctuary or in small side rooms trying to listen to the service."

Members began to say, "Let's move to a larger auditorium," but Hayford replied, "Let's not hurry. The Lord said he'd bless us here in this place, and before we move, we need to know his timing, not the strategy of human wisdom."

In order to handle the crowds, Hayford and his staff began to run multiple worship services in that small auditorium. But there were still more people than seats. Then he organized what could be called "breakouts." He asked people to divide into groups, and each group to meet in a home Sunday morning one service a month, to reduce the crowds at the church center. Meanwhile, the corporate worship services drew even more people, brought on, in part, by the newcomers invited by participants in the home groups.

Later, when Hayford had clear leadership from God to build a larger auditorium, the church's leaders said, "Good, now we can all come back together for worship, instead of having these home-based meetings." So, for a number of years, home-based groups became a lower priority for the church.

Today, Hayford and the church leadership are actively advancing participation in home cell groups. As they discovered two decades ago, small groups provide not only a durable context for Christian growth, but also an effective means for sustaining personal care for the body.

My interview with Dr. Criswell will register most strongly with those readers who are more rational and cognitive. But the same kinds of experiences have been recorded from the radical, hard-core Pentecostal side as well.

I remember, for example, listening to an evangelist from Latin America who believes that God speaks audibly to him. He reported, "One evening, before the sermon the Lord said, 'I wish to heal people tonight. And I wish for you to give the invitation for them to come and be healed.'"

He replied, "That's wonderful, Lord, immediately after my sermon, I will issue an altar call with the confidence that people will be healed."

But the voice of the Lord said to him, "No, not at the end of the service. Invite them now." He replied, "Lord, I haven't even preached yet. How will there be enough faith if we call them forward now?" Then the Lord rebuked him and said, "I am telling you to call the people to come for healing right now."

So he stood up and he said, "The normal thing for me to do at this point is to preach the Word. I believe that the Lord wants me to give you an opportunity right now to come forward and to be healed." And the people streamed forward. The healings were so obviously miraculous and spontaneous that the audience was reduced to jelly. They fell down as if to say, "The Lord is great, the Lord is good." The Lord showed up, even though the evangelist never got to his sermon!

A final example is in order. A number of years ago, my family and I attended First Church of the Nazarene in Pasadena, California, where Dr. Earl Lee, a former missionary and former school administrator, was senior pastor. Among the many strengths of his ministry was an outstanding youth program, which one of my children particularly needed at that time.

A typical Sunday would find me, my wife, and our six children occupying the front row of the balcony, with my children on the edge of their seats, watching and learning from Dr. Lee.

Now, if ever you could say that there was a personality that was antithetical to homiletic practice, Dr. Lee was that person. I believe in the course of the year that he may have preached two "proper" homiletic sermons—with a text; a well-developed introductory

Alternatives to "Sunday at 11:00 A.M."

Until recently, 11:00 Sunday morning has been the most likely time for newcomers, especially unchurched ones, to visit a church. If a church offers multiple services,* then the late-morning service is typically the most crowded, even without first-time guests. The reason for this popularity can be traced to several factors ranging from tradition to sociology, such as friends going together to church and then lunch or brunch.

Increasingly, however, churches are experimenting with nontraditional times for repeat services or for alternate worship styles. Here are several models:

Redeemer Presbyterian Church (P.C.A.), New York, New York. Launched in 1989, the church draws the majority of its people from Manhattan. More than 70 percent are single, and the average age of worshipers is about thirty-five. They meet in the auditorium of a college. (Mailing address: Rev. Tim Keller, Sr. Pastor, 271 Madison Ave., Suite 1208, New York, New York 10016, phone 212-808-4460, FAX 212-808-4465)

11:00 A.M. Sunday (700 people)**
    formal liturgical service; traditional music
4:00 P.M. Sunday (200 people)
    liturgical service (slightly less so than 11:00 A.M.) with question and answer time held afterward (same sermon as at 11:00 A.M.)
6:30 P.M. Sunday (600 people)
    informal service, contemporary/jazz music led by worship band (different sermon from earlier services)

St. Stephen's Episcopal Church, Sewickley, Pennsylvania. The church, founded in 1797, draws most of its people from the immediate area, a suburb north of Pittsburgh. The average age of worshipers is about thirty-eight, and a fourth of the parishioners are single. (405 Frederick Avenue, Sewickley, PA 15143-1522, phone 412-741-1790, FAX 412-741-7360, denomination: Episcopal, Sr. Pastor: William "Mike" Henning)

7:30 A.M. Sunday (30 people)
    Traditional—no music
8:45 A.M. Sunday (400 people)
    Contemporary, different sermon, geared to families
8:45 A.M. Sunday (200 people)
    Contemporary, meets in parish hall, geared to young families
10:00 A.M. Sunday (350 people)
    Contemporary, same sermon as 8:45 service
11:30 A.M. Sunday (70 people)
    Traditional, but with same sermon as 8:45 service

Community Baptist Church of Alta Loma, Alta Loma, California. The typical parishioner is thirty to forty years old and lives in nearby Rancho Cucamonga, a suburb of Los Angeles. The church was started in 1978 and has planted nine daughter churches. (P.O. Box 490, Rancho Cucamonga, CA

91701-0490, phone 909-945-5001, FAX 909-948-3174, denomination: Conservative Baptist, Sr. Pastor: Dr. Rob Acker)

5:30 P.M. Friday (300 people)
7:00 P.M. Friday (200 people)
8:00 A.M. Sunday (300 people)
9:30 A.M. Sunday (600 people)
11:15 A.M. Sunday (550 people)
     Contemporary service—identical for all five services

Hope Chapel, Hermosa Beach, California. About 50 percent of attenders are single, and the majority live in nearby Redondo Beach. Average age of worshipers is about thirty-two and the church was started in 1971. (2420 Pacific Coast Hwy., Hermosa Beach, CA 90254, phone 3100-374-4673, FAX 310-374-8223, denomination: Foursquare, Sr. Pastor: Zac Nazarian)

7:00 P.M. Friday (450 people)
5:00 P.M. Saturday (200 people)
7:15 P.M. Saturday (150 people)
8:00 A.M. Sunday (300 people)
9:30 A.M. Sunday (150 people)
10:45 A.M. Sunday (450 people)
7:00 P.M. Sunday (300 people)
     Contemporary style—worship band and music team (all services identical—except 9:30 A.M. Sunday, when the worship team is different, and the location is a community center two blocks away, and on Sunday evenings, which is primarily singles)

Other More Recent Experiments

Prince of Peace Lutheran, Burnsville (Minneapolis), Minnesota, sponsors four weekend services, each with a different worship style. They are currently testing out a fifth and sixth service at 12:00 noon and 7:00 P.M. on Thursdays.

Community Lutheran Church, Las Vegas, Nevada, has four Sunday-morning services (7:30, 8:45, 9:45, and 11:00). Two services are traditional and two are contemporary in worship style. At 7:00 P.M. on Sundays, they offer a service with country-western gospel music and liturgy.

*Researcher John Vaughan, in tracing the history of large churches, indicates that multiple services are not a recent historical development. For example: "Spain's Cathedral of Seville, begun in 1402 and completed in 1519, is reported to be the largest Gothic building in the world. This cathedral has seven naves, thirty-seven chapels, and eighty altars. Fifty masses are celebrated in it each day." John N. Vaughan, *The Large Church* (Grand Rapids: Baker, 1985), 44, quoting Andrew Bieler, *Architecture in Worship: The Christian Place of Worship* (Edinburgh: Oliver and Boyd, 1965), 43–46.

**Worship attendances, which include both adults and children, are rounded to the nearest 100 and represent an average for 1993.

remark; transition remarks; points one, two, and three with proper forms of support; and a summary. He held the academic credentials necessary to do so but chose not to. In the course of being a real leader to this great established congregation, he had learned that there was something more important than the form of the sermon— the response of the people's hearts to the burden of the Spirit.

Dr. Lee would open his Bible and read a verse or passage. Then he would pull out a newspaper clipping, a missionary's prayer letter, a page torn out of a devotional guide, or any number of other things. Everything he did had meaning and value, but it couldn't be confused with the more traditional oratorical three points and a poem!

He kissed babies, he gave mid-service altar calls for prayer, he inserted a minihomily. Before we knew it, the hour was gone. We had been exposed to thirty or forty verses of Scripture, to five or six heart-touching observations, and to a dozen people whose lives were changed or were being changed. It was as though heaven had parted, and we watched God's Spirit move through that audience, taking care of people and their needs. It was a marvelous kaleidoscope of worship practice. Some two thousand people were present, but the shepherd seemed to speak to each of us, nudging us along the way of holiness and life.

Our children were wonderfully touched by Dr. Lee's ministry. As our family would walk to the car, one of my sons or daughters would touch me on the arm and tell me that he or she didn't want to miss the next week. Why? There was life in that worship service! During that year I realized that the experience of corporate worship is something far greater than a publishable sermon or homily. It almost seemed that preaching, even great preaching, was beside the point. When I was a child I heard a traveling evangelist say something I've never forgotten: If you can get a person to Jesus, that person will be all right.

That's just what God used Earl Lee to do—bring people into the presence of God. That's the essence of celebrative worship, with or without a proper sermon.

Meta-Church and Worship Style

Meta-Church technology is transparent to worship style. Does it require you to have a seeker-sensitive service like at Willow Creek

Ginghamsburg United Methodist Church

7695 South County Road, 25-A
Tipp City, OH 45371
Phone: (513) 667-01069
FAX: (513) 667-5677
Denomination: United Methodist

Senior Pastor: Michael Slaughter
Contact: Jimmy Jones
Attendance: 1400
Total Cell Groups: 147

How to Fit a Big Vision into Small Worship Facilities

The two-room, white-clapboard country church building was constructed in 1876. Back then, the town of Tipp City, Ohio, was distinctly rural. Today this meeting place of Ginghamsburg United Methodist Church is still twenty miles from any major town—Dayton.

In 1979 when Pastor Michael Slaughter arrived, there were ninety worshipers (including children) wondering how to fill the rest of their sanctuary. By 1993 some thirteen hundred worshipers were crowding into a facility that has a recommended seating capacity of 287!

How? Pastor Slaughter has learned not to let the seating capacity of a church building limit the size of harvest God seems pleased to reap through the church. Each weekend convenes three Sunday-morning worship services and one Saturday-evening service. In addition, practically any day of the week, at all hours, evangelism and discipleship are taking place away from the church building through care groups, support groups, Stephen Ministry, worship teams, service teams, or other forms of small-group care.

"Probably the thing that has best caused ministry to go forward at Ginghamsburg Church has been our ability to exploit our facilities," says Slaughter. "Many churches today talk about maximizing the use of their facilities, but a true movement of the Holy Spirit is not dependent on buildings."

"We initially met resistance in going to additional services," says Slaughter, "because people, especially in a small church, want to maintain that feeling of comfort they've always had." Slaughter decided that the key to change involved the size of the church's vision. "We began showing people the big picture of why Jesus built his Church," says Slaughter. "As our people focused on the call of Christ, and not on their own personal preferences, they came to understand that what pleases Jesus is not necessarily comfortable, but it affects destiny."

Through multiple building use for corporate worship, and through home, store, and even warehouse use for small-group ministries, the church continues to reach a harvest without waiting on the funds or time required to construct larger facilities.

Says Slaughter, "We need to keep risking and keep going forward with a God-sized vision. We can't stop until all the lost are found, and all the oppressed are set free."

or an open-church style as in some Vineyard Fellowships? Neither. The Meta-Church works equally well in a Greek Orthodox setting, a Pentecostal setting, an incense-burning high Episcopal setting, or a Baptist setting! It doesn't ask, "What is your liturgy?" but "How do you produce it, and why do people respond the way they do?"

> Meta-Church technology is transparent to worship style.

Meta-Church thinking informs leaders how to coach and multiply worship teams, not what worship style to use. It works because it makes sense, not because certain high-visibility churches are using it!

Sometimes people mistakenly assume that if they make the transition to Meta-Church thinking, they'll need to get rid of their liturgy. That is not correct. Meta-Church technology will give them the ability to produce *more* liturgical services—as well as more nonliturgical services (if they so desire). Meta-Church organization shows a church how to have more of whatever they're now doing.

The Meta-Church paradigm, being indifferent to worship style, holds no investment in one particular style of service. An emphasis on staff-coached, lay-led small groups is not dependent on seeker services, an open church, or any other variety of worship style. Community can be formed in a small-group system regardless of worship style. Rather, Meta-Church thinking helps a church reach a larger harvest. It doesn't tamper with a denomination's theology of liturgy, emphasis on absolution, level of rationality, or level of emotion—assuming the liturgy is centered on Jesus Christ, who was declared to be the Son of God with power by the resurrection.

As John Kieshnick, senior pastor of Gloria Dei Lutheran Church of Houston says of the three worship services sponsored by his church, "Meta-Church ideas work whether it's 'high liturgy, low liturgy, or no liturgy.'"

Meta-Church thinking looks at the essence of what it takes to make a community work, and worship style is irrelevant to the social dynamics of community. How David danced in the streets of Jerusalem was relatively irrelevant (except to his soon-to-be ex-

Gateway Cathedral

200 Boscombe Avenue
Staten Island, NY 10309
Phone: (718) 966-4500
FAX: (718) 966-8577
Denomination: Nondenominational

Senior Pastor: Daniel Mercaldo
Contact: Tim Mercaldo
Attendance: 1000
Total Cell Groups: 40

Pageants That Attract Outsiders and Refresh Insiders

It's said that Christmas comes only once a year. But in 1993, at Gateway Cathedral, Staten Island, New York, it arrived with a "Christmas in August" party and went away only after eleven public performances (and countless rehearsals) of the Christmas story.

No one was glad to see the season end, however. The church has learned how to produce pageants on a scale that attracts *eight times* its average Sunday worship attendance—and can do so without its actors or support personnel having to grumble, "Never again!"

Tim Mercaldo, associate pastor for celebration arts at Gateway, has learned to be a producer of worship teams, rather than a coordinator of individual performers. Each year's "Celebrate Christmas!" pageant (and each summer's "Celebrate America!" production) involves up to 30 percent of the church's regular attenders, all in some kind of team role. Children's celebration arts clubs supply singers and dancers. Junior-high and senior-high groups do likewise on a more advanced level. A wide range of vocal groups allows room for all kinds of singers, from those professionally trained to those whose voices are not as well developed. Technical positions likewise build on a team motif, offering slots for everyone from newcomers to electronic wizards.

"The team idea has helped us discover and attract a lot of talented people," says Mercaldo. "But it's helped do something even more important: It's enabled every team member to receive nurture and emotional support. Our leaders intentionally make time for prayer and personal care on a small-group basis. Through these touches, their people have stayed spiritually refreshed, even during physically exhausting rehearsal times."

As a result, Christmas 1993 was a very joyful time around Gateway Cathedral. Those involved with the pageant delighted in being able to redeem the arts for Christ. The pastoral staff, who closed each pageant with a call for decision, rejoiced in the full house that each performance drew. The follow-up teams praised God for an enormous number of pageant visitors who have no identifiable church home, and who indicated that they would welcome further contact from Gateway. The rest of the church baked cookies for the intermissions and brought their friends to enjoy the pageant.

It looks like Christmas will come to town lots of times during 1994 as well!

Cell Visibility in the Celebration

✓ Sermons legitimize lay care
✓ Bulletin or announcements highlight cell ministry
✓ Pastoral prayer implies/includes cell-based ministry
✓ Cell leaders and/or apprentices play visible role in the celebration
✓ Other:_____

Figure 25

wife). The fact that the processional was a very exciting event is what really counted. But there would have been no Jerusalem celebration had the tribes not come up from their respective towns (see 2 Samuel 6).

Meta-Church technology contributes to the re-tribalization of Christianity in the sense of creating clans through artificial extended families. The spiritual kinship groups of the cells, and everything else can be perceived as some form of cell assembly, cell congregating, or support for cells (see figure 25).

Meta-Church thinking helps a church reach a larger harvest.

What about Multiple Services?

Here's what I see increasingly happening: Churches are figuring out ways to do their Sunday-school and adult-worship services simultaneously so that they can use their facilities in a single period of time—an hour and a half basically—to bring a group of people in, worship, educate the children, and then move them off. That way, the whole facility can be used for the next group of people.

In most cases, it's a church's site, not the pews (or chairs) and classroom space that makes the difference in how many people who are seeking the Lord can come. Your parking area determines your capacity. A church can simultaneously worship and educate only the number of people who can park in the parking lot (except, of course, urban churches and churches with atypical circumstances).

Fellowship Alliance Chapel

199 Church Road
Medford, NJ 08055
Phone: (609) 953-7333
FAX: (609) 953-7465
Denomination: Christian &
   Missionary Alliance

Senior Pastor: Martin Berglund
Contact: Dennis Episcopo, Associate Pastor
Attendance: 900
Total Cell Groups: 40

Preaching Teams Help Maintain Growth Momentum

In December 1991 Senior Pastor Marty Berglund became bedridden with what would be eventually diagnosed as the Epstein-Barr chronic fatigue syndrome. The church Berglund had planted nine years previously, Fellowship Alliance Chapel in southern New Jersey, numbered seven hundred worshipers who were accustomed to Berglund's preaching for all three services.

As the church entered 1992, it became clear that Berglund would be unable to preach regularly. So he introduced, with the elders' approval, a team idea that would eventually solidify into a four-preacher system. He and an associate pastor were the constants; the other two spots were filled with a small group of "regulars": an assistant pastor, the church business administrator, a nearby evangelist, a seminary professor from an hour away, and on occasion one of the church's elders.

To the surprise and delight of all, the attendance once more began to grow. When it hit eight hundred, the church went to a fourth service. Rather than each speaker handling an entire weekend of services, they follow a rotation system: Preacher A covers Saturday night this week, Sunday early service next week, Sunday mid-morning service the week after that, and so forth. Meanwhile, the very strong children's and youth programs maintain their continuity by keeping the same leadership personnel at the same hour each week.

By 1993 Berglund's illness, which in some instances requires several years for full recovery, still severely restricted his weekly activities. But even had the Lord healed him immediately, he was not envisioning himself as ever doing all the preaching again.

"We've had nothing but praise for our preaching teams," Berglund says. "People feel the multiple perspectives give a broader outlook on the Word of God; meanwhile my sickness has enabled me to become more focused on setting the overall vision of the church. I'm the kind of pastor, based on the gifts God has given me, who easily allows a lot of other people to minister."

Another benefit is that the church can now continue to build as many multiple services as it wants, without being limited by staff energy level. "Even without my sickness, I couldn't have done four services," says Berglund. "But with preaching teams, virtually anything is possible."

In some cases, churches have enough parking, but not a big enough auditorium. Many churches today, though, are learning to use technology so effectively that those in the back row of the video-overflow chapel can see better than those in the sanctuary on the sixth row. Similarly the sound is rich and conveys every emotion. It's as if the video observer were at the live setting. I hear pas-

> Security is not found in your personal performance, however excellent, but in producing other performers and leaders.

tors express fears that overflow services are an inferior product, but most participants would beg to differ!

The all-in-one-time-slot approach may not be necessary at present in strong Sunday-school churches, but as a church adds its third, fourth, fifth, sixth, and seventh services, they can be self-contained within a sixty to ninety minute period, without necessarily having Sunday school before and after.

Will children in those churches receive the kind of Christian education they need? The answer depends on whether the church has children's cell meetings during the week, and whether their moms and dads are in cells designed to enable parents to be good Christian educators of their children—adults who socialize and talk about their faith in cells and develop the verbal skills necessary to share their faith with their children.

Staffing the Red Zone

What, then, are the implications for the church staff that oversee celebration- and worship-arts ministries? The goal of the minister of worship (or whatever you call your key Red Zone staff) is to broaden your leadership base—to build talent. Security is not found in your personal performance, however excellent, but in producing other performers and leaders.

Remember, what you're looking for is not music in itself but the ability to guide the audience's experience during an hour, which could include music. At the same time, use an ensemble-incubator

Ensemble Incubator

Between 10% and 30% of those attending any church could be involved in some form of Celebration Arts, including children, too!

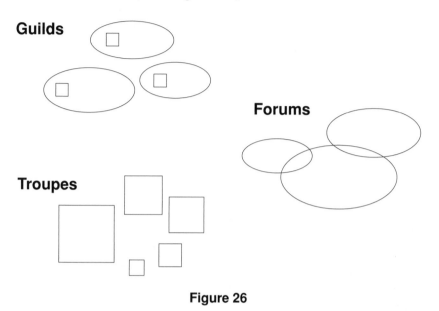

Guilds

Forums

Troupes

Figure 26

concept to expand to a full musical program. The more choirs and groups, the more people will come in many cases.

Based on the concepts described above, if staff members can visualize worship celebrations as being produced by a network of cell-group leaders, then they will be aware of the management needs required by these roles. Your perspective on what kinds of technical and performing teams are involved in producing and prompting corporate worship will shape your sense of both priority and of who needs touching.

Meta-Church infrastructure for the Red Zone is relatively uncomplicated once you envision workable forms for how to make things happen. The typical pathway for cultivating celebration-type leadership is a progression of talent development, from training to performance, that may be generically described as an *ensemble incubator* (see figure 26).

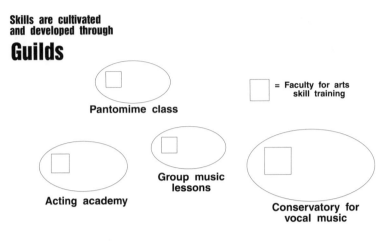

Figure 27

The components of the ensemble-incubator idea are threefold: *guilds*, where people receive training from music lessons to acting classes (see figure 27); *troupes*, which are actual performance or production teams and ensembles (see figure 28); and *forums*, which are the gatherings involving a live congregation or audience (see figure 29).

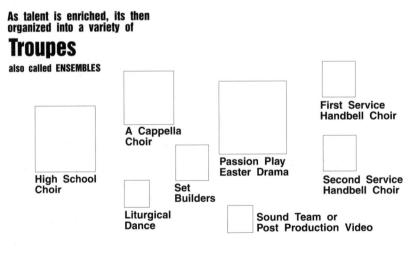

Figure 28

**These groups receive motivation
and opportunity to perform at**

Forums

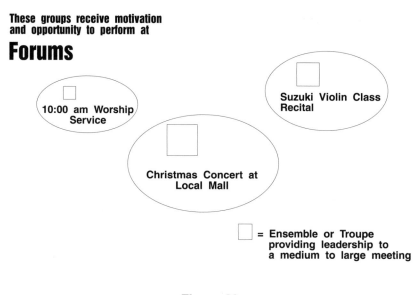

**10:00 am Worship
Service**

**Suzuki Violin Class
Recital**

**Christmas Concert at
Local Mall**

= Ensemble or Troupe
providing leadership to
a medium to large meeting

Figure 29

Be careful not to confuse the above *description* with a program-matic *prescription*. The ensemble incubator may or may not represent an actual meeting, just as, in other Meta-Globe zones of the church, the VHS may or may not be a separate meeting of the leadership community (see figure 30).

If the primary vision caster, in conjunction with the rest of the church staff, gets a mental picture of cell-produced worship services and then visits the worship-events production staff meeting, he is able to say, "Bless you!" and "What you are doing is right!" as various lay leaders shepherd their people through the ensemble-incubator process. The role of the minister of worship, then, is that of a subvision caster—the head of the tribe of Levi working alongside a Moses. He or she will offer inspiration and direction within the ensemble incubator in the same fashion that the primary vision caster (usually the senior pastor) communicates with the entire church. The minister of worship will be trying to inspire people to outdo themselves and to become a contagious and infectious force

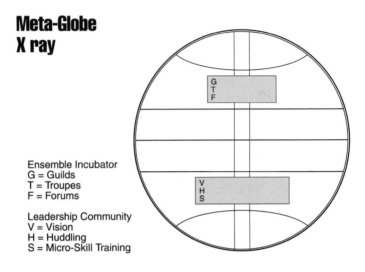

Figure 30

for worship leadership and personal growth. This idea represents a far greater agenda than being a chancel-choir organist!

Therefore, don't hire any more music directors; you can usually get volunteer artists to do that for free. Hire worship-service and pageant producers and make sure they have an impresario flair about them; that is, do they know how to create a solid, flowing sense of worship that is put together and produced by various worship teams? Your Red Zone staff, as they work to develop excess talent, will become facilitators, not bottlenecks, to kingdom growth.

What about Ministry Fatigue?

A prime source of ministerial fatigue occurs when the people of a church have greater expectations of a staff person's personal availability for them than that person can physically deliver. Regrettably, most pastors were trained, both by example and study, to engender such expectations. Most pastoral leaders and staff operate under a certain interpretation of the shepherd model: "I will personally touch the flock."

What's an alternative for the Red Zone or any other zone? Revise your estimate of what is really required of you. Ask yourself and the Lord, "Do I have a greater need to care for the flock than they have to be cared for?" "Am I working like this because they need this, or because I need it?"[1] In too many cases, the church doesn't really want the aggravation of waiting on you, of seeing you always tired, and having you always at the last 5 percent of your strength!

Faithfulness is not measured in terms of fatigue. Rather, it's determined by whether people are cared for! See to it that they're cared for by farming out some of the caring—make sure all worship production is done in a context of small groups that contain an element of nurture. The result: You won't be so tired, and you'll be able to focus your energy on developing volunteer leadership.

In a smaller church, the minister of worship may wind up both producing (the L role) and leading one or more groups (the X role)

> Faithfulness is not measured in terms of fatigue. Rather, it's determined by whether people are cared for!

If the distinction between these roles isn't clear, you will tend to see yourself as too available to lead and, therefore, you won't develop the strength of other leaders through other teams.

Where's the Lay Talent?

Any church, in any circumstance, has room to improve what God has already put in its midst. With prayer, energy, and more advance planning, any church can spruce up its worship service.

Start by making one-on-one contacts within the church to ask for help. Perhaps you've got people who know more about dramatic production than you've dreamed. They may warm a pew on Sunday, but during the week, they put on plays at the junior-high school or with the junior league. Find the two or three people in your congregation with the most zing and know-how and say, "What can we do to improve the quality of our worship experience?" Lift up the worship so it is more meaningful to the people who are coming.

Learn to listen carefully to feedback, even if it challenges your preconceptions. Sometimes the improvement of worship has more to do with child-care arrangements, wafting bathroom or kitchen odors, or fixing the microphone than it does with anything preached or sung!

Some churches will say, "We don't have enough talent." When I've looked around, I've found that there are reasons why. Music in many churches is seen as entertainment not as organization or talent development. Apply the perspectives described in this book and begin to look on each choir or other group as an organizing unit into which people can be inducted, find meaningful service, build enjoyable camaraderie and fellowship, *and* be trained, both by apprenticing and modeling, for leadership—such as when you organize another service or another choir.

I used to be the principal of the largest preschool in our county. We had two kindergarten teachers. One of them was gifted with a beautiful voice. The other was Mrs. Frog; she had a hoarse, raspy voice, was forever getting emotionally choked up, and couldn't sing at all. When it came time for show night, the hoarse, nonsinging teacher's class out performed everyone in sight because, from the very beginning, she knew she could not carry the performance. As a result, her kids shined and sparkled. The woman who knew how to sing well and loved to sing did a great job, but unfortunately it came across as a solo. Her voice dominated while her kids mumbled along behind her.

If both ladies were music directors, many churches would bypass Mrs. Frog and hire Mrs. Nightingale in a minute. If they did, however, they'd weaken their whole program because all they'd get out of her would be songs and song directing. They would get her ability and passion for personal production but not the capacity to produce worship services.

As management author Stephen Covey emphasizes, there is a pivotal difference between production and production *capacity*. An organization that focuses on production maximizes itself fairly quickly, but the organization that diverts some of its attention to increasing production *capacity* has the ability to produce far more. That's why we emphasize things like making sure all of your groups are led by leaders who are cultivating an apprentice because that's increasing your church's production capability: You're doubling your leadership capability.

> The role of Red Zone leadership will become that of preparing worship leaders, rather than of simply leading worship.

Churches of the future will give the ministers of worship [Ds], and the various coaches [Ls] and group leaders [Xs] who serve in the Red Zone a much wider franchise and assignment than that of preparing worship services. Increasingly, the local church will be seen as the place where the talent capable of leading the worship services is developed. The role of Red Zone leadership will become that of preparing worship leaders, rather than of simply leading worship. And when leadership development and worship ensembles are paired together, a church can provoke celebrative worship in ways beyond your wildest imagination.

Questions for Discussion and Application

1. According to this chapter, what makes worship celebrative? Why is that important? How do cells contribute to celebrative corporate worship?

2. List five advantages to the idea that a minister of worship's goal (or whatever you call your key Red Zone staff) is to broaden your leadership base—to build talent.

3. What can you do next to transform your corporate worship celebrations into a cell-produced convention of cells?

10

Strategic Uses of Church-Planting Teams, Cross-Cultural Missions, and Auxiliary Activities: Orange Zone

> The leadership development needs for Orange Zone
> groups are often not unique; the Orange Zone is a place
> to apply principles from the other zones.

Meta-Church observations are a tool for helping leaders think through certain relationships that could be developed further in the churches they serve. The Meta-Church offers a new way of perceiving the task these leaders face.

One starting point is to make all meetings visual. That's where the Meta-Globe comes in: Through appropriately visualized data, the Meta-Globe helps pastors and staff look at how their churches are configured. As a result they can better determine what needs to happen next in the life of the church.

Meta-Globe concepts, field-tested over about five years in several hundred churches before being released in *Prepare Your Church for the Future,* are designed to offer a simple, coherent model applicable to virtually any church. The last of the zones to be developed in that schema was the Orange Zone. The Orange Zone has therefore "migrated" in its purposes more than any other zone.

The Orange Zone is where ministries are placed that cannot be easily classified in the other color zones. That is, if an activity doesn't seem to contribute to the membership enlargement of the particular local church, it goes into the Orange Zone. Hence the Orange Zone received the nickname, "the miscellaneous zone."

Applying this principle of noncontribution-to-membership-enlargement means the following for most North American churches:

- A *hosted congregation,* such as a Korean-language congregation that uses the buildings of an all-English-speaking church, is Orange Zone. Why? With separate membership rosters, one group's attendance has no influence on the other. (A "language" Sunday-school class or congregation considered part of the parent church's membership would be Yellow Zone, however.)

- A *new-church development,* especially the hive-off variety, might come from the Yellow Zone (as the "womb") but would be moved to the Orange Zone as soon as it was declared to be the launching point for a new congregation.

- *Direct missions involvement,* such as sending a twenty-five-person team of teenagers to build missionary houses in the Amazon Basin, is significant to the parent church in terms of visibility but doesn't do much for the growth (membership enlargement) of the local church. Therefore, this too is classified as Orange Zone.

- *Missions education,* as a through-the-year activity, also fits the Orange Zone, as do *missions board activities* in most cases. If a missions group is primarily focused on finance, it goes into the Purple Zone, though colored orange.

  Similarly, some smaller churches conduct much of their missions work through committees that relate to denominational agencies; while the Orange Zone is a legitimate location for such committees, they often gravitate toward the Purple Zone, though maintaining their orange color.

Church of the Apostles

3500 Pickett Road
Fairfax, VA 22031
Phone: (703) 591-1974
FAX: (703) 591-1983
Denomination:
 Episcopal Church

Senior Pastor: David R. Harper
Contact: Richard Gomer,
 Associate Rector for Pastoral Care
Attendance: 850
Total Cell Groups: 50

Not One, but Many "Missionary Committees"

Many pillars that once helped support the missionary enterprise have become weakened in recent decades. Denominational loyalty, for example, is slowly vanishing; people of the 90s tend to support foreign missions not as a duty but because they've had hands-on experience with a missionary or at a cross-cultural mission site. As a result of such changes, many churches are looking for new models of how yesteryear's passion and involvement can be instilled in parishes of today.

At Church of the Apostles, located just west of Washington, D.C., the majority of the church's missionary endeavors, from spending the church missions budget to sending out short-term missionaries, has been decentralized to a number of groups, each of which focuses on a different geographic region of the world.

"These people do 95 percent of the actual work—setting up overseas contacts, communicating with the congregation, and recruiting new group members," says Richard Gomer, an associate rector. During 1993 there were five such committees, called outreach groups. One, led by a former state department diplomat, focuses on Latin America. Other territories are the Middle East, Africa, and Europe. Yet another targets northern Virginia and works with local missions in ministries such as offering meals to the poor through local motels.

"There are lots of advantages to being so decentralized," says Kelly Kahler, staff contact for what is known as the Mission Commission. "These groups know how to elicit more participation than the church office can! They tap into the gifts, backgrounds, and experiences of those in the group, so that they do everything from writing articles in the church newsletter to convening a potluck supper at the church building where they show slides from a recent mission and generate new interest. People will often join an outreach group as a result of hearing about one of the missions."

"During the course of a year, about one hundred fifty church people are involved with one of the groups or its activities," says Herb Pearce, who chairs the church's outreach program. "It's worked well. The people here all feel empowered; they feel an ownership in what we're doing with missions."

- *Denominational linkages,* such as a delegation to a denominational convention, are labeled as Orange Zone if the group is relatively separate from the church's governing body. In churches with a more connectional church structure, such as a Presbyterian church where denominational participation typically occurs through the presbytery, denominational activities are placed in the Purple Zone, though colored orange.

- *Community services* are assigned to the Orange Zone if they use church facilities, *and* if they have business connections to the church's budget or office, *and* if they are not calculated to enlarge the host church's membership. Most of these groups can be identified with "presence" or "service" mission: bookstores, elementary schools, retirement homes, adult day care coordinated through community agencies, Alcoholics Anonymous meetings that do not involve any church members, youth hostels, homeless shelters, pregnancy crisis clinics, kitchen usage by Meals on Wheels, and the like.

  Preschools are also Orange Zone unless they have a clear purpose of drawing young nesting-stage families into the church; in that case, the school can be placed in the Yellow Zone.

- *Beyond-your-constituency services* also fit into the Orange Zone when they reach beyond the constituency of the sponsoring church. For example, many church-based adult Bible institutes offer classes that cater to a totally churched clientele: committed Christians from the host church *and* from other churches outside the local church constituency. Similarly, Orange Zone radio and television ministries usually seek to give spiritual food to people in other parts of a city—or other cities. (If the media ministry broadcasts locally, and effectively draws new people to the church, then the ministry is functioning as a Yellow Zone outreach but is retained in the Orange Zone because of the donor and financial management associated with such ministries. The visual object depicting a broadcast ministry is sized according to the teams involved with the actual production and follow-up, not according to the listening audience.)

Community Church of Joy

P.O. Box 6030
Glendale, AZ 85312
Phone: (602) 938-1460
FAX: (602) 938-9210
Denomination: Evangelical
    Lutheran Church in America

Senior Pastor: Walter Kallestad
Contact: Tom Eggum
Attendance: 2600
Total Cell Groups: 100

Using Groups and Giftedness (Not Guilt) to Motivate Missions

Many churches think cross-cultural missions are best handled through a national office. Their attitude is, "Let's contribute our moneys to the denomination, and let them handle the ministry of missionary work."

Such is not the case for Community Church of Joy in greater Phoenix, Arizona. "Missions involvement starts here. We get our own people directly involved in outreach and mission opportunities," says Tom Eggum, director of outreach and missions since 1984.

"One of my goals is to develop a church-wide awareness of the outreach that we ourselves are gifted to do either across the street or across the sea," he says. Eggum, with support from senior pastor Walt Kallestad and the rest of the pastoral staff, has focused his challenge on the church's cell groups and cell leaders.

As a result, a number of other already-existing groups have begun to include a greater missions emphasis in their regular group life. For example, an intercessory prayer group that had been covering Asian countries for several years decided to take a short-term mission trip to Korea, Hong Kong, and Vietnam. In addition, many nurture-type small groups have added community mission projects to their group activities.

Several specially formed short-term mission teams from Community Church of Joy have traveled to Russia, Central America, and South America. In preparation for its overseas service, each team met on a regular basis to support and encourage one another.

Also, local outreach mission teams regularly minister at places like Life Station, an on-premises food and clothing distribution center. Others go into south Phoenix on a regular basis for ministry to homeless people. "Some of our people are particularly gifted in ministering to those who are less fortunate than we are," says Eggum.

Who keeps this momentum building? One key is the Mission Commission—a leadership team that regularly meets to develop outreach and mission ministries, as well as to nurture and support one another. "We work very hard to communicate to people that their motivation in being involved in outreach or missions activities can come from a desire to share out of grace and giftedness, not out of guilt," says Eggum. "We look for people who have a heart for missions first. Then we help them develop the 'how' of what they will do to serve."

"Orange Zone" Is *Not* a Negative Label

The Orange Zone, then, can be defined as any meetings or activities that don't directly contribute to the growth of the sponsoring local church. The possible Orange Zone member groups, though numerous and diverse, are fairly easy and clear-cut to peg: any ministry that may build the kingdom of God overall but is not targeted to enlargement of the sponsoring church's membership.

In some ways, then, the Orange Zone is a "catchall" domain. If a group is not governance related (Purple Zone), worship-celebration related (Red), fishing-pool related (Yellow), or cell-group related (Green and Blue), then it probably belongs in the Orange Zone.

There was a time, when I was still experimenting, that I recommended "pejorative" assignments to the Orange Zone: Any group that was not open to newcomers got listed as Orange Zone. Or if a group, such as a Sunday-school class, was designed to help with a church's growth but was in fact not doing so, then it could be shunted over to the Orange Zone, studied, sorted out, repaired, and then when blockages were removed, returned to the Yellow Zone, Green Zone, or other zone, as appropriate. In short, if a caregiving structure didn't seem to have apparent outreach operations, a church could say, "We can't see how you help us bring in and care for new members, and therefore you go to the Orange Zone."

This pejorative-assignment approach has turned out to be more complicated than useful. Instead, through diagramming numerous churches in recent years, far greater benefit emerged through placing cells in their natural zone on a "good intentions" basis. Thus a Bible class, even if closed to newcomers, would be Green Zone if it had sixteen or fewer people, Yellow Zone if seventeen or more people, or Purple Zone if restricted to elected leaders only. So, in recent years, the Orange Zone has increasingly been emptied of all negative connotations. The net result is that the Orange Zone is less complicated and has no stigmas attached to it.

In addition, a new concept has emerged: If a church can visualize how a class or meeting *could* be used as a fishing pool, outreach tool, mezzanine, or care unit, then allow it to be placed in the color zone representing its intention—where you'd like it to be—not the color zone of its track record. Thus, whenever a choice becomes

New Song Community Church

Office: 4065 Oceanside Blvd, Suite T
Oceanside, CA 92056
Meeting site: Breeze Hill
  Elementary School
Phone: (619) 940-1500
FAX: (619) 940-8144

Denomination: Conservative
  Baptist Association
Senior Pastor: Hal Seed
Contact: Scott Evans
Attendance: 300
Total Cell Groups: 30

Church Planting with Meta-Church Tools

"Our ability to respond to the great needs in our church and community is limited only by our number of available care givers," says Hal Seed, describing the church he launched in September, 1992—New Song Community Church, Oceanside, California.

"I was first motivated to consider church planting when I heard about the Meta-Church," explains Seed. "I was on staff in a traditional church where decisions-by-committee and disciple-making-through-Sunday-school were the norm. The problem was, church members weren't experiencing life change as described in the New Testament, and unchurched people weren't being attracted." Thus Seed and his wife were drawn to the Meta-Church vision of a church fueled by teams, relationships, and a high conversion rate.

From day one of the new church, Seed used the Meta-Globe (see chapters 7 and 14) as a reference map in designing and evaluating the young church's people flow and ministry systems. "Because we could literally see the big picture through our visualizations of the Meta-Globe," he says, "our leaders could understand the need for corporate worship, for small-group care, and for fishing ponds as the means by which we funnel people into caring relationships."

"We measure all our plans against their place on the Meta-Globe, and as a result have moved forward with balance," says Seed. For example, as the church got started, Seed recruited some "mature brothers" from other churches in his denomination to serve as an advisory board (Purple Zone). A paid programming director coordinates the northern hemisphere, such as the programming team (Red Zone); the associate pastor oversees both the equatorial zone (Yellow Zone) and the small groups of the southern hemisphere (Green Zone); and Seed recruited a local counselor to handle the church's care net and counseling needs (Blue Zone).

The fruit, at the church's one-year anniversary mark, included ninety people who have confessed Christ as Lord, eight care groups called Friendship Groups, eleven task teams, and a worship attendance of 270. Even more exciting are the prospects for the future: "Virtually all our growth has come from unchurched people," says Seed.

"This church-planting experience," Seed says, "has shown me why Jesus never asked his disciples to pray for a harvest, but rather for harvest-workers to go into the field (Matthew 9:37)."

available between two zones, the "non-orange" option is usually chosen. An adult Bible school is assigned as Yellow Zone because it *might* bridge to a whole community and *might* be positioned to have an outreach and intake function and *might* become a fishing pond for recruiting members of cells. Only if that school is for training believers and members would it remain, by definition, Orange Zone.

The "quick summary" of the Orange Zone's population is this: new-church development, missions, and other auxiliary ministries—with no disparaging implications!

Systems-Thinking Applied to the Orange Zone

How, then, does one determine and address the leadership-development needs for an Orange Zone meeting? Here are some questions to ask:

- *Can the D-L-X formula be applied?* At first glance, it may seem that the D-L-X structure won't work for the management of radio, television, or bookstore ministries. Many churches, however, are now organizing volunteers into teams to produce and manage these areas. Similarly, the D-L-X approach can be helpful to most mission activity, such as the raising up of short-term teams to assist missionaries overseas and to work in service ministries, such as the staffing of a crisis-pregnancy hotline or clinic.

- *Are spans of care kept manageable?* Leaders of everything from political-action groups to denominational liaison committees can burn out if they spread themselves too thin by trying to keep up with too many workers.

- *Are apprentice leaders being trained?* Suppose a church-sponsored day-care program has been classified as Orange Zone. Are future leaders being raised through apprenticeship roles? The same question could be asked of an Orange Zone adult Bible institute or a church-planting project.

- *Are relationships nurtured?* Whether it's a team heading an adopt-a-people awareness program or the volunteer staff of an in-house church library, are the people involved making time to nurture and care for one another?

- *Could a stronger caregiving or evangelistic bias be built into the ministry?* Chapter 16 will explore the larger questions of: Could this ministry be repurposed? Should it continue? and How important is it to the overall vision and mission of the church? On a much simpler scale, perhaps only slight tweaking will empower the ministry to more directly contribute to processing people through cells.

   Perhaps, for example, an Orange Zone day school could be "yellowed" by creating a fishing-pond effect at the parent-teacher level. Perhaps the litter-cleanup task force could erect a sign that invites the community to this wonderful, civic-minded church! Perhaps the council on racial harmony could do more than build awareness in the church; maybe it could design events that would draw new people, of whatever ethnicity, into the groups of the church.

In short, the leadership-development needs for Orange Zone groups are often not unique; the Orange Zone is the place to apply principles from the other zones. In many cases all that differs from other zones is the specific assignment or mission that Orange Zone groups are seeking to accomplish.

Special Comments on Foreign Missions and Church Planting

Donald McGavran and Win Arn's thesis that the planting of new churches involves the most effective tools for reaching the unreached,[1] illustrates one of the many powerful effects of creating new social units.

Their statement can be demonstrated both historically and across the globe. For example, every denomination that has risen to the forefront of North American Christendom, including Methodist and Southern Baptist, has been involved in a church-planting movement.[2] Yesteryear's leaders of great churches, from Charles Spurgeon[3] to Dallas Billington,[4] established a host of mission churches, both in their respective cities and around the world.

Further, according to large-church researcher John Vaughan, "Many of the world's largest churches are specialists at church planting. More than half of the twenty largest congregations in the world have an army of satellite groups."[5]

More recent developments in North America are no exception. Rick Warren's Saddleback Valley Community Church, Mission Viejo, California, started sixteen daughter churches during its first eleven years. One of Canada's largest churches, First Alliance Church in Calgary, Alberta, has parented or grandparented ten new churches since 1965. Many present-day large churches have produced a host of offspring churches. Among the parent churches are Thomas Road Baptist Church in Lynchburg, Virginia (Jerry Falwell); Calvary Chapel, Santa Ana, California (Chuck Smith); Vineyard Christian Fellowship, Anaheim, California (John Wimber

> No single church can reach everybody. Therefore a need exists to multiply the number of available units.

and Kenn Gullikson); and Church on the Rock North America, Dallas, Texas (Larry Lea).

Meta-Church thinking puts a high priority on the multiplication of small units led by people with a passion to serve human need. That focus easily translates into new-church units under a number of circumstances:

- If a ministry becomes centered more than five miles beyond the church's meeting site (in urban areas, closer than that)

- If a ministry takes on a personality different from that of the people leading the current church

- If a ministry constantly develops new volunteer leaders and encourages them to take responsibility for an evangelistic harvest

- If a ministry reaches a group of people who could not readily join with the parent church due to differences in language or culture.

The Meta-Church's greatest contribution to church planting (and to all other strategy areas) is a perceptual one: What light does systems-thinking bring to the role of new churches in the larger task of expanding the Christian movement? The answer is that the human species is made up of a wide variety of language and cultural streams, social and economic stratifications, geographical boundaries, and political movements. No single church can reach everybody. Therefore a need exists to multiply the number of available units in order to handle the large number of people groups and communities within a general population.

Meta-Church observations, when applied to the church-planting enterprise, often give impetus to the starting of new units. They also do something else: They offer a viable pathway for breaking the 100-person attendance norm that many new churches struggle to overcome.

The secret to the expansion of Christianity as a movement is to deploy more laborers. The key is not only new congregations but new units. It's a harvester-based approach. The more units, the more harvesters who can be effective. The best way, then, to prepare for a greater harvest is to prepare more care leaders.

A small unit is able to exploit a niche; a large unit depends on a large number of smaller units contributing to its mass. The secret of overall growth is to deploy more leader-led units, of the kind of talent available in greatest number [Xs], and to place those units within easy reach of a susceptible population. One of the many advantages of a church plant is that it can often be near a possibly responsive population. This strategy will typically reach more

> The secret to the expansion of Christianity is
> to deploy more laborers. It's a harvester-based approach.

people than the alternative approach of presuming the presence of one large target segment or one rare leader who can singlehandedly attract and carry large numbers of persons.

In addition, sometimes a church reaches out to a people with little expectation that they'll join the parent church. Suppose, for example, a group in your church shows the love of Christ to your neighborhood through social-service activities like cleaning the bathroom of the local gas station, managed by a person from India, and nobody at your church speaks Gujarati. Or perhaps you have a group that travels to an inner-city area and sponsors after-school reading classes. In both cases you'll probably have to create or find a new congregation (indigenous satellite unit or new mission church) to meet the spiritual needs of these people.

An existing church has two inherent limitations to reaching its community: (1) Its already-defined "personality" characteristics open a door to only a segment of the total potential market, and (2) its existing location determines the distance from which it can draw people. Both of these limitations can be overcome by the planting of new churches; each church planter will develop a church with a different personality in a different location. For an existing church not to plant additional churches will probably leave much territory unpenetrated and unharvested.

The birthing of new churches is similar to the expansion of McDonald's franchises. When Ray Kroc's hamburger chain began its expansion in the early 1960s, one McDonald's per 500,000 people was all the market could handle. Later on, the public showed a readiness for 1 per 100,000 people, then 1 per 50,000, and eventually 1 per 25,000.

What made that difference? Positive experiences with fast-food restaurants in general led to a popularity and rise in the industry, which led to a higher demand for McDonald's products. As market

> If an existing church does not plant additional churches, it will probably leave much territory unpenetrated and unharvested.

openness increased, McDonald's kept increasing its market share by continuing to plant its franchise units in smaller and smaller population segments.

That's what the Christian church does as the Holy Spirit opens new harvest fields. What counts is the susceptible harvest. The elements of servicing that harvest are geographic (location), incarnational (touch and availability), and personality-based (magnetism between a particular population segment and the church's leadership). New churches that emphasize multiplying their number of lay-led cells should employ all three harvest elements with a susceptible target population.

Market Segmentation Demographics

Sometimes, before a church can launch a new church development or service unit, it must first become aware of those groups who live within the target area but are beyond the normal scope of current reach. In order to identify these segments of the population, the church group will need special training or assistance in market segmentation demographics.[6]

This kind of analysis can be obtained from several groups or books that specialize in this area of marketing. The steps for such a process are summarized in the accompanying chart. After doing that basic analysis, you will be better prepared to develop a specific strategy for the new mission church.[7]

Steps in Analyzing a Target Community's Marketing Segmentation Demographics

1. **Prayerfully understand what you're trying to accomplish.**

   "Market segmentation is the process of classifying the population into groups with different needs, characteristics, or behaviors that will affect their reaction to a religious program or ministry offered to them."

   Conceptualize the kinds of ministry you think you could offer and the types of people who would respond best.

2. **Prayerfully determine what core information you need and how you'll use it.**

   You could study dozens of different variables in how a population is divided—age, gender, household size,

---

marital status, presence and age of children, family life cycle, racial- or ethnic-group identity, social class, personal felt needs, use of free time, worship attendance at local church sites, predicted demographic changes over the next few years, and many more. *If you don't know what you want, you may find yourself incapacitated by an overwhelming sea of interesting facts.*

Information sources include public libraries in the target community, regional collections of census information,[8] U.S. government publications and statistics, almanacs, magazines, local elected officials, and private vendors (who sell both information and tailored analysis).[9]

3. **Prayerfully identify those groups God is calling you to reach and strategize how you'll reach them.**

"Target marketing is the process of selecting one or more of these segments to focus on and developing ministries and marketing plans to meet the unique needs and interests of each chosen segment."

4. **Prayerfully show how what your new church will offer is better or different from other existing ministries.**

"Positioning is the art of developing and communicating meaningful differences between one's offer and those of other organizations serving the same target market."

The three quotes are from: Shawchuck, Kotler, Wrenn, and Rath, *Marketing for Congregations: Choosing to Serve People More Effectively* (Nashville: Abingdon, 1992), 167.

Next Steps for Your Orange Zone

The category of the Orange Zone is an immensely helpful one because it enables leaders to ask, How do these ministries relate to the growth and health of the sponsoring local church as well as the overall kingdom of God? The wide population of this zone is very purposeful; it invites examination and experimentation. It can often raise more questions than it can answer, as though waiting to see what church leaders will do with Orange Zone activities and where they'll take them.

Here's the Meta-Church foundation: Any church that's preparing for the future must become good at convening people into groups. Such a church has to know how to leverage clergy productivity through volunteer leadership development. It must focus on the central question: What kind of volunteer leaders are we producing?

If we follow Meta-Church thinking very far, we learn that virtually all the ministry work of the church is done through groups and teams—a basic work unit of five to fifteen people. Thus the more individuals you commission to group leadership, the wider the range of people you wind up ministering to.

Since there will probably always be mysteries and new insights of the Holy Spirit's working for your church to fathom, the Orange Zone can be a helpful tool through which to bless the formation of additional types of new groups and then to partner with God in coaching the groups' multiplication potential from there.

> Here's the Meta-Church foundation:
> Any church that's preparing for the future
> must become good at convening people into groups.

Questions for Discussion and Application

1. Why does the Orange Zone exist? How is it helpful to a church?

2. What ministries in your church would be classified as Orange Zone? Why? Are you surprised to find so few—or so many?

3. What Orange Zone activities are you involved with? How could those groups contribute more intentionally to the growth of the cells in your church—or in cases of new-church developments, to the growth of cells in other churches?

11

Strategic Uses
of Middle-Size Groups:
Yellow Zone

> When Christians genuinely reach out, target and build
> bridges of affection and love to other people, and offer a
> social context in which newcomers can be accepted and
> assimilated, a church can't help but be evangelistically
> effective.

The greatest benefit of the Yellow Zone is that it can help "massage" a movement of ready individuals toward and into a church. This concept is called *people flow*. It occurs when a selected segment of a population moves from unawareness to increasing awareness as it comes to see participation in a particular church as a possible resource in the quest for solutions to life's problems.

In recent history, middle-size groups (congregations) have often served as an initial point of contact for people flow. Thus many churches would say that meetings similar to those in the following chart are their primary tool for building bridges toward the *outside* community, and for promoting acquaintance making and general fellowship *within* the church community. In analyzing such meetings according to size (celebration, congregation, or cell), such groups tend to be 25 to 175 people, which best fits the middle-size category.

Typical Congregation-Size, Yellow Zone Groups

1. An outreach-minded women's seminar on "How to Build a Strong Marriage."
2. A community-service seminar, "Understanding the Needs of Your Aging Parents" that exposes participants to the host church as a source of help.
3. A church-sponsored nursery school designed to draw new families into a church.
4. A large adult Sunday-school class (sometimes called an adult Bible fellowship) that invites newcomers from the community.
5. A church's youth group that regularly attracts unchurched teens.
6. A "resurrection breakfast" to which church people bring their neighbors to hear the personal witness of a well-known Christian athlete.

Thus congregation-size groups can be of great benefit to a church. They are generally best at:

- Bridging: Offering a nonthreatening link between the outside community and the church, both for transfers and for non-Christians.

- Fellowship: Providing a forum for the fellowship of those who already know each other.

- Mezzanine: Creating a launch point for new-member classes and for awareness of ministry opportunities in larger meetings and smaller groups.

- Fishing Pool: Functioning as a cell reference bureau—a forum in which small-group leaders can fish for prospective members.

Must a church fill its Yellow Zone? No. If the cell as a nurturing and caring place becomes increasingly significant, then the role of the middle-size group will be challenged. A healthily functioning cell is able to deliver people all the way to the place of worship without the intermediate step of casual fellowship's being essential. According to Meta-Church organization, then, the celebration and cell are foundational, while the congregation is optional.[1]

According to Meta-Church organization, the celebration and cell are foundational, while the congregation is optional.

Leadership Present in Congregation-Size Groups

In Jethro II terms, the leader of a congregation-size group is the Roman numeral C—someone who can facilitate a crowd of approximately one hundred people. Various people who use the Jethro II jargon have suggested that C could also stand for: centurion, congregation, or clergy-like. Jim Dethmer calls Cs catalytic, charismatic, crowd-drawing people.

Why such terms? Those who head congregation-size groups tend to have a strength of personality and enough star quality that they can convene and hold the attention of a large group. They tend to feel comfortable in the spotlight and they enjoy the entertainment and attraction role that is necessary to keep people interested. Consequently many Cs perceive little need to delegate ministry or to coach others in ministry.

This center-stage performance of the C leader doesn't mean, however, that small groups and other lay leadership are absent from the Yellow Zone. Sometimes, for example, small groups are intentionally connected with a Yellow Zone meeting. Figure 31 shows the role of small groups in congregation-size events.

Many times a C works with a leadership team, as figure 32 represents. A large Sunday-school class may be run by a cadre of officers. A women's seminar may have an executive committee or council that does the planning. A church that offers regular high-visibility evangelistic events may have a different planning team for each, or one team of high-energy people who dream up new outreach ideas, "sell" them to existing groups within the church, and move on to dream other dreams.

Yellow Zone Events Usually Involve Small Groups

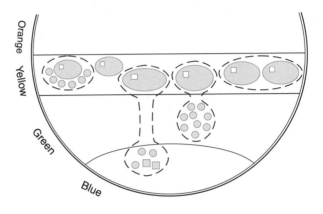

Figure 31

Two Types of Yellow Zone Leaders

In the typical congregation-size group, the kind of people who rise to the top and become leaders or officers tend to be consensus oriented. Another group of individuals, far more entrepreneurial in nature and far more impatient with process, tend to accept assignments only if such assignments are short-term and targeted in terms of accomplishments they can quickly see. These leaders can achieve the results they want, get out of the activity, and not have to maintain it.

In the typical church the consensus-style leaders gain more of a hearing: They're present at church activities more often, and they hang around whether required to or not. By contrast, the entrepreneurial person becomes discouraged with the slow machinery of board process but would probably do the work if given a short-term assignment.

If a church staff is open to this entrepreneurial style, the church can gather much momentum and new life by allowing these short-term bursts of energy. Catalytic volunteer leaders are simply not going to wait in line for an assignment to be handed to them! They can be challenged, or if they approach church staff to ask permis-

Vineyard Community Church

P.O. Box 46562
Cincinnati, OH 45246
Phone: (513) 671-0422
FAX: (513) 671-2041
Denomination: Vineyard

Senior Pastor: Steve Sjogren
Contact: Randy Emelo
Attendance: 2800
Total Cell Groups: 120

Building Bridges from Church to Community

The Friday-evening traffic in Cincinnati, its worst of the summer, backed up cars for a mile from the intersection where Vineyard Community Church's building is located. In ninety-degree heat, church people went into quick action. They iced down four hundred soft drinks, and posted signs along the road: "Free Drinks Ahead." As cars came to the stop sign, members of the Vineyard team asked, "Would you prefer diet or regular?"

"Diet or regular what?" came the skeptical reply.

"We're giving away free sodas to show people God's love in a simple and practical way."

Some motorists smiled, and some shook their heads in disbelief. But lots of people took the soda, and thought hard about the church.

In less than an hour, the church team had given away every soda, and received positive coverage on a local radio station.

The philosophy behind this event is what founding pastor Steve Sjogren calls servant evangelism. "If we can lighten some of the pain people are going through, and serve our way into their hearts, maybe we can get their attention," he explains.

These servant-evangelism points of contact are not an end in themselves. The pastoral staff invests an equal amount of energy in creating an affinity-based network of small groups, so that those who are drawn into the church family will feel at home and begin growing in Christ as soon as possible.

Ministry themes and activities tap into a wide variety of interests, from pool playing and motorcycle riding to Bible studies and prayer groups. Almost half the adults in the church are actively involved in one of about thirty different affinity-based groups.

The Vineyard Church pastored by Sjogren typically launches some one hundred creative outreaches each year, touching about 100,000 people annually at present.* Worship attendance has grown in eight years from thirty-five people to 2800, with six weekend services. During that same time, the church has planted six other Vineyard Fellowships in the Cincinnati area.

*For a list of more than one hundred "Servant Evangelism Projects that Work," see the appendix by that same title in Steve Sjogren, *Conspiracy of Kindness* (Ann Arbor: Servant, 1993), 211–26.

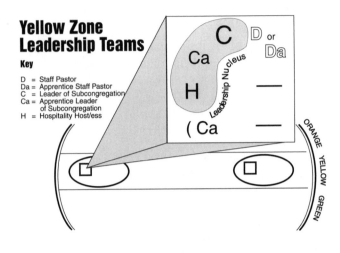

Figure 32

sion, they must be responded to in a very short period of time lest the window of willingness pass and another opportunity for capitalizing on people's availability is lost.

When commissioning leaders, one size does not fit all, especially for the leadership of congregation-size groups. Some leaders work best through committees, and others through assignments. Both modes are legitimate, and both can feed the church with new opportunities and prospects. A wise pastoral leadership will learn to capitalize on *all* the gifts God sends to that church.

Affinity Discovery as an Important Part of Yellow Zone Events

When linking people together, it's important to respect the amount of affinity they sense for one another. Any group is far more likely to be healthy, happy, and durable if the people in it have had a say in who they want to get to know. This sense of chemistry is quickly apparent to most individuals. After just a few minutes of conversation together, people will quickly decide whether or not they're willing to generate the energy necessary for

Valley Christian Church

6700 160th Street W.
Rosemount, MN 55068-1901
Phone: (612) 431-5858
FAX: (612) 431-5453
Denomination: Christian Church

Senior Minister: Jim Conner
Contact: Jim Conner
Attendance: 350
Total Cell Groups: 11

Out of Sunday School Room Doesn't Mean Out of Answers

The traditional system for adult Sunday school at Valley Christian Church, Rosemond, Minnesota has worked fairly well for most of the church's thirteen-year history. By 1990 it involved about 115 men, women, and children grouped into three large classes.

Unfortunately, the size of the church's facility had begun to restrict the number of additional people who could attend. For that and other reasons, adult Sunday school had not grown for three years straight, while worship attendance and membership had increased by 15 percent annually.

"During this time I had been learning a lot about the benefits of developing smaller-size home groups," says Jim Conner, senior minister. "I knew they were God's answer to the future needs of the church, especially since the kind of people we were reaching tended to be resistant to the idea of attending two events on Sunday mornings, such as both worship and Sunday school. Their church background hadn't given them an appreciation for that tradition."

Conner, working with other church leaders, discussed the problem at length and came up with a proposed repurposing of the Sunday-school ministry. Adult education would be shifted to Wednesday evenings, and a small-group ministry that met in homes would be launched.

Adults could elect to participate in one or both. "If you preferred a more cognitive approach to discipleship, you could choose the Wednesday-night class option; if you preferred a more relational approach, you could join a small group," Conner says.

The idea, introduced on a one-year trial basis, went so well that only minimal lobbying arose for returning to the original setup. "As we began the changeover," explains Conner, "the miracle I prayed for was that we wouldn't lose too many people. Instead, the satisfaction rate went far beyond what I had dared to dream."

The combined participation now far exceeds 1990's tally of 100 people in all classes. Instead, the Wednesday night count jumped immediately to about 150, and had inched upward to 165 by the latter half of 1993. The small-group ministry went from zero to approximately 110 people in ten groups during those same three years.

Says Conner, "The worship service is still the main first exposure for newcomers, but our groups, especially the home cells, have considerably improved our assimilation rate for those visitors."

future development of a relationship. Give four or five people a chance to interact together, and each will have little trouble lining up who he or she is most excited about seeing again. This characteristic is simply a quality of human nature.

You may be able to estimate what kinds of persons will connect with each other, but with adults, you are wisest to avoid assigning one person to another. When you let them sort out who they would like to hang around with, you allow them to make their own affinity declarations. For example, the notion of "life stages" tells you that if you give two or three young nursing mothers an opportunity to be together versus being with other adults (and it won't take you long to figure out who the nursing mothers are), you will find that they would rather congregate and talk about the issues that are preoccupying their lives at that point in time. Thus since you want to facilitate a foundation on which mutual caring will occur, you need to let these moms choose those potential friendships. People come to church for many reasons, but they stay if they find a friend. Be constantly concerned about how to bring people into intimacy so they don't get lost or feel left out in the process.

Certain techniques, popularized and systematized by Lyman Coleman, director of Serendipity House Publishers,[2] are generically called acquaintance-making exercises. I explain and illustrate them further in *Prepare Your Church for the Future*,[3] but the basic idea is this: If you put three or four people toe-to-toe, and give them a simple "safe" or minimally self-disclosing assignment, each person, in

> People come to church for many reasons,
> but they stay if they find a friend.

just a few minutes, will come to a decision ranging from "I would like to get to know this person better" to "Let me out of here!"

If you were to place in that foursome somebody who had the responsibility of recruiting people into a small-group setting, you would significantly facilitate the acquaintance-making process. If you form and dissolve several of these groups over several weeks' time, you're setting up a high probability that many workable matches will surface.

In many church contexts, people do not know how to get acquainted with each other without assistance. It's a learned skill, and Yellow Zone activities can not only legitimize it, but they can also serve as fishing pools for recruiting and referring people into smaller groups.

Cautions for the Church Staff

As the number of congregation-size groups increases, church staff keep from suffocating by:

- Not leading the C-size groups themselves. If they are currently leading one or more C-size groups, they identify Ca's (apprentices), and pass the baton so that volunteer leaders can have the privilege of leading these groups.

- Working with other C leaders to produce lay-led groups that in turn can create more C-size events—if indeed the church needs more C-size events. As with all other leadership roles, apprentice leaders significantly speed up the process.

- Meeting with C leaders to coordinate Yellow Zone personnel issues, budgets, and facilities-usage permissions.

- Communicating a constant churchwide vision that says, "The way you integrate into the fellowship here and keep from feeling like a stranger, is that you find relationships and care within the context of small groups."

Summary of Training Themes for Yellow Zone Leaders

- Distinguishing Cs from Xs. As I explained in chapter 3, it usually doesn't work for leaders of larger meetings [Cs] to supervise cell leaders [Xs]. That is, church staff [Ds] would be wise to supervise the leaders of ten-person meetings (cells) separately from the people who supervise the teachers of one hundred-person classes (congregations). Why? Two kinds of thinking are involved, and very few people can mix them without creating a turf-protection conflict between the one hundred-size group and the ten-size group. One set of skills knows how to entertain and attract people one hundred at a time; another leads to coaching people in groups of ten.

- Acquaintance facilitation. One of the primary needs in training Yellow Zone leadership involves both philosophy and
skill. It involves applying and answering this question to a
particular church culture: What kinds of social acquaintance
work—icebreakers and "seeding" of Xs and Xa's—are most
helpful for placing as many people as possible *near* a small-
group leader in order that they might be drawn, by affinity,
into involvement with a small group?

- Clarifying the game plan. Ministry leaders tend to do their
own thing if they're neglected; they're often willing to take
part as team members in the overall goals of the church if they
have an idea of what that larger picture is. As standing groups
meet week after week, they take on certain predictable characteristics of a subcongregation—a church within a church. One
of those traits is that, over time, they tend to develop their
own leadership appointment or election, they form consensus,
they hold "town meetings," and they meet together for long-
range planning. The danger is that they become insulated
among themselves.

- Alliance building. Skilled staff people who know how to build
alliances with various department leaders (i.e., preexisting
Yellow Zone groups) can be helpful to a church's health and
growth. The key is getting the leaders of these large church
units to see that they (1) have a potential ministry to one
another by meeting in a huddle, (2) have a potential ministry
to the small groups of the church by providing acquaintance-
making grounds, and (3) have a potential ministry of teaching
and interpreting the game plan of the church on behalf of the
senior pastor.

Combining Yellow and Green
Leads to Unavoidable Evangelism

When a group's leadership genuinely reaches out, targets others,
builds bridges of affection and love to other people, and offers a
social context in which newcomers can be accepted and assimilated, a church can't help but be evangelistically effective.

That process usually cannot be accomplished by medium-sized

Eastside Foursquare Church

14520 100th Avenue N.
Kirkland, WA 98083-0536
Phone: (206) 488-2500
FAX: (206) 488-6587
Denomination: Foursquare

Senior Pastor: Doug Murren
Contact: David Lanning
Attendance: 4500
Total Cell Groups: 150

Stirring Up the Gift of Evangelism

Senior pastor Doug Murren believes that each year 2000 to 3000 people put their faith in Christ through the ministry of Eastside Foursquare Church in greater Seattle. "We exist primarily for outreach—for converting the unconvinced—and so we spend as much or more energy on community evangelism as we do caring for the already gathered," says Murren.

Although Murren himself is gifted in evangelism, he has developed a series of church structures, from large- to medium- to small-size groups, that enable everyone to be an evangelist. "We are called as Christians to bring people to Christ—to be Andrews," says Murren. "We've built this concept of mission, which we call 'Bringers and Includers,' into the very identity of the church."

The weekend services are the most visible forum to which members can "bring and include" unchurched people whom they've befriended. About 3 percent of the people at any given service are first-time visitors.

An equally strategic forum are the eighty or so felt-needs-based or high-visibility events offered during the course of any year. These middle-size groups allow people to bring and expose their guests to the church on a non-threatening and nonmembership level. Some of these subcongregations attract people according to age, such as the groups for people 50-plus or for college/career singles. Others center around life-stage, such as the Moms and Moppets ministry.

"We see these subcongregations as becoming fishing ponds to develop the most vital unit of our church, which is the cell group," says Murren. His goal is to make sure that an increasing number of small groups are available so that, as people become comfortable with the church and draw near to God, they have a place where they're going to be cultivated, nurtured, and loved.

Eastside's mission-first emphases permeate all sizes and types of groups in the church. They enable everyone, not just Murren alone, to be evangelists.

Murren estimates that 90 percent of the church's constituency attributes a personal invitation from a friend or relative to their initial involvement in the church—whether it was to a celebration, a congregation, or a cell. "We want, at every point, to stir up the gift of evangelism," he says.

groups alone, however. Small groups are an important part of the equation. The small group is effective because it allows church members to come alongside new people and, without condemning them as erroneous or unacceptable, extend love to them. That show of care enables newcomers to develop a sense of dignity, worth, and trust, such that they can feel at ease and relaxed.

In a very natural progression, they soon drop their guard. That individual is soon caught within a pastoral-care network of loving human beings. The link then becomes the binding social context in which the Holy Spirit is freed to do a convicting work, knitting the hearts of people into the social fabric of what is becoming first of all a community of love, second a community of faith, and third a community of truth. In many cases people must sense the love of the people of God before they will move toward trusting God. Small groups, as intentional social contexts, assimilate, which results in conversions as people are loved into and through the groups.

The Role of Large Sunday-School Classes

In Southern-Baptist circles, from the 1920s to the 1950s, it was well understood that if a pastor cultivated the Sunday school, his interest was rewarded with a hearty support for the worship service. A good 80 percent of the worship attendance would be fueled by Sunday schools coming to worship.

The standardization of Sunday school, which built on the heritage of such historical developments as the Wesleyan class meeting,[4] was popularized and theorized by such luminaries as Arthur Flake,[5] Louis Entzminger,[6] and Elmer Towns,[7] and deserves great honor and respect. North America's Sunday-school movement has been responsible for winning millions to the Christian faith, instructing them, and then equipping them for service.

Over time, however, Sunday school has changed in most churches. To the extent Sunday schools have adopted certain public-school methods and curriculums, they typically lose their community dimension and produce a rather sterile institution that exists today as a teaching association. This fails to fulfill most biblical standards for the body of Christ.

As I point out in chapter 18, if churches hope to see vitality returned to Sunday school, it will not so much be by improvement of

Village Church

5725 County Road #11
Maple Plain, MN 55359
Phone: (612) 479-3433
FAX: (612) 479-2793
Denomination: Evangelical Free Church

Senior Pastor: Kevin Meyer
Contact: Gregg Bergman
Attendance: 550
Total Cell Groups: 35

Using Volunteer Teams to Plan Churchwide Outreach Events

When Village Church in Maple Plain, Minnesota, celebrated its tenth anniversary, attendance was hovering around one hundred. Then, as new pastor Kevin Meyer led the church into its second decade, worship attendance began to increase by about one hundred new people every year. By 1993 nearly six hundred people were passing through the doors of the church facilities each weekend.

Meyer realized early on that without an emphasis on small groups and team-produced ministry, the growth momentum could not continue, and quality care could not be ensured. In each phase of the church's growth, therefore, he encouraged lay ministry through small groups.

He also began to experiment with using teams of lay volunteers to plan congregation-size events, such as three strategic, churchwide outreach events each year. These have ranged from everything from mother-daughter banquets to classic auto shows. In recent years these have been supervised by associate pastor Gregg Bergman. "These events may be staff-motivated," says Bergman. "But they are organized and led by teams of lay leaders."

"Using teams of lay volunteers helped us in our goals of developing our lay leadership and creating a greater sense of ownership," he says. To their surprise, this process met another goal as well: The staff has found that using lay teams to produce medium-size events aids them by providing an entry-level opportunity to recruit, identify, and develop potential leaders. In fact, many of the new lay leaders are recruited by the existing lay leaders. "Nowadays, half the goal is to get the event going, the other half is to discover new lay leadership talent," says Bergman. In one case a woman in the church showed such strong leadership skills in organizing teams of people for these outreach events, that the staff asked her to oversee the entire adult education ministry in the church. She committed to a two-year stay in this position, and it has worked tremendously well.

"At Village Church, delegation doesn't mean 'do it yourself,' but rather, 'your job is to develop a team who will help you do it,'" says Bergman. "Everything is team-dependent around here."

the curriculum as by the increase in the number of hugs and prayers, the laying on of hands, and the confessing of sins one to another—all of which are an essential part of true Christian community.

The vision of a cell-driven church is certainly not antagonistic to a healthy Sunday-school system, especially if Sunday school is viewed as an on-premises cell system (see discussion in chapter 18), or if the Yellow Zone dimensions of a Sunday school are perceived as fishing ponds for cell-sized groups or classes.

The public-school paradigm heavily influences how North Americans think about Sunday school. The school model provides a useful framework for enabling churches to divide the labor

> If churches hope to see vitality returned to Sunday school, it will not so much be by improvement of the curriculum as by the increase in the number of hugs and prayers, the laying on of hands, and the confessing of sins one to another.

between professional (clergy, such as a minister of education) and volunteer (teachers and departmental superintendents).

But when a church's worship attendance or Sunday-school attendance reaches three hundred or so, the social supports for Sunday school frequently disappear under the press of program. Longtime church observer Lyle Schaller calls this transition the "Rotten Beaver vs. Silver Mink" award,[8] to indicate what happens to Sunday-school workers who no longer receive the support or affirmation they need. Feeling neglected, they burn out, and next-generation teachers prove hard to recruit. The title "Sunday-school teacher" moves toward pariah status.

This situation poses a great danger for other cell groups in a church, as they come alongside the Sunday school. If the existing Sunday school isn't fixed, and small groups become positioned as an alternative, then a resentment can grow because resources are scared away. The biggest problem is scarcity of touch, whether in a Yellow Zone Sunday school or other Yellow Zone gathering. The big challenge is to have a high-morale team of teachers who feel both loved and touched.

The first and most obvious contribution of Meta-Church thinking regarding a Sunday school system is to assure a social support system for the faculty of Sunday-school classes. Meta-Church thinking helps church leaders say, "Every Sunday-school class should be treated like a group. Every teacher, therefore, should be treated like a group leader. Thus if our church's group leaders need encouragement, stroking, affirmation, supervision, and prayer, then so do our Sunday-school teachers."

As a result, the departmental superintendent no longer becomes the person who leads music at the opening assembly before the teachers squirrel off on their own to teach their classes. Instead, the purpose of the departmental superintendent is to encourage a group of teachers (Xs by an L leader). The nurture and encouragement of those people, the debriefing with them, the visiting of their classrooms all become an important function not to be left to chance. Then the emotional support of teachers will rise, and morale will be enhanced.

Using Yellow Zone Groups Strategically

C. Peter Wagner[9] and others have spoken of intimacy as the characteristic hallmark for the small group, fellowship for the middle-size group, and worship for the very large group. For churches that have congregation-size ministries, their Yellow Zone can do far more than be a place for the fellowship of the saints—a Christian "Cheers" plan where, as the theme song to the popular TV series says, people are attracted to a place "where everybody knows your name."

An intentional use of Yellow Zone events does that and much more. It can draw newcomers into the church, offer a place of fellowship for those already in the church, and serve as "placement office" for pointing people to close, caring relationships through smaller groups.

Questions for Discussion and Application

1. Based on this chapter and the previous one, what's the difference between an Orange Zone event and a Yellow Zone event? Why is that distinction important?

12

Strategic Uses of Small Nurture and Ministry Groups: Green Zone

> The churches needed for the future will be centers of
> evangelism, discipleship, and pastoral care because
> they've learned how to provide quality care in small,
> humble structures of ten people who meet together.

A Meta-Church is a church in transition. The term Meta-Church is a way of saying, "You, as a leader, need to change your way of thinking about 'church' so that the church you serve can undergo the metamorphosis necessary to handle the challenges that lie ahead."

To what or where is the church transitioning? A Meta-Church is moving away from pastor-driven, one hundred-size groups and toward lay-driven, ten-size groups. These small groups meet as individual units and then together as a big worship-celebration convention. Meta-Church concepts lead to the understanding that the churches needed for the future will *not* grow solely because of their pulpits, stellar musical performances, or tremendous building facilities. Rather, they'll be centers of evangelism, discipleship, and pastoral care because they've learned how to provide quality care in small, humble structures of ten people who meet together.

> The Green Zone of the Meta-Church is where the cure
> and care of souls can best occur.

In the traditional congregational paradigm, the church-wide worship service (celebration), along with medium-size groups (congregation), are both seen as requirements, with cells being perceived as elective. This system organizes around hundreds in order to worship with, and reach, thousands. There appears to be a revolution underway, called the celebration-cell paradigm (or Meta-Church), which says that by organizing by tens, a church can provide such intimacy, encouragement, nurture, accountability, growth, love, and quality care that ten thousands can be reached without anybody's needs being overlooked.

The Green Zone of the Meta-Church is where the majority of these nurture groups and ministry teams will accumulate and be developed. This is where the cure and care of souls can best occur.

The Meta-Church, therefore, is primarily interested in getting people involved in a nurturing group of about ten people, and then in bringing those cells of people into corporate worship. Everything else serves to feed that rhythm between the cell and the celebration.

The "Greening" of the Church

Cells are a consequence of an emphasis on leadership development. Therefore, to make the Meta-Church transition, a church's staff should concentrate on this objective: We want more leaders for cells. Everybody is to be cared for in the context of a cell led by a leader to whom the staff is connected. No matter what methods or programs are selected, a Meta-Church's foremost goal is to strengthen the lay ministry necessary to multiply the number and quality of ten-size groups. Such is not the case today. Most churches today, if depicted on the Meta-Globe, would be colored mostly red, plus a little green.

By contrast, churches of the future will be about two-thirds green and maybe one-third red (see figure 33). In such churches, cell-group involvement will help people feel that they're part of their

Great Churches of the Future

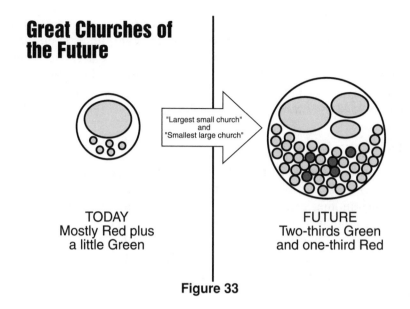

"Largest small church"
and
"Smallest large church"

TODAY
Mostly Red plus
a little Green

FUTURE
Two-thirds Green
and one-third Red

Figure 33

area's "largest small church" as well as its "smallest large church." Their church life will center on a network of small units that discover spiritual gifts, develop leaders, receive converts, and contribute to worship services. The most abundant type of group will be the nurture groups and task forces that populate the Green Zone.

Is there a role for small groups in the other zones of the Meta-Globe? Of course. By and large, all the ministry of a church is done through small service units, groups, and teams. But unless the zones are proportioned such that great emphasis is placed on creating new Green Zone groups, a church won't have enough energy available to take in new people, and there won't be a larger harvest. As chapter 1 emphasized, the core motivation of a Meta-Church is not a desire to build a large church. The motivation is a Christlike compassion for people's needs and a desire to obey God by harvesting everyone he wants harvested.

People need care far more than they need excitement. Unless large segments of a church's constituency accept the nurturing of souls as their primary responsibility—as a more important role than anything else they do—then that church won't experience the quality of care that's needed.

This chapter, with its emphasis on developing leadership for Green Zone ministry, will help you give the care function enough significance so that volunteer leaders will see it as a dignified role, worthy of commanding their best actions, efforts, and prayers. This chapter will also help you identify and simplify the nurturative roles in your church, both present and potential.

Meta-Church Maturity

A church's Green Zone is made up of nurture groups and ministry teams. Thus any small group whose primary goal is nurturative, one-another care belongs in the Green Zone. (The exception is if the group has a psychologically intensive dimension, such as a support or recovery group, in which case it's Blue Zone.) Ministry teams likewise are classified as Green Zone unless they're directly related to governance (Purple Zone), to large worship services (Red Zone), to missions and auxiliary (Orange Zone), to congregation-size groups (Yellow Zone), or to classic pastoral care (Blue Zone).

Nurture cells, in a church's early stages, help close its *back* door. They reduce the percentage of people who drop out or fall through the cracks because they were unattached, unnoticed, or uncared for. As a church becomes more developed, nurture cells become a *side* door—a point of first contact. In fact all the world's very large churches, with attendances above twenty thousand, are being built primarily on conversion growth, side-door entry, and cell care rather than on transfer growth and front-door entry.

> Nurture cells, in a church's early stages, help close its *back* door. As a church becomes more developed, nurture cells become a *side* door—a point of first contact.

Where do prospects for Green Zone groups come from? As figure 34 illustrates, eventually cells feed themselves—they learn to develop new contacts among unchurched neighbors, friends, and acquaintances. In addition, both Yellow Zone events and Blue Zone meetings are strong sources of prospects for Green Zone cells. From the Yellow Zone, cells "dribble down" as a result of assign-

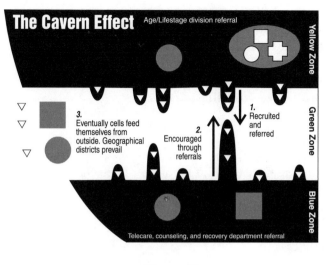

Figure 34

ments and associations made in mezzanine groups. This pattern is more pronounced when the church is smaller. From the Blue Zone, cells feed from referrals and associations made in recovery and support groups. This pattern is more pronounced as a church becomes very large. The process includes the following:

- *Entire* recovery and support groups (Blue Zone) transition into nurture groups (Green Zone).

- *Individuals* from recovery and support groups (Blue Zone) join nurture groups (Green Zone).

- *Telecare groups* (Blue Zone) refer individuals to nurture groups (Green Zone).

The long-range goal is to increase the number of nurture groups and ministry teams. You want people to make acquaintances and then come into the Green Zone groups because they will be with people who have impressed them favorably—people they want to be with. The curriculum you use, as long as it's consistent with your church's doctrinal beliefs, is a secondary issue. The name by which you call your groups is almost immaterial—as long as it rein-forces the purpose for your groups.

**Popular Names for Green Zone Groups
That Emphasize Nurture**

Term	Popularizer
Tender Loving Care (or TLC) groups	Dale Galloway
Shepherd groups	Ralph Neighbour, Jr.
Serendipity groups	Lyman Coleman
Covenant groups	Roberta Hestenes
Home groups	John Vaughan and others
Sunday school	many people
Growth groups	many people
Koinonia or Fellowship groups	many people
Bible studies	many people
Small groups	many people
Cell groups	many people

How to Resource Cell Leaders

Leaders of Green Zone groups not only need the supervision that comes from being part of a manageable span of care (see chapter 3), but they also need a training regimen—an ongoing nourishment that gives them the various "food" groups they need. These nutri-ents may be summarized by the words *vision*, *huddle*, and *skill*—or abbreviated with the acronym *VHS*.

The *vision* involves big-picture faith and encouragement issues like, "Where is God leading this church?" "Why is your ministry crucial to how we're getting there?" and "Who are the role models that we can cheer and follow?" Vision, as figure 35 indicates, is often expressed through the game plan, hero making, and the party line.[1]

3. Hero Making

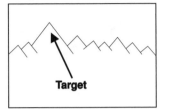

1. Game Plan

2. Party Line

Figure 35

The *huddle* builds on the concept of adult learning summarized in chapter 5: Adults learn best when they have an assignment and therefore a problem they're committed to solve: "Jordan, I've got a question I can't handle out of Romans" or "Colin, are you still feeling frustrated with how Shelli and Dave keep outtalking everybody in the group?" According to Meta-Church thinking, the best teachers and coaches aren't the ones who know the most, as much as they are the ones close enough to the situation to best understand the questions being raised. Figure 36 summarizes the areas that can be addressed through huddling—whether sitting down at a table together, or catching one another on the fly.

Finally the *skill* training depends on the needs that are present. How would the group leaders in your church answer this question: "What skills do you need in order to be a more effective cell-group leader or apprentice?" Any answer is fair game, from "I need help in bringing closure to a Bible-study discussion" to "I need to understand the life cycle of small groups in general, and my group in particular!"

Supervision through Encouragement

Relationships to address

- Leadership nucleus?

- Other rising leaders?

- Growing Christians?

- Seekers?

- "Open Chair" prospects?

- ECR's (Extra Care Required people)?

- Any re-seating needed?

- Any re-visioning needed?

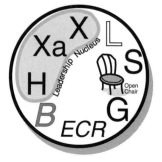

Figure 36

In keeping with comments elsewhere about avoiding a programmatic approach to leadership development (see chapters 1, 4, and 17), I recommend treating VHS components the way you would deal with vitamins in a diet. Every meal doesn't contain every vitamin—and probably doesn't need to. By analogy, then, each VHS element doesn't have to be present every time your leaders meet. Over the course of a month, though, are they exposed to generous amounts of inspiration and big-picture perspectives (vision)? to encouragement, report taking, feedback giving, and problem solving with someone who is supervising their ministry (huddle)? to opportunities for developing and improving the microskills needed for their particular type of group (skill)?

If volunteer leaders aren't receiving regular doses of these "vitamins" through the standard "food groups" offered at your church, then what needs to happen so they do? You might modify existing leader training menus, or you might create a special leadership community meeting.

The best ways for professional staff members to leverage their time is by becoming specialists in developing group leaders. A church's success, over the long run, will be largely determined by its skill in organizing these VHS-axis activities.

How does a pastor install a VHS-type meeting? What are some tips that can help a staff minister avoid pitfalls? After watching or talking with literally hundreds of clergy who have launched a VHS, I believe I can suggest how you might avoid the most common errors.

- In my experience, the most widespread mistake is for a pastor to think, "Everyone will be very glad that we're adding an intentional leadership community to church life." Often, it reduces the pain felt by *some* volunteer leaders, but it adds a great deal of agony to *many* others who perceive it as a threat and thus show little appreciation for it. In addition, a VHS community sometimes complicates the lives of the pastoral staff before it eventually simplifies and leverages their priorities.

- Another problem arises when pastors forget that the church they serve is a living organism. I recommend that a church not be hasty to launch VHS as a program. Instead, the wiser approach is to identify the VHS functions that are currently in place and to discover the regularity with which they are occurring. You may be surprised, for example, to find that in your youth ministry, children's ministry, or women's ministry, you already have relatively intact systems that look very much like a VHS but have never been recognized as such before. By showing this kind of care and sensitivity, you're less likely to destroy helpful foundations that are already in place.

- Another potential trouble spot arises when a pastor tries to impose supervision on previously existing ministries. The discussion of transitioning an existing church in chapter 16 offers a number of specific suggestions in that regard.

- There is one last factor that often leads to frustration, especially among baby boomers (those born between 1946 and 1964) and younger. The pastoral staff, in positioning the VHS meeting, must continually show how it addresses the felt needs of the participants. The "what's in it for me?" question, if unsatisfactorily answered, can quickly translate into nonparticipation.

> A church's success, over the long run, will be
> largely determined by its skill in organizing VHS-axis activities.

How often should you schedule a VHS-leadership community meeting? There is no rule. Our surveys, involving hundreds of churches, lead me to advise this: "Have vision, huddle, and skill components at least monthly, and more often if you can." Many suburban middle-class congregations find it best to plan a meeting on a semimonthly basis. Here are some examples of the more commonly occurring formats for those churches that create a specific forum for resourcing their volunteer leaders:

- "Instead of doing a VHS sequence, we do VSH, so that the huddles can linger afterward or go out for coffee if they want to."

- "We have a once-a-month vision session, followed by a huddle session and then two weeks later we have a skill session followed by a huddle session. So we're huddling twice a month but we're only visioning and skilling once apiece."

- "We need more time for huddles, so we do our vision teaching for the first session of each month, accompanied by a little bit of skill. Then in the second (and final) session for that month, we take the whole night for huddling."

- "We've decided to do skills as a course, which we run for eight weeks, with a different skill taught each week by a presenter from the nearby university or from the human-resource development profession. A member of our church discovered these people, and so we're using them for our skill component. The senior pastor, alternating with staff pastors, handles the vision component. Every week the participants break out around tables for some kind of huddling."

The variations are almost endless! What matters is not *how* you do it, so much as *that* you do it. If people come, and it does them some good, then it's probably a helpful use of the church's time and energy.

Sometimes a pastor says, "We just can't hold a VHS on a semi-monthly basis. We have so much traditional programming. We have

such a load on our staff. The best we can do is monthly." My reply
is to ask a series of questions. "How motivated are your people?
How skilled are your people? How much huddling are you getting
done? Are your people bright eyed when they go into the meetings?
Are you seeing results? If yes, then monthly is working for you."

Summary of Recommended VHS Goals

A helpful goal for almost any church is to establish a leadership
community with the V, the H, and the S components arranged so that
at least 80 percent of your leaders—Xs, Xa's, and Ls —will be able
to take part in them on at least a monthly basis. The mechanics of
how a church reaches that goal will vary due to a host of local factors. Figure 37 shows the various roles in a healthy cell and their
linkages to the rest of church life, such as the leadership community.

In addition, at least twice, maybe three times a year, it's both
important and helpful to hold a lay-ministry recognition day or
weekend. These are occasions where you make as much ado over
cell-group ministry as you do over mothers on Mother's Day, over

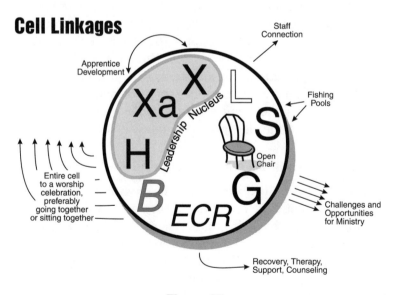

Figure 37

the Pilgrims on Thanksgiving, or over prayer warriors on the National Day of Prayer.

Dale Galloway, senior pastor of the 5500-person New Hope Community Church in Portland, Oregon, calls these high-visibility events superbowl weekends. He precedes these superbowls with a special seminar that inducts new people into leadership. It's a kind of Xa extravaganza. It's a refresher course for Xs and an introduction and orientation course for Xa's. He offers a Friday-night, and all-day Saturday seminar for Xs and Xa's, and then on Sunday he brings the group leaders in front of the whole congregation to commission and pray over them, to celebrate them, to announce them, to hear testimony, and to make all kinds of other recognitions that together make an important statement about the ministry of lay pastoring.

Every year New Hope varies the form a little, but the general net effect is that it provides an opportunity for Xs, who have spent the last several months on the lookout for potential Xa's, to help these rising Xa's make a commitment and publicly formalize it. After the weekend, all kinds of new lay-pastor groups are launched, the clock starts ticking again, and soon, within a few months, another new crop of Xa's are ready to step forward at a superbowl weekend.

Finally, most church staffs find it helpful to create two documents or policy statements. One deals with how to contract, enroll, or commission a cell leader or apprentice because the clearer you are on how someone becomes an X or Xa, the more likely you are to deal with expectations and standards in a positive, preventative manner. The second instrument is a training manual that includes report forms. This document will explain the training and supervision process for cell leaders and apprentices at your church.[2]

The Role of Ls and Xa's in Leadership Development

When a cell-group leader needs help with a problem in the group, to whom does he or she turn? The person who has responsibility for coaching that cell-group leader is known as an L in Jethro II language (see chapter 3). Churches use many kinds of names for such persons: coach, coordinator, cluster leader, section leader, care leader, zone servant, and team captain. At issue is not what this person is called, but what he or she does. The most important job of the L is to see to it that there are rising cell apprentices [Xa's] in the various groups being supervised. I have observed in numerous cases that where the apprentice role [Xa] is weak, so is the coaching role [L]—and vice versa.

Where do Ls come from? How do they take on this role? What causes them to excel at it? My observation of several dozen churches has led me to discover that the notion of an "apprentice L" rarely works. The phrase "acting L" is a more accurate description of what most churches end up putting into place. Why? The vast majority of Ls emerge from being a successful X and, in particular, of being recognized by their peer Xs as being a natural leader and counselor to them (see figure 38). What you want to find out is: If you put five Xs at a table with a problem-solving assignment, to whose opinion do most of the Xs defer?

The typical next step, then, is for that person to continue leading a cell group [as an X] *and* to coach cell-group leaders [as an L]. That person is thus functioning as an acting L. That person becomes a full-fledged L when he or she is responsible for only *one* group—a handful of cell-group leaders and possibly their apprentices as well. For full-fledged Ls, the huddle group *is* their small

Identifying Coaches

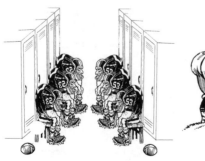

If the official coach were away, who would the players want to deliver the locker room talk?

If the quarterback lost his voice, who would the team look to for calling the plays?

Figure 38

Our Lord's Community Church

11400 North Portland
Oklahoma City, OK 73120
Phone: (405) 755-6522
FAX: (405) 755-6946
Denomination: Reformed
  Church in America

Senior Pastor: Jack Dabney
Contact: Marcia Gautier,
  Community Group Minister
Attendance: 600
Total Cell Groups: 27

Creating a Bias toward Birthing New Groups

Testimonials are the most powerful way in which small-group care and outreach are being multiplied at Our Lord's Community Church, Oklahoma City, Oklahoma.

Janie Wall, a longtime member, frequently tells the story of the four different groups she participated in that each went through the process of birthing a new group. Kathleen Edwards is contagiously excited about how the one core group she led has now multiplied into five different groups. Marcia Gautier, the church's minister of community groups, coordinated an entire worship service (a "cell-ebration") that praised God for the benefits of small-group ministry. And Jack Dabney, the senior pastor, has challenged small-group leaders to speed the birthing process by each raising up two, three, or even four apprentice leaders.

"We don't allow the word *division* at this church," says Gautier. "And we don't talk about splitting groups or breaking them up. New groups multiply God's grace. And that's exactly what he's done."

In 1990 the church's few nurture-type small groups were by and large closed to newcomers. By 1992 the church could count twenty-four open groups, fourteen of which were multiplications. By the end of 1993, fully one third of the adults in the church were involved in a community group. Without the process of cells birthing other cells, this growth rate could likely not have occurred.

"Through prayer and waiting on the Lord, we have established a climate that encourages multiplication of our cell ministry," says Dabney. "Over the years, we've given great love, care, and discipleship to our own, but we've had little experience in outreach. So the biggest obstacle we faced was the mindset of our people."

The fruit is already evident. In November 1993, of the forty people received into membership, thirty were already in community groups. "We're experiencing an explosion of disciple making," says Gautier. "And in the process, we're drawing more new people to the church than ever before."

The possibilities for future growth are now virtually limitless because the leadership load is being shared among a very wide group of people, and a technology is in place for making sure that care will continue to be effective and intimate. Instead of letting a growing group strangle in its own success, the church regularly develops enough new leaders to be able to spin off additional groups and thereby multiply the church's total number of listening posts and ministry centers.

group. The management of five cell leaders, the visiting of their groups, and the nurturing of the apprentices [Xa's] in all those groups generally requires an L's full ministry time and energy.

Thus the itinerant L prays that God will release the giftedness of the persons in each group who are able to take on the apprentice leader's role [Xa]. That coach also spends a lot of time mulling and praying over, "I wonder if so-and-so is gifted in this way."

There's both an art and a science in the discovery of nascent leaders. The science, based on experience gathered in several places, says that probably four out of five groups are going to have a future leader within their ranks. The art is hearing the whisper of the Holy Spirit.

I remember overhearing a conversation between a very skilled group leader who had L potential and another leader. The skilled leader was serving as an X-group leader at the time, and due to his skills, was constantly sending out leaders to create new groups. He and I were in a conversation with a group of staff members and other cell leaders in the church. He said, "Yes, I have two people who are going to make very fine leaders for the future. One of them knows it and one of them doesn't know it yet." The woman who headed a Blue Zone group, and had even written a book on recovery from abuse issues, immediately became concerned about boundary issues. She jumped into the conversation and charged, "Don't say that. You're violating that understudy. You're manipulating him. You can't say that he's going to be a leader when he doesn't know it yet. God has to call him."

Undaunted, this artful rising L said, "You're right. I'll tell him that God has called him."

I'm not poking fun at the issue of divine call. Rather, I believe that a person's gifting often indicates God's calling. It's very conceivable that someone with the gift of discernment might discover God's action in that understudy's life even before the person himself does.

Designating someone as an apprentice leader is simply an issue of getting that person ready to serve. I was consulting with a Pentecostal church in San Jose, California, for example, and I met a young Hispanic who was a group leader there. He told me this story of how he had moved from apprentice to full leader: "I was a mem-

Trinity Episcopal Church

1415 Halsey Way, Suite 320
Carrollton, TX 75007-4455
Phone: (214) 245-3400
FAX: (214) 245-3472
Denomination: Episcopal

Senior Pastor: Dr. Bill Atwood
Contact: Focus Ministry, (800) 944-1067
Attendance: 250
Total Cell Groups: 50

"Side Door" Growth Builds the Worship Service

Unlike many new churches, where a newcomer's first contact is through the worship service, an Episcopal church plant in Carrollton, Texas, has learned how to build the worship attendance from a more durable, fast-growing base: home cell groups.

Bill Atwood, founding pastor of five-year-old Trinity Episcopal Church (and of the two churches he planted at the same time), says, "At least half of our recent worship-attendance growth is a result of people's involvement in the small-group ministry. In addition, many of our people would not have made it through our church's rough times, when we had some very divisive forces at work, without a cell-group system."

In order to build such a strong small-group system, Atwood has pursued a different set of priorities than those in a traditional church. "Most of my time is spent in vision casting and overseeing the lay coaches, and less and less of it is spent giving direct care to the lay leaders," he says. "But that's possible because all we have are cells and Sunday mornings."

He has developed extensive training modules, both written and video, for his lay leaders. These resources have been in more than two thousand churches across twenty denominations. Since the earliest days of the church he has also held a "Supercell" monthly meeting (dinner, vision, huddling, skill building) solely for his leaders. They met weekly in the early years; currently, once a month.

The net result is that Trinity Episcopal, as all churches, sees people come and go. But, in contrast to most traditional churches, Trinity Episcopal has found a binding social context that preassimilates people, and the "stick rate" is high enough to keep the church knit together during hard times, and powerful enough to accelerate the growth rate during other times.

Under Atwood's leadership, the "side door" of small-group ministry has become the church's most important point of entry and assimilation, building the worship service, and even surpassing the traditional "front door" entry to the worship service.

ber of the group and I was so hungry for understanding the Word of God, that I would stay after each of the meetings and quiz my group leader on the Bible. After several months of staying each time until nearly midnight, asking questions, and digging through the Bible with the cell leader, he said, 'You should be my apprentice leader.' I asked what's involved, agreed to serve, and had a wonderful year of growing in my faith. The leader then learned he had cancer, and in a matter of weeks, died. I wasn't sure I was ready to head the group, but the elders met with me and encouraged me to do it, and it's working well. The widow of our former leader has started another group, and I'm leading the group by myself—with help from my apprentice."

The same thing happened in Knoxville, Tennessee, in an Episcopal church that serves a very professional-class community. One of the group leaders died. The next Monday night when the VHS group-leader meeting occurred the apprentice, who was one of the attorneys of that town, showed up and sat in the chair of the deceased leader. Nobody from the church ever wrote this apprentice leader a note saying, "Now you're the leader." He had been prepared for leadership and was ready to step into it.

The notion of succession and progression is inherent in the apprenticeship role, which is why I avoid the term *assistant*. Someone may remain an assistant forever, but to be an apprentice means that you're preparing to step into your mentor's shoes.

The apprentice role is critical to every cell-size group because (as observed in chapter 2) a church's greatest need, in most cases, is a lack of available leadership. The first task of the newly raised leader is to appoint another apprentice. At every meeting of the group, the apprentice should do something "leaderly"—recruiting a greeter, seeing that the Bibles are passed out, or opening in prayer. Similarly, the apprentice needs leadership responsibilities between meetings—making sure the absentee is called, going with someone to pick up the Bible-study guides, and so forth. But the apprentice's foremost responsibility is to help start a new group.

Remember, the most likely site of new growth in any church—from a one hundred fifty–year–old traditional congregation to a two-year-old innovative church plant—is a new group where everybody feels like they're starting at the same place together. In cell

Fairhaven Church

637 E. Whipp Road
Dayton, OH 45458-2203
Phone: (513) 434-8627
FAX: (513) 434-0822
Denomination: Christian &
   Missionary Alliance

Senior Pastor: Forrest Schwalm
Contact: Jim Corley
Attendance: 1200
Total Cell Groups: 75

Birthday Parties for Cells that Multiply

People are motivated when they receive recognition and appreciation, and cell-group leaders are no exception.

Lanny Burton, a small-group leader at Fairhaven Church in Dayton, Ohio, experienced that principle in an unusual way. He says, "One evening, when I walked into our church's Vision, Huddle, and Skills meeting—which we call VHS meetings for short. I saw a large colorful bouquet of balloons at the far end of the room." From past meetings, he knew the balloons signaled that a leader would be congratulated on the birthing of a new cell group. What he didn't know was that he was the honoree.

"So many balloons were present that I assumed several leaders were being honored," Burton recalls. "But to my surprise, the celebration was solely for me. It was the way our associate pastor, Jim Corley, encouraged me and gave God glory for the way he has worked in my life and in the lives represented by our cell group."

Lanny Burton became a Christian through the outreach of Fairhaven Church, and as soon as the church launched a cell-group ministry, he became involved. "Through the ministry of small groups, God has transformed me from a discouraged, small-faith person to someone who can effectively lead a cell group and trust God to grow a group," Burton says.

"Making heroes out of ordinary people creates a new culture for others to follow," says Corley. "Potential leaders see average people succeeding as cell-group leaders and decide they can also."

"Lanny," says Corley, "was at first a reluctant leader who often became discouraged. Now his peers know him as someone who has come from the ranks, and has successfully birthed two cell groups. He has learned to trust God, himself, and us to succeed."

In a short time, motivated leaders like Lanny have created an entire network of successful cells where people can grow and find a place to belong. The number of off-premises, lay-pastored small groups has gone from 0 percent in 1991 to more than 25 percent of the church's constituency by 1993. This growth comes in addition to an ongoing strong Sunday-school program.

At this rate, balloons will be a regular sight at leadership meetings for some time to come.

systems that are growing and flourishing, generally at least 20 percent of all groups are new within the previous twenty-four months. As Meta-Church perspectives take root in a church, that percentage can grow to 50 percent, even with the inevitable fallout that comes from people who move away, drop out, or discover that their spiritual gifts are best used in another context.

The Cell Leader and the ECR

Every church has terribly wounded people, also known as extra-care-required persons (ECRs), who show up in about one out of every two nurture groups. Their souls need healing, and they've sought out or been referred to a Green Zone type of group. Unfortunately they may not behave acceptably. A common pattern, for example, is that ECRs will confess the sins of others—their husband's, wife's, children's, senior pastor's, or cell group leader's(!)—in ways that the Bible calls talebearing or complaining.

The demands that ECRs place on a group often require the group leader to provide close monitoring and managing with high levels of assertion and firmness. The cell leader [X] must deal with it, usually with help from a supervisor [L], or the group will sicken and die.

In dealing with an ECR, there is no room for self-righteousness or haughtiness by others in the group because at one time or another virtually everyone, even the leader, wears the hat of an ECR. An attitude of humility needs to convey, "They're the needy one this season; I might be the needy one at a later point. We'd better treat people well here."

Previously, I helped popularize the term EGR, which stood for extra-*grace*-required person.[3] In recent years I've observed, however, that too many people used the idea of EGR pejoratively. ECR's are often conscious of their condition and are pained by references to themselves as being an extra-grace-required person. Hence the kinder term, ECR.

The Cell Leader and Spiritual Abuse

Is it possible that small groups led by lay people will lead to spiritual abuse? The answer is yes—just as it's also possible for small groups led by professionally trained counselors or ordained minis-

Beulah Alliance Church

17504—98 A Avenue
Edmonton, AB T5T-5T8
Phone: (403) 486-4010
FAX: (403) 489-4577
Denomination: Christian &
    Missionary Alliance

Senior Pastor: Keith Taylor
Contact: Keith Taylor
Attendance: 1250
Total Cell Groups: 100

Long-Term Members Find Benefit in Small, Caring Groups

Beulah Alliance Church, Edmonton, Alberta, was about seventy-five years old when senior pastor Keith Taylor arrived in 1991. At that time, worship attendance was about seven hundred, and it zoomed to 1250 by the end of 1993.

The changes leading to and required by this growth were well received, by and large, especially since so many segments of the congregation found their stability in the church's small groups and classes. "It's our desire to develop a community of caring people," says Taylor, "and we are seeing many men, women, teens, and children come to value the experience of small groups." The staff has regularly promoted the vision for leadership development through small groups, using a wide variety of means, from sermon illustrations to dramatic vignettes during the worship services.

Even long-term, well-connected members, who typically have many friends and feel generally cared for, are sensing the importance of group life at Beulah. One such longtime attender, for example, was skeptical about the importance of groups, but in loyalty to the pastor's vision, he found a group. "When I joined, I didn't sense a personal need for the support and care of the members of that group," recounts Frank (not his real name). "Then the birth mother of our adopted daughter informed us that she was dying of a form of cancer that was genetically transferable. Our daughter went in for tests and learned that she was also infected with the disease in its earliest stages."

As the daughter went through treatment and was ultimately cured, Frank and his wife experienced a great deal of trauma. The group provided them with meals, prayer, hospital calling, and support. As a result, Frank now enthusiastically supports the need for small groups. "I can't tell you how much the support of my small group has meant to us during our time of need," he says.

"Our worship services and talented staff remain the primary attraction point for those who visit Beulah Alliance Church," says Taylor. "But as we become more purpose driven, and less program driven, we anticipate that the greater number of new people will be reached through the 'side door' of groups like Frank's."

ters to lead to social and psychological abuse. People are sinners and have the potential to abuse one another. Fortunately, a number of publications discuss spiritual abuse in terms that can help a church look out for and identify abusive situations.[4]

Why are small groups susceptible to spiritual abuse? Because people tend to conform to norms. Such behavior shaping occurs in sports teams, artistic groups, church committees, youth groups, and just about every other regular small-group gathering of people, in or out of a church. The question is: When does such conformity go to a point where it violates the personhood of individuals? The answer is: when it invades their boundaries, shames them, condemns them, and causes them to carry a burden greater than they are supposed to bear under God's rule.

What safety precautions can be taken against abuse? There are several: the awareness that abuse exists; a rising literature to help define abuse; the fact that you are meeting with the group leader for supervision on a continuing basis; the presence of coaches [Ls] circulating through to watch the groups and keep their "ears to the ground"; and the proximity of an informed community of mental health workers who can be invited from time to time to teach your people how to recognize mental illness, how to recognize the need for referral for counseling, or how to tell whether something you're doing is beyond your ability. In short, supervised groups are less likely to fall into abuse than groups that are left on their own.

What about doctrine and curriculum in cell meetings? How does a pastoral staff convey an appropriate degree of control over what is taught in cell groups? There are numerous, almost endless, options. A group leader can (1) guide a discussion based on a video of the sermon; (2) go through a written outline geared to the weekly sermon text; (3) offer a uniform lesson on a seven-year cycle; or (4) select his or her own materials based on an approved curriculum list.

If you have older, more mature Christians who are used to picking their own curriculum, and you can trust their theological judgment, then ask them to tell you what they'd recommend using, look it over, and assuming you agree with it, say, "Hey, that's great!"

If you have new Christians who need theological and doctrinal guidance, then perhaps have them discuss the sermon by talking

Prince of Peace Lutheran Church

2115 Frankford Road
Carrollton, TX 75007
Phone: (214) 245-7564
FAX: (214) 242-7101
Denomination: Lutheran Church,
   Missouri Synod

Senior Pastor: Stephen Wagner
Contact: Wyman Bess
Attendance: 800
Total Cell Groups: 70

Spiritual Gifts as Key to Ministry Placement

"When you become a member here, you're asked to take a very long test on the topic of spiritual gifts," says Robert Balduc, a member at Prince of Peace Lutheran Church, Carrollton, Texas. "Initially I was confused and hesitant about the reason why, especially since I'm a lifelong Lutheran and I was simply transferring my membership from an out-of-state church."

When Balduc got the results back, he began to see the big picture. "They told me my strengths," he says. "They showed me the different ministries where I could best serve Jesus Christ here at this church."

Today Balduc is actively and joyfully using his gifts to lead a small group and to coach three other group leaders. "In most churches, the need for volunteers is basically a roll call for whoever feels guiltiest or whoever is afraid to say 'no' to the pastor," he says. "At first I thought it was novel to describe ministry positions according to spiritual gifts needed. Now I see a direct link between spiritual-gift usage and a sense of excitement about service to Christ."

Balduc's experience has been replicated in hundreds of lives at Prince of Peace. "As we administer spiritual-gifts surveys, we help people get a feel for what God has blessed and equipped them to do within his body," explains staff minister Wyman Bess. "We've learned by experience that people burn out or lose interest when a ministry doesn't seem to fit their gift profile. Those who find great fulfillment are often the ones God has blessed and equipped for that ministry."

The focus on spiritual gifts has been applied at every level, including the leadership board. As Bob Kopitke, a member of the executive board ministry, says, "A church serves best when you start from the bottom up, making sure your people are focused and moving correctly, rather than worrying about the top down—how do we make sure we're managing people, and they're doing what they're supposed to do?"

Kopitke has likewise matured in understanding his own spiritual gifts. "As I focus myself more specifically in those areas, I'm more effective and comfortable in my work because I'm where the Lord has gifted me to be."

Are all testimonials so positive? "There are certainly times when we become aware of people who are perhaps inappropriately slotted," says Stephen Wagner, senior pastor. "If the role shift involves a long-term office holder, we might be in for a difficult transition! However, as we see the effectiveness of people and the results of their ministry, very soon the success stories serve as a healing balm to the pain or tension that might exist in another area."

"As I think back over the history of our church," summarizes Wagner, "would I again go through the pain to get from where we were to where we are today? Absolutely, I would."

through a set of questions that the church office provides. The content, as long as it's orthodox and fits the profile of your church, is far less important than the fact that people are seriously pursuing obedience to the Word. Thus exactly what is taught, as long as it

> You'll lose more people through the cracks if you don't sponsor a cell system than you'd lose through neglecting people.

fits your biblical parameters, is far less important than the fact that something from Scripture is taught.

More cautious readers may be thinking, "But can we really trust people with the souls of others?" Someone trusted *you* with that responsibility. Why be so hesitant about allowing others that privilege? Remember, if the group falls apart, it may re-form around other leadership. You'll lose more people through the cracks if you don't sponsor a cell system than you'd lose through neglecting people. Over time your cell leaders will credential themselves simply because they produce recognizable disciples of Jesus Christ.

The Cell Leader and Spiritual Gifts

I've learned from observation that there is far more that takes place at a meeting called a Bible study than study of the Bible. The participants in that group receive whatever spiritual gift mix is represented by the group and its leadership. It is easy to see that in one Bible study the emphasis will be on teaching the Word of God, in another on using insights from Scripture to help people in need, in another to compassionately pray through the Bible text at hand, and so forth.

While all the group leaders may see that the same verses are covered, one does so as a teacher, one as a wisdom counselor, one as an exhorter, one as a mercy giver, and so forth. (See the listings of spiritual gifts in Romans 12:6–8; 1 Corinthians 12:7–11, 28–31; Ephesians 4:11–13; 1 Peter 4:8–11.) In short, the giftedness of the leader, and of the others in the group, shapes the way the meeting is handled.

Sometimes people gifted with teaching are bothered when they hear that a Bible study doesn't always pack in a thirty-minute lesson. They don't understand that thirty minutes of hugging, crying, advising, rebuking, showing mercy, or praying can be just as much a lesson, if that's what the Holy Spirit needed to do through that group on that particular day. The role of the cell group is to focus on Bible application, even more than on Bible content—if the two must be put at odds with each other. After all, what is the purpose of convening people in small nurture groups? It's so they'll be encouraged and their faith will be strengthened. God's people need strong faith and clear consciences. The tools to use are truth spoken in love, a lifestyle of obedience in trusting God, and an expectation that God will assist as his children ask and seek him (Ephesians 4:24–5:2; 1 Peter 2:1–10; Matthew 7:7–12).

Prewiring People for Facing Crisis

Several years ago when I had surgery, the nurse put a catheter in my arm, taped it down nicely, and didn't plug it in to anything. I asked, "Why have you just put some plumbing in me that I don't see any apparent need for?" She replied, "It's much easier to find the vein now, than if we need to in an emergency." I questioned her further. "If we need to give you medication rapidly, we'll have you already prepared to receive it." I appreciated that preparation because I might not need it, but if I did, the extra few seconds could make the difference in a successful recovery or even survival. Similarly, if a church will prewire its people for care, then when crisis comes, everybody will be ready. The fact of life is that people have wounds and need everything from Band-Aids to emergency direct pressure.

How, then, can your church prewire people for facing crisis? Make sure they are lodged in a group in which the love and gifts of the Holy Spirit are active. Then when the inevitable crisis occurs in their lives that group—just like my already-prepared intravenous tube—will be ready and available to infuse whatever nurture and care is needed. The most important tools that a church's professional staff can give their people, as they face the future, is the assurance that the basic, fundamental components of Christian

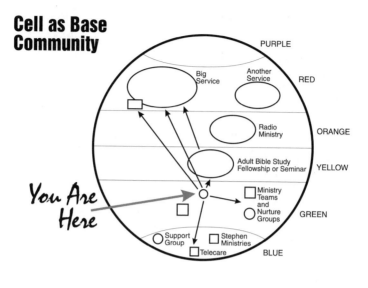

Figure 39

community are not accidents but are purposeful. The loving touches that people require in order to make God flesh among them must occur with such regularity that God's people are prepared for the shocks and jolts of life. The nurture cell is the most basic form of Christian community, and is the foundational building block of the church of the future (see figure 39).

Every time a paid professional encourages a volunteer leader to share the ministry by getting people to love one another in Jesus' name the church is being prepared for the future. A church's staff must jealously guard their own priorities so that they can focus their energy on one assignment: Creating more groups who are creating more group leaders. The resulting explosion in the number of Green Zone cells can "crisis proof" a church by making it able to handle the times of personal dismay, turmoil, or crisis that come because the memory of a hug and the attitude of turning to God is ever near to each person's mind. Such is the result of pouring energy into developing leaders who, in turn, ensure spiritual-gift-driven care in small, nurturing, manageable ten-people units.

Questions for Discussion and Application

1. Why, according to this chapter, is populating the Green Zone such a strategic emphasis in a Meta-Church?

2. What are the Green Zone groups in the church you serve? List four examples.

3. What are the leadership development needs of the Green Zone leaders in your church? What are the most important next three steps your church can take? How will you help accomplish them?

13

Strategic Uses of Small Critical-Care Groups: Blue Zone

The Blue Zone is not a permanent place for participants to stay. Rather, it's somewhere to grow through and grow out of.

Why does the Blue Zone exist? This domain draws together the many church situations that would traditionally be handled by an ordained minister, a professional licensed clinician, or a layperson with special training in counseling or other forms of crisis care. Upon identifying all the individuals and groups that could be described as Blue Zone, most boards and pastoral staffs are surprised by how many such needs are represented in their church. In churches with attendances of four hundred and fewer, Blue Zone concerns typically draw as much as half the pastoral staff's time and energy.

Further, most churches do not know how to organize Blue Zone ministries in such a way that a gifted volunteer leader can partner in the need-meeting opportunities they represent. Instead, as in the oft-cited adage about a football game, a handful of people (the pastoral and office staff) are in desperate need of rest, while a far larger group (the cheering church membership) are in desperate need of exercise (see figure 40).

Figure 40

In many cases the "fans" aren't even aware that there is something significant they could do out on the playing field.

Varieties of Blue Zone Ministry

The Blue Zone's content, summarized on the Meta-Globe in figure 41, includes:

- Traditional pastoral care, from hospital and shut-in visitation to intercessory prayer.
- Psychologically intensive ministries, including all forms of counseling, as well as recovery and support groups.
- Telecare ministry—a safety-net concept in which teams routinely phone each household of the church to offer prayer support and care.

Thus, the Blue Zone is not a permanent place for participants to stay. Rather, it's somewhere to grow through and grow out of. Why is the Blue Zone such a transitional arena?

Blue Zone Overview

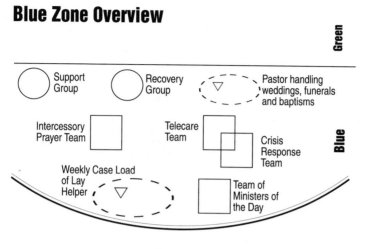

Figure 41

- Medical crises, funerals, weddings, baptisms, confirmations, and the like are generally short-term or one-time events.

- Suicide threats, bereavement after a death, church office walk-ins, and governmental social-service requests, likewise generally represent a one-time need for each individual involved.

- People in 12-Step recovery or support groups can graduate and move to Green Zone growth groups as their recovery progresses.

- Sometimes an entire Blue Zone group, such as a Parents-of-Adolescents support group, will become a Green Zone nurture group.

- Telecare callers and crisis response team interactions often help refer people into an appropriate group elsewhere on the Meta-Globe.

- Counseling subjects may likewise be introduced to suitable groups.

Telecare

As churches enter the future, a telecare system can no longer be optional. Because this is a newer form of pastoral care, it needs a

New Hope Community Church

11731 SE Stevens Road
Portland, OR 97266-7597
Phone: (503) 659-5683
FAX: (503) 774-1133
Denomination: Independent

Senior Pastor: Dale Galloway
Contact: Church Growth Institute
  at the above address
Attendance: 5500
Total Cell Groups: 500

Support Groups as a Significant Entry Point to Church

Dale Galloway, pastor of New Hope Community Church in Portland, Oregon, believes support groups can be a powerful force in drawing people to the church. Under the right leadership, one small group can multiply and duplicate until it becomes a major need-meeting force within the larger body of believers.

"I had a secretary once who never got my work done," Galloway explains. "I'd come into my office and she'd have someone at my desk leading him or her to Christ. Another time I'd arrive and she'd be counseling someone on the telephone, praying with that person. One time I looked for her and found her in the sanctuary with a whole family, praying with them for the healing of their mother."

Galloway prayed about the situation and decided that his secretary never finished her assignments because she had such obvious ministry talent. So he asked her to oversee some of the church's small-group ministries.

"Along with commissioning her to oversee this area, I asked her to take over a newly formed group for adult children of alcoholics, which we called New Life Victorious." What Galloway didn't know was that his secretary herself had gone through years of recovery for personal alcohol abuse.

Ten years later that one group has spawned or inspired more than sixty-five New Life Victorious groups with over 750 people actively involved. Their topics include divorce recovery, cancer recovery, marriage, sexual abuse, and overeating. Galloway says the possibilities of future topics are limitless.

"I believe that the only way to effectively do pastoral care these days is through small groups. No pastor can give the kind of care that a small group can," Galloway says.

(For another case study on New Hope Community Church, see "Seven-Day-a-Week Opportunities for Children," on page 289.)

bit of special explanation. Basically, telecare is a safety-net concept in which teams routinely phone each household of the church to offer prayer support and care. Its effect has been proven in dozens of churches across the continent: There is no doubt that a network of intentionally installed small groups enables the people of a church to feel cared for at higher levels than under the old system where they had to chase down the clergy to receive the care.

Research about Telecare

(based on a 1993 survey of thirty-five churches using telecare)

1. The most surprising and most consistent finding is that the people who are called deeply appreciate the calls.
2. The telecare callers themselves receive a blessing and they report that the experience energizes them, rather than wears them out.
3. Virtually everyone using telecare reports that this ministry has made a significant impact on the "care level" of their church.
4. Telecare boosts the prayer level of a church; the most frequently identified content of a telecare call is a prayer concern, which is sometimes prayed for by telephone, sometimes put on a printed prayer list, and sometimes relayed to the pastoral staff.
5. In most cases, little to no specific budget is required. Once in a while a church will install an additional phone line, but in many cases churches have figured out a way around that.
6. Most churches surveyed (75 percent) report that less than two hours a week of pastoral supervision is required to facilitate the telecare phoners.
7. When asked what they could do differently if they started over in launching their telecare program, the most commonly stated response was that they'd place a greater emphasis on training the people who phone.

Christian Outreach Center

1049 Harbor Drive
West Columbia, SC 29169
Phone: (803) 794-1001
FAX: (803) 739-0511
Denomination: Assemblies of God

Senior Pastor: Steven C. Allen
Contact: Vaifanua ("Pele") Mulitauaopele
Attendance: 500
Total Cell Groups: 46

Spiritual Cardiac Units All Over the City

"I recently spoke with a lady in our church who had been in the hospital with a heart attack," says Steven Allen, senior pastor of Christian Outreach Center, Columbia, South Carolina. "She had nothing but praise for how her care group leader had watched over her and her family. She was as happy as if five pastors had visited her!"

Since 1986 when Pastor Allen arrived at Christian Outreach Center, the church has grown from an attendance of sixty to more than five hundred today. As was true when the church was smaller, Pastor Allen is personally involved in hands-on, front-line ministry: He leads a small group, replete with apprentice leader, and he makes hospital visits, often with an understudy in tow. He, his wife, and a retired Christian psychologist each do some one-on-one, short-term counseling.

But were he to limit this ministry to himself and a small handful of people, Christian Outreach Center would touch only a small segment of those with needs. Just because their appointment books might be full, they would have no guarantee that the church's counseling needs were being adequately handled.

Instead, through books like *The Master Plan of Evangelism*, by Robert Coleman,* and seminars like "How to Break the 200 Barrier" and "Beyond 400,"** Allen has learned how to pour his energies into leadership development. "The church is built on a cell model from the Sunday school to the singles ministry," he says. "My job is to meet with the leaders of those groups. Even in the counseling arena, I've learned that the preferred way to meet the counseling needs of a church is through groups, rather than one-on-one."

"As a result, I am sharing literally hundreds of pastoral responsibilities, including counseling," says Allen. "We have mature leaders in the church now—men and women of God who are ministering out of a servant base, not a power base. And they're training others, too; their apprentices are coming up the ranks with that same heart attitude.

"I may be the chief of spiritual cardiac surgery for our church," says Allen, "but if I quit or the Lord takes me home, the ministry would go on. We now have critical-care units all over the city. Whenever a spiritual catastrophe happens, our people can be there in minutes. In the long run, that's far more important than me getting there."

* Robert E. Coleman, *The Master Plan of Evangelism* (Grand Rapids: Fleming H. Revell) 1963.
** Sponsored by the Charles E. Fuller Institute, P.O. Box 90095, Pasadena, CA 91109-5095, phone 1-800-MAP-META, FAX 818-449-6129.

The involvement of many parishioners in peer care through small groups usually raises the problem of what to do with those who need care but aren't willing to participate in a small group. In extreme cases, such as long-established, change-resistant churches, as many as 80 percent of the constituency may choose not to be in groups whose leadership receives coaching or supervision.

If church people have come to expect a clergyperson in a collar to make regular visits to the hospitals, nursing homes, and seniors groups, then a change in pattern often has the effect of yanking away from people something they've grown accustomed to over an entire lifetime. In many long-established churches, pastors may be wise to continue those personal visits, or the parishioners will do nothing but grouse and give the pastor grief.

You can do something supplemental, however, that may also decrease the expectation of a pastoral visit. I recommend putting a safety net of additional care under the entire current ministry of classical pastoral care. Part of this is the development of teams of people willing to phone the entire constituency and prospects of the church on a regular basis to offer prayer, care, and other support as needed. Such a system has been deployed in various churches across the continent for well over a decade, and has been refined through their experiences (see figure 42).

Telecare works on the presupposition that there are many advantages to team-based calling: More people receive calls, more people make calls, and thus more people are involved in the blessing that comes from this widespread system of care. The pastor's role eventually becomes that of an encourager to the calling teams.

In churches with attendances of up to three hundred people, a staff pastor would do well to do some of the phoning on a highly organized, efficient basis. The secretarial, or other volunteer office staff, could line up the pastor's call appointments in advance ("Would it be convenient if Pastor Hazlett phoned you about 7:45?"), enabling the pastor to make up to two dozen quick contacts in one evening.

The long-range goal, however, would be to train various lay callers—two, three, five, six, and soon enough the church would have a lay-led telecare team established.

Gloria Dei Lutheran Church

18220 Upper Bay Road
Houston, TX 77058
Phone: (713) 333-4535
FAX: (713) 335-0574
Denomination: Lutheran Church,
   Missouri Synod

Senior Pastor: John H. Kieschnick
Contact: John T. Lindner
Attendance: 1000
Total Cell Groups: 38

Effective Crisis Care through Stephen Ministers and Hospital Visitors

In most long-established churches, whether large or small, the crisis care needs far exceed the ability of the pastoral staff to personally attend to each situation. Fortunately, new clergy-laity partnerships are providing fresh solutions to this dilemma.

Over the last several years, trained volunteers at Gloria Dei Lutheran Church in Houston, Texas, have made hundreds of visits to hospitals, to the homes of recuperating patients, and to nursing facilities. Their goal is to extend the loving care of the church as they share their relationship with Jesus Christ.

Team members, after each hospital visit, turn in a "Visitation Evaluation Form" to John Lindner, director of Counseling Ministries. After indicating time and date information, the form asks: Did your patient desire prayer? Is there any information that needs to be brought to the attention of the pastors? Will you be visiting again? Has this person been placed on the church prayer list?

"Two registered nurses function as advisors for whenever team members need help in understanding what a patient is going through," says Lindner. "While staff pastors may be able to get there only once, our lay people can visit a second and third time, which is when the real help usually begins," says Lindner. "Further visits may also be in order as the patient convalesces at home as well."

What about other kinds of crisis needs? Since the mid–1980s, the church has deployed Stephen Ministers. Founded by pastor and clinical psychologist Kenneth C. Haugk,[*] the Stephen Series of lay ministry training raises up teams of paraclergy, equipping them to care for people affected by a wide variety of challenges and crises, or in need of referral to more professional care.

These lay volunteers receive ongoing supervision from Lindner. "The range of care our Stephen Ministers provide is just as varied as you would see in a pastor's counseling office," he says. "In the long run, without our team of twenty-five active Stephen Ministers, a lot of individuals would have suffered silently, and perhaps left the church, feeling the church was not there for them in their pain." Instead, trained volunteers are multiplying the ministry of the church. "Without them, we simply could not provide adequate ministry and care," says Lindner.

[*]Stephen Ministries, 8016 Dale, St. Louis, MO 63117-1449, phone 314-645-5511, FAX 314-645-9133.

The principles of telecare are quite basic:

1. Touch the entire church constituency regularly without shaming, blaming, finger pointing or in any way creating a truancy effect. In short, touch everyone; scold no one (see figure 43). Telecare is not even an exhortation ministry ("We hope you can come next week. . . ."); it's an extension of love ministry ("We just called to say we care, and to ask if there's anything we can do. . . .").

2. Purposely be redundant. If someone's already receiving care in a small group, call that person anyway. If someone recently received a pastoral visit, call him or her anyway. If you are confident that this family is doing well because they gave public testimony to that effect on Sunday, call them anyway.

3. Pray for the people you call. If you can do that over the phone, wonderful. If you pray as a telecare team after the

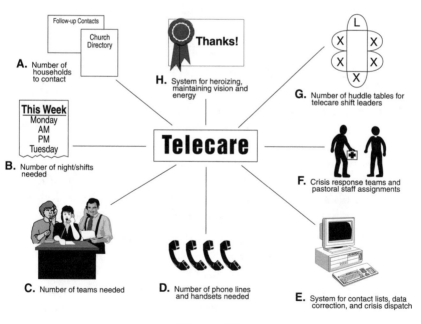

Figure 42

Telecare as Scold-Free Care

Figure 43

phoning has been completed, great. Any excuse to pray or any forum for prayer is acceptable.

4. Whatever you do, don't say anything during the call that the recipient might misconstrue as: "Nice call, but what they really wanted was my money—must be a new budget-preparation scheme." It is much better for the person to decide, on his or her own, "Imagine a church that calls you twelve times during the year whether you're a donor of record or not. It's enough to make you want to give!"

5. Listen to complaints but avoid taking sides. Genuinely extend a comment like, "I'm sorry if that happened to you," but don't make a lot of excuses, don't make a lot of promises, and don't become defensive. Sometimes the acceptance of the complaint is enough to rehabilitate a family, who will conclude, "Somebody finally listened and said

we weren't nuts when we felt like we were neglected or mistreated. We'll go back to church there. They've heard us."

6. Intensify telecare efforts during times of change within the church in order to give people extra strokes. If, for instance, you begin to implement new pastoral care methodologies such as small groups, remember that the new baby typically receives all the attention, causing an older-brother syndrome in which those who have been there the longest and endured the heat of past battles may feel overlooked. They can feel deeply resentful if they too don't receive some special attention. Telecare can dispel people's anxiety that they're being abandoned simply because they're not yet taking part in something new.

The mathematics of telecare calling are illustrated in figure 44. In short, if a team of five meets two evenings a month, it can complete about eighty calls a month.

Finally, don't be surprised when church growth is traced to the telecare ministry. Studies of people who drop out of church indicate that some drop out due to apathy and others drop out because of

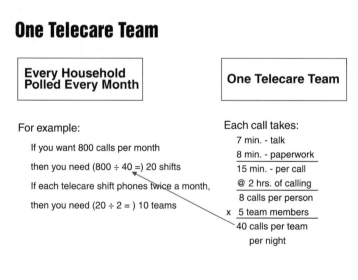

One Telecare Team

Every Household Polled Every Month

One Telecare Team

For example:

If you want 800 calls per month

then you need (800 ÷ 40 =) 20 shifts

If each telecare shift phones twice a month,

then you need (20 ÷ 2 =) 10 teams

Each call takes:

7 min. - talk

8 min. - paperwork

15 min. - per call

@ 2 hrs. of calling

8 calls per person

x 5 team members

40 calls per team per night

Figure 44

anger. A telecare caller can recreate interest in angry people if he or she will simply listen nondefensively. And if people are already coming to the church, a telecare ministry heightens the sense of churchwide self-esteem. The net result will be that people are all the more excited about their church and thus are eager to invite friends to it.

Staffing the Blue Zone

Although the recipients of Blue Zone ministry may constantly change, the leadership can be more constant, especially if given appropriate training, encouragement, and supervision. The key roles might include (see also figure 45):

- Ordained clergy and minister-of-the-day.
- Specially trained counselors and/or lay caregivers.
- Professional clinicians.
- Crisis-response team leaders (often a church's deacons).
- Veteran intercessors able to rally other people to prayer.

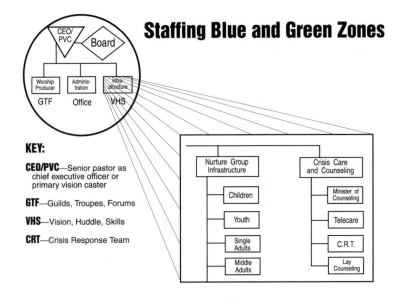

Figure 45

Types of Care

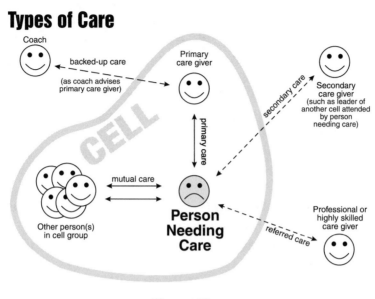

Figure 46

The net result is care that is decentralized, just as in all other Meta-Globe zones, to teams and service units of approximately ten people. The role of Blue Zone leadership is to ensure, and perhaps even track, whatever level of care is needed and provided through cell-size Blue Zone groups (see figure 46).

Church staff will serve as minister makers and team developers more than primary-care doers of one-on-one ministry. As the church matures, the staff pastor(s) [Ds] overseeing Blue Zone ministry will have a penchant for critical-care training skills, and the coaches [Ls] will typically be trained or supervised by those with clinical, licensed, or professional expertise (see figure 47).

In the Blue Zone of a maturing Meta-Church, for example, there will tend to be a minister of counseling who will be handling intake and minister-of-the-day assignments, so that needs are being met by groups in a routine way. There will also be a telecare unit, and an accompanying crisis-response unit that parallel traditional deacons' work. Sometimes there will be one or more intercessory

---

Ten Common Qualities of Recovery/Support Group Leaders

1. **Aren't Stuck:** Have a growing, personal relationship with Jesus Christ and are experiencing gains in their journey toward wholeness and spiritual health.

2. **Can Identify Boundaries:** Have a mature perspective on personal boundaries.

3. **Can Reflect Emotions:** Are able to communicate empathy and to involve other group members in peer-to-peer empathy.

4. **Understand Group Dynamics:** Know how to create a safe, grace-filled, non-shaming group environment.

5. **Are Trustworthy:** Know how to keep confidentialities, to maintain trust, and to ensure that the entire group does so.

6. **Are Vulnerable:** Are able to admit their personal weaknesses and struggles—but do not focus the group on themselves.

7. **Can Handle Conflicts:** Can help group members resolve conflicts both among themselves and in relationships outside the group.

8. **Are Secure:** Aren't easily threatened by others' ideas, emotions, or behaviors.

9. **Integrate Scripture with Recovery Principles:** Can effectively blend Bible study, practical insights, prayer, sharing, and therapeutic interaction.

10. **Have a Sense of Humor:** Know how to use humor appropriately and keep the group from becoming morose!

These ideas were refined through input from Jeff VanVonderen, Pat Springle, and Janet Logan.

---

teams. Sometimes also the church will have a cadre of volunteer counselors and volunteer people helpers. In fact, the training of indigenous, psychologically sophisticated, and prayerfully supported Blue Zone leaders is of higher priority than the opening of

Our Saviour's Lutheran Church

815 S. Washington Street
Naperville, IL 60540
Phone: (708) 355-2522
FAX: (708) 355-2553
Denomination: Evangelical
  Lutheran Church in America

Senior Pastor: Gerald W. Nelson
Contact: Sally Scaife, Church Administrator
Attendance: 1350
Total Cell Groups: 60

Providing Care through Telecare Teams

Our Saviour's Lutheran Church, Naperville, Illinois, has significantly increased its "care factor," prayer touches, and member morale through the use of telecare teams. This telephone ministry offers a safety net of redundant care designed to contact the entire church on a regular basis.

"I worked in telemarketing for thirteen years," says Sally Scaife, the staff administrator who coordinates the church's telecare ministry, "and one of the things I learned was that when you have a group of people together they support each other in good times and bad. If somebody has a bad call, the person sitting alongside can commiserate. If a person has a great call, the news enlivens everybody."

"One evening, one of our phone ministers called a lady who's going through a divorce," says Scaife. "She was having a bad night. She said, 'I'm so glad you called; I wish I could get a wonderful call like this every night.'"

"Our telecare phoner, who's knowledgeable about the other ministries of the church, said, 'Would you like help from one of our Stephen Ministers?'* She said, 'That would be wonderful.' Within two hours, a Stephen Minister was on the phone with her and has continued working with her ever since."

Another of the volunteer phone ministers came to her telecare shift tired and worn, according to Scaife. "I've had a really rough day," she said, "but I'll try to stick it out."

Two hours later, this lady came to Scaife and said, "I'm going to go home and clean my house!"

"What happened to that person who walked in?" Scaife asked.

She replied, "I've been ministered to. I made twelve calls and they ministered to me as much as I did to them. It was a great evening."

Telecare's purpose is to improve the care and prayer system of a church on a touch-everyone-scold-no-one basis. The phoning teams divide the agonies, griefs, and pains, while multiplying the joys. The team experience also enables the caller to increase his or her level of skill by working alongside other telecare workers.

More important, the people who are called deeply appreciate the contact. Says Scaife, "Our phone ministry enables people who might otherwise be overlooked to feel they are part of a larger family of faith."

* See page 228 for more background on Stephen Ministers.

Blue Zone Huddle

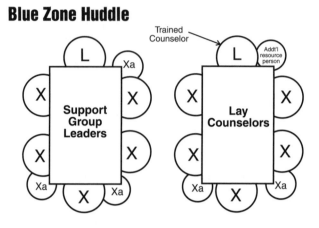

Figure 47

new Blue Zone groups. If your church has leaders, you can form new groups. Otherwise, if you focus on opening new groups, you'll constantly struggle to train enough volunteer leaders.

> If your church has leaders, you can form new groups.
> Otherwise, if you focus on opening new groups,
> you'll constantly struggle to train enough leaders.

An Example of Training Blue Zone Leaders

Imagine a staff pastor named John. He may be an exceedingly skilled volunteer with much experience as a wounded healer. Or he may be the most psychologically trained and certified person on the church's staff. The senior leadership (e.g., senior pastor or executive board) assigns John to be responsible for the church's Blue Zone ministries.

   1. He identifies everything that would be included as Blue Zone ministry. Figures 40 and 41 as well as the accompanying text, should prove helpful in doing that.

St. Luke's Lutheran

2491 San Miguel Drive
Walnut Creek, CA 94596
Phone: (510) 935-0160
Denomination: Evangelical
    Lutheran Church in America

Senior Pastor: Scott Dunfee
Contact: Scott Dunfee
Attendance: 225
Total Cell Groups: 16

From Prayer Counselors to an Entire Support Group Network

Gerda (not her real name) needed help to overcome grief about her young son who had died six years previously. During those years, many well-meaning people had advised her to "just accept and deal with it," but their counsel only made Gerda feel further injured.

Here she was, however, attending a healing service at her church, St. Luke's Lutheran Church, Walnut Creek, California. She entered the service about to give up on finding help for her pain, but she went up to the altar to ask for prayer. There, surrounded by those who were to become close friends in the coming months, she believes God began to heal her of grief. Her going forward also marked the first step in a journey that took her from receiving prayer by others, to joining a "New Hope" recovery group, to leading a recovery group, and most recently, to being trained as a member of a prayer team.

"St Luke's has developed into a 'safe place' that meets people where they are and accepts them for who they are, as we help them heal by God's grace," says Scott Dunfee, senior pastor at the church.

The goal of the church staff is to multiply the number of lay volunteers who lead recovery groups. "When the church's healing ministry began about ten years ago, the response was so large that we began to train lay people as prayer counselors," explains Dunfee. "The staff organized training seminars, taught by local professionals, to equip intercessors in understanding what they were dealing with when they offered to pray with hurting and broken people. We wanted to guard against inappropriately handling a situation and unknowingly adding spiritual abuse on top of someone's other pains. As time went on, the prayer ministry expanded into ten or so support groups."

A volunteer leader has also been trained to coach the recovery group leaders. The church staff equips and supports group leaders through ongoing resourcing, such as a monthly leadership meeting. The "huddle" portion of that meeting, however, is facilitated by a lay volunteer. "She is far more effective than I because of her personal experience with recovery issues," says Dunfee. "Lay leaders and lay coaches have truly expanded the church's possibilities for ministry."

2. He maps out his own current leadership responsibilities. Figures 45, 46, and 47 should be helpful for doing that.

   He begins by mapping out the one-on-one level: For example, his schedule for the previous month might include counseling (about five individuals per week), visitation to the hospital and shut-ins (about ten individuals per week), and crisis care (about two emergencies per week).

   Then he lists the groups he leads in an X capacity. Maybe he heads an Adult-Children-of-Alcoholics support group, a Caring-for-your-Aging-Parents Sunday-school class, and a recovery group for workaholics. Next he indicates the ways he serves in an L capacity: What group leaders does he coach? Finally he assesses how he functions as a D: What Ls does he supervise?

3. John identifies all other Blue Zone team leaders and how they are being coached at present.

   Perhaps the deacons have been organized into four geographic teams to handle crises. The north team and west team have leaders, but the south and east teams are inactive because no one has taken the mantle of responsibility. The chairman of the deacons has caught the vision for crisis care, and is willing to serve as the L.

   Perhaps the senior pastor started telecare, but the volunteer leader who agreed to oversee it isn't working out. Fortunately, she had been training an apprentice leader. It's not yet been spelled out who will serve as L to that group.

4. John begins to understand why he's so tired and ready to resign! He discovers that he is trying to provide hands-on care for almost one hundred people, and that there are serious leadership gaps among groups that represent another fifty people. Any gap created when a leader fails will come to John.

5. John remembers that one foundation of Meta-Church thinking is the idea that virtually all the work, fellowship, and care of the church takes place through groups and teams. Further, these basic units of approximately ten people are

best coordinated in little huddles of five or so. He realizes that spans of care need to be reduced to the five to ten range.

> One foundation of Meta-Church thinking is the idea that virtually all the work, fellowship, and care of the church takes place through groups and teams.

6. John decides that the most crucial issue is that of needing to develop more trained leaders. So he begins to spread the vision for apprentices. No one ministers alone. Everyone is responsible for the cultivation of an apprentice leader. Otherwise, the pipeline will always be empty (or only trickling), and disaster will always be imminent.

   His first step is to find apprentices [Xa's] for everywhere he's filling the role of a cell leader [X]. In fact he decides to recruit a minimum of two apprentices for each cell group he leads. His next step is to develop a plan for using group care to handle many of the needs he currently deals with on a one-on-one basis. He then works with his cell leaders to help them identify and cultivate an apprentice leader [Xa]. He walks them through the process of understanding the need for an apprentice, prayerfully naming potential apprentices, securing a commitment from someone to be an apprentice, training that person, helping that person recruit his or her own apprentice, and then releasing that person into ministry, with apprentice already in tow. This progression is symbolized by either the prefixes R (for rising) or U (for unknown) as in figure 48 or by "disappearing brackets." (We used the latter annotation method for years, but it proved unworkable when, with computer scanners, we began using optical character recognition to computer generate Meta-Globe databases.)

7. John now targets the spots where it is most important for him to work himself out of a job. In most cases these involve his responsibilities as an X or an I (individual).

Graphic Notations for Meta-Church Roles

1. Bare letter = Role Occupant	H, XA, X, LA, L, CA, C, DA, D

2. R + Letter = Rising or Ascending Role Nominee	RH, RXA, RX, RLA, RL, RCA, RC, RDA, RD

3. U + Letter = Unidentified or Yet-Unknown Role Nominee	UH, UXA, UX, ULA, UL, UCA, UC, UDA, UD

Figure 48

8. John also begins looking for an apprentice coach [La]. These people generally function also as Xs and at the huddle tables keep emerging as the natural leaders of the Xs.

9. Ultimately, John begins watching for someone who might become a Da, with the goal of coming on staff and replacing John (see figure 49).

John's job will never be finished. But the approach described above offers the greatest promise of sanity and fulfillment for both himself and all volunteer leaders he partners with. John and the group leaders he works with may always struggle with a motivation to be super-rescuers—to burn out by taking on too many needs. But over time, as John and his various leaders look back, they see that the dramatic shift in priorities has enabled more leaders to be involved, and more needs to be met. As a result, more people are moving toward maturity in Christ, and the level of heartache and pain in the community is noticeably less.

Leadership Career Paths

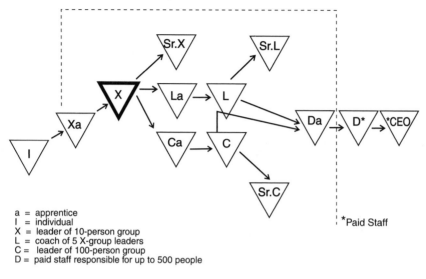

a = apprentice
I = individual
X = leader of 10-person group
L = coach of 5 X-group leaders
C = leader of 100-person group
D = paid staff responsible for up to 500 people

*Paid Staff

Figure 49

Blue Zone volunteer leaders, if trained, released, and supported, can bring a great deal of wholeness to a desperately hurting world.

Questions for Discussion and Application

1. What, in the church you serve, qualifies as a Blue Zone group? How much Blue Zone ministry is currently handled one-on-one that could be better handled by groups?

2. Why is telecare so important in a church, especially one that is experimenting with new forms of pastoral care?

3. How would you apply "John's" self-diagnosis to your own ministry?

PART 3

Transitioning Wisely from "Here" to "There"

14

Infrastructure Analysis: Mapping Your Care Structure

> The Meta-Church strategy is to develop a maximum number of Green Zone ministry teams and nurture groups, with: (1) as much Red Zone as you need for the worship needs of the cells, (2) as much Yellow Zone as you need to feed the Green Zone, and (3) as much Blue Zone as you need to care for the cell system's referral needs.

You have been exposed to the big picture of why Meta-Church ideals are desperately needed (chapter 1) and how they differ from most other ministry paradigms (chapters 2–6). You have learned the graphic notation idea of the Meta-Globe (chapter 7), and have explored how leadership development works in each different color-zone domain of a church (chapters 8–13).

Now you're ready to make a Meta-Map of your church. The map is foundational preparation for making a shift from where you are now to what you believe God is calling your church to become (chapters 15–19). My concluding challenge (chapter 20) will remind you that God has put a series of unprecedented opportunities within your reach. The net result will be to unleash and empower every available saint to minister the love of God to every person in need of Christ's love and then to enlist those people in cooperating with God's call to the harvest!

Ladies and Gentlemen, Map Your Churches!

Meta-Church organization provides you with a sense of proportion to your work. It enables you to zoom in and out, and do inventories. You can identify existing gaps, assets that need to be kept strong, and where assets need to be added so as to best contribute to the health of the whole. All of these concepts can be envisioned through the Meta-Globe and applied to your church through the creation of a Meta-Map.

Skillful use of a Meta-Map helps staff and boards understand how their churches are configured so they can track such critically important factors as where leaders and potential leaders are, where new people are, how visitors are being handled, and where long-term members are relative to more recent members. A Meta-Map enables leaders to see what happens after everyone has gathered for corporate worship: Where do they go? What tasks do they take with them? What stations in life are they occupying? Until pastors visualize those dimensions of the church life, they don't know how to walk from the pulpit to the workers' meetings and lay out the game plan of what needs to happen next in the life of the church.

Every visual symbol on a Meta-Map represents a leader to be supervised, a training site for producing an apprentice, a place where people are loved and cared for, or an entry point where new converts can be lodged. When ministry can be perceived in that way, the task of the church's leadership team becomes very clear.

In fact, one of the primary purposes of using the Meta-Globe to map a church is to help staff and boards see differently than they've seen before. Each time a church creates an event small enough that people can be listened to, a cell is present and can be nurtured. Most churches (as chapter 17 will explain further) are filled with such cell-size groups, but they are frequently underreported by at least 50 percent. When meetings and groups aren't recognized as cells, they're not cultivated for their soul-building potential.

It's critical, then, that pastors, staff, and boards change their perception of church. I believe that if the right data is selected and appropriately visualized, then we can help these leaders move to a new way of seeing the task before them.

Your map can be so clear that you will say, "That's our church!" You'll learn to read your map with the same degree of skill that a surgeon reads an M.R.I. and says, "I see what's going on here."

> When meetings and groups aren't recognized as cells, they're not cultivated for their soul-building potential.

Then you'll learn to reflect on your map just as a surgeon studies the X ray before taking out the scalpel.

The ultimate purpose for a Meta-Map is not to have a smartly colored, mechanically precise, professional-looking chart to hang on your office door, in your church lobby, or even in your board-room, though many churches do use their Meta-Map in that way. For instance, a large Meta-Map on the wall where staff meetings are held can be used to facilitate dialogue among staff members on the use of volunteers, ministry interfacing, people flow, entry points, leader development, new-ministry planning, and existing-ministry redirecting. Other churches use their Meta-Map as a communication tool with ministry leaders, showing how their area of ministry supplements and compliments the total ministry of the church. Still other churches, using colored paper stock, structure their annual reports according to the Meta-Globe.

Those ideas are helpful, but the most important advantage of mapping is the process rather than the product. The graphic conventions used in a Meta-Map have proved useful across various denominations, sizes, and settings of churches, but their primary purpose is not to force a "right" answer. The value of your map is the experience you go through in self-diagnosis, agony of prayer, and response to God.

Being precisely accurate isn't always as important as learning to see the whole and the parts, and then to see how the parts relate to the whole. In short, you want to discover what new "doors" the Lord is showing you, which you have not seen to date in terms of building your ministry on lay-pastored units of ten as the core foundation of the church.

In the long run, every leader you produce gives you the power to provide personal evangelism, discipleship, nurture, and care to five to ten more people.

Steps in Meta-Mapping

You are now ready to add specific action steps to the general overview of the Meta-Globe you received in chapter 7.

1. Identify all groups.

List every group in the church that meets at least once a month. Create a simple inventory that includes name, purpose, place of meeting, leader, and typical attendance. Only after all groups have been so identified can you move to the next step. (Seasonal groups, such as six-week Lenten prayer groups, are best understood via a separate "seasonal" map.)

2. Assign basic visual object and color.

Visual objects, analogous to computer icons, are summarized in figure 50. If a group is primarily designed for nurture and mutual self-care, depict it with an oval. Thus most Sunday-school classes, covenant groups, tender-loving-care groups, and so forth are ovals (and *tend* to be Green).

If a group's purpose is that of ministering to others beyond the group itself, the group is represented by a rectangle. The range of these task groups includes worship ensembles (red), the officers group of a large adult Bible fellowship (yellow), a food bank (usually green), or an intercessory prayer team, hospital-visitation team, crisis-response team, Stephen Ministers, or telecare team (all usually blue).

Governance groups (usually purple) use a diamond (a tilted square) to represent the group's task focus. Examples would include a pastoral staff meeting and probably any board that gives oversight to other separate ministries.

3. Decide function—surface or axis.

Since an emphasis on leadership development is so central to Meta-Church organization, all leadership teams are graphed on the

Basic Visual Objects

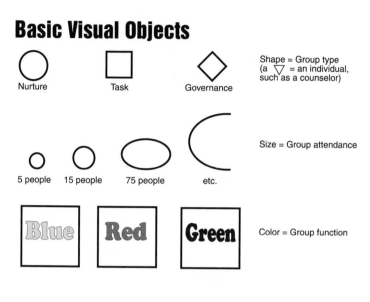

Figure 50

axis—an imaginary pole or elevator shaft running through the center of the Meta-Globe from top to bottom. All other groups go on the "surface" of the Meta-Globe.

Figure 51 illustrates various axis details. Note that two of the most crucial leadership communities are the Ensemble Incubator—a worship production structure placed on the axis of the northern hemisphere; and the Vision, Huddle, and Skills meeting—a coaching and supervision structure, placed on the axis of the southern hemisphere.[1]

In order to create a Meta-Map, a church must decide which of its meetings are for leaders (and potential leaders). Those gatherings go on the axis.

4. Determine zone and conjunctions with other groups.

In most cases orange-color groups will go in the Orange Zone, blue-color in the Blue Zone, etc.—but not always. Here are some factors to consider:

Axis Details

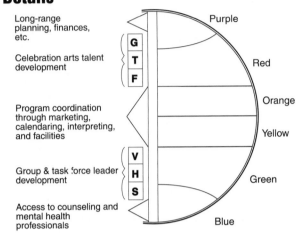

Long-range planning, finances, etc.

Celebration arts talent development

Program coordination through marketing, calendaring, interpreting, and facilities

Group & task force leader development

Access to counseling and mental health professionals

G
T
F

V
H
S

Purple

Red

Orange

Yellow

Green

Blue

Figure 51

Group Size

Current Meta-Mapping practice says that by the time a group reaches seventeen people, it no longer functions as a small group (see figure 52). No published research I have seen proves seventeen to be a cut-off point, but much experience suggests that intimacy in a group is hampered when you exceed ten members. Also, when more than ten people are present, the group begins to function like a class. Before the group grows to fifteen or sixteen, several members will report feeling left out or overlooked. At seventeen and above, almost nobody reports feeling that the group still has the care and personal touch of when it was smaller. Thus seventeen is an upper limit.

On a Meta-Globe, then, if a group size is greater than seventeen people, it will be placed in the Purple, Red, Orange, or Yellow Zones. Smaller groups (four to sixteen people) can go anywhere, and ministry teams can be virtually any color.

Commonly Occurring Situations

Figure 53 illustrates options for depicting large and small groups near each other. For example, altar prayer counselors can be a blue

Group Sizes on the Meta-Globe

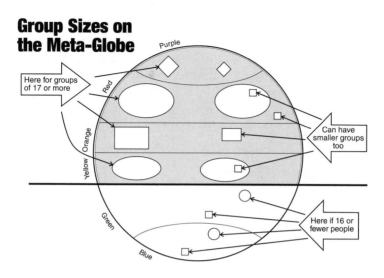

Figure 52

Related Big and Small Groups

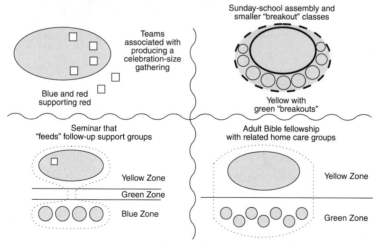

Figure 53

rectangle *inside* a celebration-size red oval; parking-lot attendants can be a red rectangle just *outside* a celebration-size red oval. Sunday-school departments might be yellow with green inside, representing a departmental assembly that has breakout classes. Or, if a large adult Bible fellowship has smaller groups associated with it, you might draw an encompassing dotted line to show the loose connection between the Yellow Zone class and the Green Zone cells.

5. Keep it simple for now.

Meta-Mapping conventions have proved to be a helpful notation system for analyzing the care structure of a church. Although they involve a certain amount of arbitrariness, they have been field-tested and refined through a broad range of denominations, church sizes, and church settings.

Advanced mapping concepts can add to the understanding of your Meta-Map—but use them only after you've mastered the "basics." For example, figure 54 explains some special conventions, such as an equal sign at the 3:00 position, representing an open door and signifying that a group is intentionally open. This "open door" mark goes primarily on small ovals and rectangles; diamonds are assumed to be always closed by definition.

Additional Uses of Basic Visual Objects

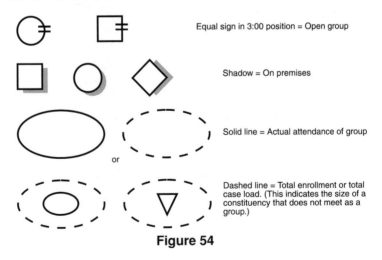

Equal sign in 3:00 position = Open group

Shadow = On premises

Solid line = Actual attendance of group

Dashed line = Total enrollment or total case load. (This indicates the size of a constituency that does not meet as a group.)

Figure 54

Users of my previous book on the Meta-Church, *Prepare Your Church for the Future* (especially chapter 10, "Think Panoramically with the Meta-Globe"), may be interested to know that only two major refinements have been found necessary since its publication. We no longer recommend a "Gray Zone" for highlighting finance-related issues. Most churches did not find that color helpful; instead finance-based governance committees are mapped in the Purple Zone. Also, some Orange Zone group assignments used to be viewed with negative connotations. That is no longer the case; we've refined the Orange Zone to be much less complicated and with no stigmas attached to it.

6. Be aware of typical blindspots.

Based on the more than four hundred churches that have conducted team planning through Meta-mapping, we're able to list the areas in which confusion is most likely to arise:

- Don't try to fit the name of a group inside its symbol. If you do, the groups with the longer names will seem to be the more important! Instead, print the name near its symbol and draw an arrow to the oval, rectangle, or diamond.

- Don't combine two or more groups under a single icon. That is, avoid drawing one oval and labeling it "Tender Loving Care," when in reality Dr. Buteux, the veterinarian, holds one group in his office, Mrs. Stanley holds one in her home, and the office volunteers hold one in the church kitchen. Unless you identify each group, you'll hide the magnitude of their attendances and leadership-development requirements. With worship-arts groups, then, be sure to indicate that a rehearsal meeting is distinct from a performance meeting. The reason for this is that care and nurture are more likely to occur at the rehearsal.

- Don't try to create a finished, precise, polished map on the first pass. Better to do a very simple, very rough map first; continue to work from greater toward lesser issues. Then, as a final step, ask a detail-oriented person to create a finished copy.

7. Summarize what you have learned.

Where does mapping lead you? Whether your church develops a
Meta-Map on its own or receives outside resourcing,[2] remember
that if a church leadership team is struggling to understand how to
classify its groups, then chances are that many important discoveries and decisions are in the offing, such as those summarized here:

Advantages to Mapping

Mapping will help you . . .

1. See the leadership requirements of your church.
2. See the proportions and gaps.
3. See new opportunities and goals-in-motion.
4. Focus your church's attention on the "forest" (not on one
   or two trees).
5. Interpret to your church where you are going and why.
6. Hold your attention as you pray over and plan key areas.

What kinds of insights are typically drawn from the Meta-
Mapping process? Here is one of the findings common to many
churches' experiences. I don't offer a checklist of "most frequent
discoveries" because the greatest value comes when you find them
yourself!

In the Yellow Zone, for instance, some churches are amazed that
so much activity occurs in medium-size groups. Same with the
Orange Zone. Or they discover that most of the medium-size
groups operate more-or-less autonomously of the church staff. That
is, the pastors don't have any effective way of connecting with,
supervising, or shaping the life of these subcongregations. Similarly, in many cases the majority of a church's small-group ministry
is linked to the subcongregations in such a way that the staff
doesn't have an effective connection with these small groups.

How do churches respond in that case? Some decide to repurpose
certain groups, especially those in the Yellow Zone and Orange
Zone (see chapter 16), so that they offer a greater contribution to

cell health and evangelism. Others desire to legitimize a staff connection with small groups directly and not merely through subcongregational leadership.

8. Know where you're headed.

It is important to know the desired emphasis. How much of each zone is enough? The Meta-Church strategy is to develop a maximum number of Green Zone ministry teams and nurture groups, with: (1) as much Red Zone as you need for the worship needs of the cells, (2) as much Yellow Zone as you need to feed the Green Zone, and (3) as much Blue Zone as you need to keep the cell system's referral needs taken care of.

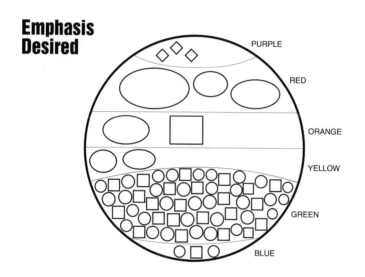

Figure 55

This strategy is depicted in figure 55.

When introducing Meta-Church theory, the first step is to help people see church as a system with interrelated parts. Everything is consequential. If you change or improve one part, you'll no doubt affect another part. Any time church leaders operate without examining how each part feeds on and contributes to other parts, they're not behaving systemically.

Indeed, when church leaders start asking, "Okay, what is the primary function of this, and how does it relate to the other functions?" then that church is poised for some important discoveries, and some very intentional forward progress.

Questions for Discussion and Application

1. What, according to this chapter, is the desired emphasis in a mature church's Meta-Map? What is the rationale for that goal?

2. What previous systems have you used for pictorially mapping your church? Did your system help you pinpoint leadership needs? group purposes?

3. If you were to map your church, using the Meta-Globe as described here and in chapter 7, which color zone would be the "fullest"? Which would you like to be the most intensely populated? What might some steps be to get from where you are to where you want to be?

15

Essential Foundations for Introducing Change

If these attitudes toward change pervade all you do in the church, you're now ready for some very specific implementation steps.

Imagine the day when every member of the church you serve is so caught up in the love of Christ and of other Christians that the church consistently cares for one another, it inducts new people into the faith, it cheers the formation of new leaders, it develops new cells, and it brings these cells, ten by ten, into the corporate worship experience to rejoice in the presence of God. That is the Meta-Church vision of tomorrow's church. Now, how to do you get from here to there, especially in light of your present traditions?

Lyle Schaller, author or editor of more than eighty books, summarizes his thirty-plus years of church consulting with this observation: "The number-one issue facing Christian organizations on the North American continent today" is "the need to initiate and implement planned change."[1] Thus, to say that most churches don't handle change very well would be an understatement!

This chapter offers advice gleaned from the experiences of existing churches who have begun to install a new social architecture, the Meta-Church, designed to maximize clergy-laity partnership in ministry.

Pastors' Priorities

This book is not specifically about personal spiritual renewal. But on numerous occasions it has emphasized the need to be in touch with the Lord, especially through listening prayer. If God visits you during the reading of this book, you will return to your ministry much better than when you opened the cover—but not necessarily because of the ideas or teaching on these pages! This book, on purpose, is not primarily a how-to manual. I presume that most church leaders already know more things to do about improving their ministry than they now have the time or energy to put into place.

Instead, this book suggests a new perspective on your ministry— a refocused sense of knowing where you're trying to go. Most pastors stay so close to the trees that they lose an overall sense of the forest. Most church leaders do a great job of filling in the pieces if they just know what the grand march is. It's the building of frameworks that's the key to Meta-Church thinking.

If Meta-Church observations can get you to redefine your role, that's as permanent a form of learning as I know. By contrast, fact-based learning is one of the least permanent.

So, armed with a fresh understanding, remember that it's not the information you're exposed to that matters but the information you commit to act on: "By the grace of God, I will *do* this." Faith kicks in, something clicks, and you're ready to go. After all, faith is simply a perception of what's next on God's agenda. Therefore, the most foundational outcome of this book begins as a pastor or program staff person makes the shift from being a hands-on minister to

> It's the building of frameworks that's the key
> to Meta-Church thinking.

being the maker of ministers. In the sheepherder imagery used in *How to Break Growth Barriers*, the change is from "shepherd of the sheep" to "dispenser of shepherd's crooks."[2]

I recommend to senior pastors, including those in single-pastor churches, that they make incremental increases until 80 percent of their time is spent in leadership-development activities. In other words, suppose the typical full-time staff member currently spends one day a week working on leadership development—such as working through spans of care (figure 5), identifying apprentices (figure 6), huddling with existing leaders (figures 36 and 47), developing measurable work goals (figure 16), and preparing sermons on lay-empowerment themes (figure 17). Six months from now that staff person should be investing two days a week in these kinds of pursuits. Six months after that, three days a week, and six months later, four days a week. Within two years, almost any church staff can be spending 80 percent of his or her energy on leadership development. The remaining 20 percent will go to direct ministry and administrative sorts of issues.

During those two years, however, another shift is occurring. In the language of Jethro II, most staff members begin their journey by wearing the hat of X *and* L *and* D. Over time they will train others for the X role, and begin to function primarily as an L and D. Their eventual goal is to establish so many L-X clusters that they work primarily as a D. The outcome is that these staff members become far more productive. Now they're multiplying themselves through twenty or thirty lay ministers instead of trying to do the work themselves.

Transition with Minimal Fanfare

These changes in pastoral priorities will be far more effective, in most cases, if not accompanied by any fanfare. In terms of the church program, you won't be doing very much differently, and most of the church won't see any difference in your approach to ministry unless you parade it.

You're simply conscientiously applying leadership-management strategy to every single group. You're brightening the colors. You're meeting with leaders more regularly. You're improving what you have. You add new groups whenever you find new talent, but you wait until these leaders are ready to do so and want to do so. You probably won't even need a board resolution to accomplish any of these changes!

I strongly advise against a crusading announcement, "We are going into the Meta-Church," because all that does is invite trouble. Instead, say, "We are going to be intentional about encouraging lay ministry to a greater extent than we have up until now. We want to improve the resources of our volunteers as they do their ministry." Who can argue with improvement? Few people, if any.

Reluctant Advocacy

Experience has shown that a particular attitude is critical to any leader's emotional survival of a Meta-Church transition. Called *reluctant advocacy*, this posture enables you to offer a positive notion and plan without the assertiveness that causes people to fear that you might destroy or dismantle existing ministries and values.

Reluctant advocacy has three components: achievement, preservation, and avoidance (APA). Although figure 56 summarizes them in that order, church leaders can mix the components in whatever way that best helps them interpret proposed system improvements that don't increase inappropriate anxiety. APA enables a leader to couch the language of change in terms that display the benefits and caution appropriate balance.

For example, after your board retreat, you might give this report to the church as a whole, "What we learned most from discussing *The Coming Church Revolution* was how to appreciate the good things we have. We also learned to dream of some things that will improve the kind of people we are, provided that we are very careful not to damage anything that God has blessed." In this case the *preserve* statement came first, the *achieve* statement was in the middle, and the *avoid* statement completed the thought. That sentence is phrased so cautiously that your most change-oriented people might find their stomachs turning! But most parishioners will say, "Great, you're still sane. Now, what is it you want to do?"

What you have done is to communicate that in the process of excelling and improving you don't want to devalue anything that the church has enjoyed in the past, or anything that they think is worthwhile, while getting on with the business of excelling and improving.

Formula for Interpreting Proposed System
Improvements (without increasing appropriate anxiety)

$\oplus$ **A**chievement Statements

$\ominus$ **P**reserve Statements

$\ominus$ **A**void Statements

Figure 56

In a church where everything is done decently and in order and according to tradition, a church leader might follow the order PAA: what we're going to *preserve*, and then what we are going to *achieve*, and then what we are going to *avoid*. In a church with a very negative congregation, the leaders may need to reverse the two A's: what we're going to *avoid*, and also what we're going to *preserve*, and then what we're going to work on *achieving*.

The overall mix, no matter how you present it, still offers one-third conservation (preserve), one-third caution (avoid), and one-third improvement (achieve). It enables a leader to respond in a way that generally will not alarm people.

Dealing with Resistance

The concept of force-field analysis (FFA), taken from social psychology, is a little like listing pros and cons. FFA looks at someone's goals and says, "This is where you are today, and this is where you'd like to go. What forces are propelling you toward your desired future, and what forces are preventing you from achieving or moving easily to that desired future?" (See figure 57.)

Those who go through an FFA exercise discover that most resistance can be overcome by the way in which you interpret and

Force-Field Analysis

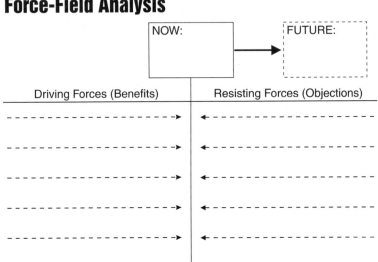

Figure 57

install your desired future. That is, you learn that many objections are brought on largely by the way you handle the interpretation and implementation process. If you carefully take into account the anticipated objections and incorporate them into your plan, most of the objections simply dissolve. People say, "I can tell you've done your homework well," or "I think I can get behind that."

> Many objections are brought on largely by the way you handle the interpretation and implementation process.

People who start out as cautious resisters and objectors become allies in implementation if you take their concerns into account. When you honor the resister, and when you treat people well, they will be your allies. But if you try to put down their ideas, they become your enemies. Remember, resistance is not bad. It can be helpful because it points out blind spots in your goals. You can even thank people, up to a point, for pointing out the weaknesses in your ideas. Then use FFA to dissolve that resistance or convert it to a benefit.

> The sheer number of people a pastor or board works with is not nearly as important as the fact that he or she includes the "right" people: the opinion makers of the church.

Identifying Movers and Blockers

Pastors and church boards often underestimate the amount of lay leadership represented in their churches. Often, when introducing changes in how a church will offer care to its people, many pastors and boards apply the law-of-large-numbers thinking: "If we just announce our intentions to enough people, we'll get enough to go along with us." Such thinking is logically faulty. They don't realize that the sheer number of people a pastor or board works with is not nearly as important as the fact that he or she includes the "right" people: the opinion makers of the church.

In every society, the majority of people decide how they feel about a given issue by deferring to the influence and convictions of someone else.

- "How am I supposed to make up my mind—I haven't asked my wife!" says a husband whose wife typically chooses a narrower range of acceptable options than he does.

- "Before we decide, we want to see what Lorna and Jim think," say parents who appreciate the impact that veteran youth sponsors have had on their teens.

- "How will this affect our Discovery groups?" asks someone who respects John's view that cell groups are the pivotal ministry in the church.

How can church leaders detect which men or women are the movers and which are the blockers of congregational public opinion? One procedure involves a simple survey. Convene the pastoral staff and board of a church and ask everyone present to write down three names for each of the following two situations.

First, imagine that something is going on at your church that needs to be stopped. Who, if given the assignment to prevent it from happening, can you trust to carry it out? Who, like an offensive line, are the blockers that can prevent undesirable movement?

Second, suppose you want something to be accomplished at the church. Name three people (either new names or repeats from your first list) who, if given an assignment, could make it happen. Like ball carriers, these are your movers.

In situations where I've conducted this poll, I then diagram the responses. I draw two intersecting circles, labeling one "movers" and one "blockers." The overlapping area is for people who are both movers and blockers. We read through the lists of movers, and put each name in or out of the movers circle, depending on whether that person is present at our meeting. We follow the same pattern with the blockers circle. Next we tag each name if it appears on more than one person's list. John, for example, might be a blocker according to four people and Mary a mover according to three people.

As we look over the results, we note that some people appear on both lists. For instance, Zed may be both a mover to ten people *and* a blocker to eight! Further, we observe that certain highly influential people—like Luis, a mover with a seven, and Thelma, a blocker with a twelve—aren't at our meeting. I usually caution against the presumption that pro and con absentees will cancel each other out.

In the above-described meeting, it turned out that all but two of the movers and blockers known to the group were sitting there in the room. This meant that those present were basically the leaders of the church. It so happened that a cousin of Luis was in the room, and I knew that if the group could sell it to the cousin, he would carry the word to Luis. And the pastor assured me that he and his wife knew how to reach Thelma.

We decided, therefore, that whatever decisions were made, they'd first need to be interpreted to Luis and Thelma, and their feedback solicited and responded to before anyone would announce the board's decisions to the entire church. This plan of diffusion worked, and five years later the church had accomplished each of its objectives without any major divisiveness.

In short, attempting to launch goals without knowing who your major opinion leaders are is an exercise in frustration. Some people absolutely have to be in on the planning, or they'll scuttle the idea.

- Do you know who the movers and blockers are in your church?

- Or do you need to take a survey that includes both the long-time, generally older members (the "senior formerberries") and the newer, well-acquainted members (the "junior new-berries")?[3]

The effective pastor will find out who the truly respected opinion leaders in the congregation are, and will then build the necessary alliances with these key members. Doing so will make any minis-

> Some people absolutely have to be in
> on the planning or they'll scuttle the idea.

ter's leadership task easier and more influential. As a result, the church will make more and better disciples of Jesus Christ.

If these attitudes toward change guide all you do in leading the church, you're now ready for some very specific implementation steps, which will be outlined in the next chapter.

Questions for Discussion and Application

1. Name the most recent major change introduced at the church you serve. Was it done with fanfare? Would a "silent" approach have worked better? Why or why not?

2. What are the advantages of a reluctant-advocate positioning? Offer a specific example of how you could use the APA formula to introduce something new at your church.

3. Who are the movers in your church? The blockers? Both? Why is it important to build alliances with them?

16

Major Phases
of a Transition

> You are the best judge of what God is calling your
> church to do and be. Consider the following, then, as the
> accumulated observations of those who may be a bit far-
> ther down the path than you.

In the event you happen on this chapter without reading the rest of the book, you need to know that Meta-Church perspectives are relationship based, not program based (chapter 4). The Meta-Church doesn't advocate a particular curriculum (chapter 5), a particular worship style (chapter 9) or a particular brand of small groups (chapter 12).

As the opening chapters of this book observed, it's inaccurate to talk about "making the transition to Meta." That expression is redundant because Meta means transition. Instead, the change is to a ministry that's shared between pastors and volunteer leaders. The resulting new effectiveness far transcends the "pull" power of preachers and musicians standing on a sanctuary platform. It also enables ministry to be multiplied far beyond the availability and personal gifts of the pastoral staff.

In short, when you get to Meta, you won't be there! The Meta-Church is a journey, not an end point. If there is an end point, it's people becoming joyful and whole under the care of godly leaders who are helping them form their lives into base communities that come together for worship celebration. As Ephesians 4:12–13 says, pastors are "to prepare God's people for works of service, so that the body of Christ may be built up until we all reach unity in the faith and in the knowledge of the Son of God and become mature, attaining to the whole measure of the fullness of Christ."

As chapter 1 also emphasized, our focus is on principles, not methods. We're trying to observe what the Holy Spirit is doing, not independently inventing something new. In the words of chapter 1, Meta-Church technology, like that of an X ray, is a diagnostic tool that enables someone to peer through the surface of things. It doesn't tell you how to treat what you see; that's a different matter. You still must apply judgment to decide what to do with what you learn. The following comments are the closest this book comes to suggesting a series of programs or sequence of events. They represent the experience of hundreds of churches and are the progression that seems to work best for them.

You are the best judge of what God is calling your church to do and be. Scripture speaks of wisdom as the application of divine truth to human experience—insight from God based on experience (Job 12:12, 15:8–10; Proverbs 1:7, 16:31). Consider the following, then, as the accumulated observations of those who may be a bit farther down the path. They are offered with the assumption that you are already installing the relational and political foundation with key leaders described in chapter 15.

Track I—Existing Churches, Recently on the Scene Pastors

In keeping with the recommendations of the previous chapter, gently deploy the following change process more as one-on-one counseling than as a roll-out-the-drums campaign. Proceed carefully. Pray as never before. As chapter 2 affirmed, go forward only as fast as you can go on your knees.

1. Meta-Globe mapping. Visualize all groups and meetings that meet at least once a month during the majority of the year. Represent these groups, according to size and func-

tion, through Meta-Globe mapping, as described in chapters 7 and 14.

2. Jethro II mapping. Carefully identify the "wiring" that brings group leaders into contact with the staff and boards of the church. Diagram these links by using the Jethro II concepts presented in chapter 3.

3. Apprentice mapping. Intentionally approach the leader of each group or ministry to strengthen the rapport and communication between the pastoral staff and the team leaders. Notice who has an apprentice, who grasps the concept of apprentice development, and who doesn't have a clue what you mean! Invite them, from whatever starting point, to explore the apprentice model as a way for their ministry to increase the number of leaders available to it.

4. Telecare. Implement a safety net that ensures redundancy of care, such as a telecare system (as discussed in chapter 13). This undergirding framework will increase the care that the entire congregation receives. Introduce it nonprogrammatically. Campaigning is inappropriate because it often raises more fear of loss than hope of gain. You don't want to increase the congregation's level of anxiety with announcements. Your goal is church renewal and lay leadership development. Even so, telecare (or whatever you choose) may represent the first system change that people begin to see. The purpose is to increase the level of caring, so that people noticeably appreciate the extra strokes they're receiving (figure 58). Then you're ready to look at additional work but not until this new contact net is spread.

5. Transfer growth. Expand the search for leadership to involve transfer members. Depending on the amount of "baggage" these people bring, including any unresolved morale issues they may have, plug them into entry levels of apprenticeship.

6. Internal fishing ponds. Enhance your leaders' network of acquaintance-making contacts, thus turning the church into a perpetual bridge-mezzanine event (see chapter 10). The

Extra "Strokes" Make a Big Difference

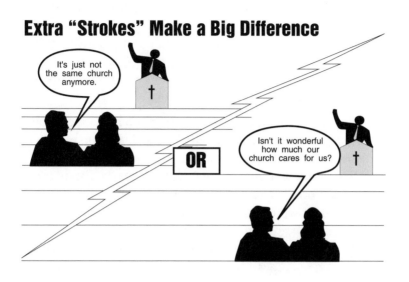

Figure 58

most prominent fishing ponds might be: new-members classes, existing receptions for newcomers and visitors, and existing subcongregations (large adult Sunday-school classes and a large women's ministry among others). In these, with enriched acquaintance mixers, group leaders and their apprentices will be dispersed throughout the existing networks of the church.

7. Staff realignment. Analyze the entire church for span-of-care inequities. If you haven't started reassigning staff responsibilities to balance the leadership development and supervision load, begin to do so. Do you observe an equity here in terms of the care of volunteer ministers? You may need to do some reapportioning. Also, new staff roles may now become apparent.

8. External Fishing Ponds. Promote programs that target population niches. Start planning the church year with an eye on having wonderful services of divine worship that

are celebrations and other high-visibility events that will serve as bridges from the community into the church. Are church people becoming excited enough that they invite friends? Are there enough guest events and other felt-need topics offered that target certain population niches of the community?

9. Vision, Huddle, Skill. As you bring about change through a negotiated process, eventually all the energy and movement will create a demand for calling a formalized leadership community meeting where huddles meet on a regular basis, and pastoral leaders can do overall vision casting (see chapter 12). If you launch this final step too soon, you may bruise yourself and the church unnecessarily. The VHS function is a kind of "neatening" up of things that have been emerging all along. For example, as you installed apprentices, that was an appropriate place to begin apprentice training. VHS grows naturally as a culmination of the process.

Track II—Church Planters, Long-Tenured Pastors

Founding pastors, very long-tenured pastors, and other special cases have the privilege and responsibility of being able to introduce change and obtain goals much more quickly. The consensus process is usually much quicker for them, and the transition process tends to be a little simpler, such as in these steps:

1. Meta-Globe mapping. Map the meetings and groups presently in existence and keep monitoring your progress by updating that map.

2. Early Vision, Huddle, Skills. Identify existing leadership community functions (vision, huddling, and microskill training). Give yourself credit for whatever is already in place. Then install missing VHS functions, especially huddling, so that as you commission people you can put them into a planning and feedback group.

3. Hoops system. Create a training manual[1] and a commissioning document that clarifies how people start ministries. Also include report forms.

4. "Find-X" system. Develop a way to discover gifted leaders and plug them into the apprenticeship process.

Sacred Cows

Every church, no matter how young or old, has certain sensitive points that are likely to provoke pain when touched.

In one survey I oversaw, we polled several hundred people who had guided their churches to a more cell-based emphasis by asking what areas of transition seemed most painful to the church. The most-mentioned domain of the church was the Red Zone—and in particular, the way worship services were perceived by the longer-term attenders. The most frequent kinds of change involved music (use of volunteer musicians, instrumentation, musical style), order of service, and treatment of visitors.

Our surveys asked these church leaders to offer suggestions to others, based on their experiences. Of the choices we offered on our surveys, these were the most-selected:

- Before you make changes, be certain your key leadership is sold on the vision.

- Be sure to interpret to the church why you're making these changes.

- Be sensitive to how change causes discomfort and discontent.

There's a lot of pain in those comments! Consequently when it comes to worship, I recommend that you not suddenly fire anyone and that you not change anything about those aspects of the music ministry now controlled by those with the purse strings. Instead, if you can, hire someone extra to develop leaders for graded choirs, sacred and contemporary drama, movement, dance, pageants, plays, children's theater, and the like. This approach automatically rules out classic technicians or performers as potential key staff. It guarantees that you'll wind up choosing a different kind of candidate. With that new person alongside the older person, you can develop a broader musical program.

Other Warnings from Experience

1. A strategy that is not helpful for a staff member to attempt is to try to impose supervision on leaders of existing subcongregations. A more effective transitional approach might be to assign a staff member to do liaison with all the subcongregations, and then assign other staff members to coach the small-group work.

2. Whenever possible, avoid the word *change*. Early, eager adopters may give you the impression that everyone is excited with the radical, dramatic perspectives embodied in the concept Meta-Church. As you assume the mantle of a reluctant advocate, as discussed in chapter 15, train yourself to use the many less jarring words for change listed in figure 59.

Alternatives to the Word "Change"

VERBS

- Adapt
- Adjust
- Amplify
- Assist
- Brighten
- Develop
- Enhance
- Enrich
- Experiment
- Freshen
- Help
- Improve
- Incrementalize
- Innovate
- Intensify
- Leverage
- Massage
- Modify
- Nudge
- Polish
- Preserve
- Refine
- Sharpen
- Strengthen
- Tweak

ADJECTIVES

- Appropriate
- Becoming
- Befitting
- Intentional
- Proper
- Sensitive
- Suitable
- Other _____

Figure 59

3. Be very purposeful about what you mandate. Wherever possible do *not* outline when or where groups may meet, who will be in the group ("this ZIP code" or "that age group"), or even the type of group ministry. Whenever possible you want to release and trust volunteer leaders to do that. Don't shackle them with unnecessary restrictions! If you mandate anything, insist that whenever possible: (1) group leaders will be nurtured, (2) groups will not close, (3) groups will multiply, (4) group leaders will be discovered from within, and (5) nurturing apprentice leaders is a priority ministry. If there's anything prescriptive about the Meta-Church System as a leadership-development schema, it's that every leader will develop an additional leader.

Repurposing

Figure 60 illustrates what can happen after you envision, and therefore better understand, a function in your church. You may decide to repurpose it.

Repurposing

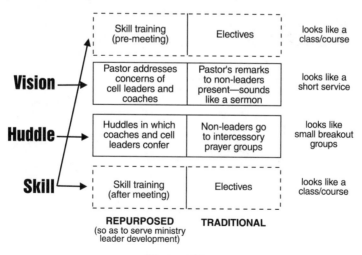

Figure 60

When I was consulting with a church that had a tired Sunday-evening service, I suggested they repurpose it so that it could double as a VHS time for their cell leaders. Two functions were already present—vision (during the preaching) and huddles (the intercessory prayer groups that followed). Earlier experience with classes before the service made it easy to add optional microskill electives before and after. Voilà! Nonleaders still had their needs and expectations met during what looked like elective training before a short service followed by small-group prayer. At the same time, cell leaders were coached and supervised through V, H, and S functions.

The Meta-Globe proves to be a helpful tool in visualizing how church ministries might be repurposed so as to make a greater contribution to cell health. The idea is to enhance a group by pushing it over boundaries from one Meta-Globe zone to another. Figure 61 illustrates that:

- An example of Purple Zone to Green Zone would be a board or committee that's repurposed to be a ministry team or task group.

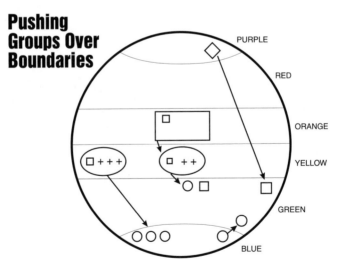

Figure 61

- An example of Orange Zone to Yellow Zone would be a church-sponsored day school that becomes a fishing pool for drawing people to church events. These, in turn, feed newcomers into cell groups.

- An example of Yellow Zone to Blue Zone would be a seminar on codependency that becomes a reference point to fill support groups.

- An example of Blue Zone to Green Zone is an adult-children-of-alcoholics group that experiences recovery and becomes a nurture group.

Why make these changes? Because you have realized that God's agenda is bigger than your plan, bigger than your denomination's plan, and perhaps even bigger than any plan seen to date in North America. Your role is to let God be God, and then figure out how to fit into his plan. Using the Meta-Globe to repurpose or bring about intentional change is a way to better see those plans to which the Holy Spirit is calling you.

The results of how you respond may develop into a foundational new approach that is a hundred times more effective than our current methods and experiences a harvest of maturing disciples.

Questions for Discussion and Application

1. Why does this chapter caution so heavily against a "methods fixation"?

2. Which "track" seems more appropriate for the church you serve? Why? What "sacred cows" must you be careful not to trample in the change process?

3. What is the most appropriate next step for your church? How can you be involved?

17

How Fully
to Cellularize?

> The Meta-Church asks what is preferable, but acknowledges that certain inevitable realities don't fit the ideal. It tries to discern the degree to which group leaders are in fact convening their people, and the degree to which coaches are in fact working with group leaders. In the process, it nudges the system toward that optimum.

What term would you use to describe the following church?

- It's not a church *with* a cell department so much as it is a convention *of* cell groups.

- It's a church so decentralized that its heart is clearly the cell—the center of evangelism, discipleship, and pastoral care.

- It's a church no more similar to a program-based, traditional church than a butterfly is to a caterpillar.

I fully agree with my long-time friend Ralph Neighbour, whose seminal book *Where Do We Go From Here?* begins like this: "The traditional church worldwide is slowly being replaced by an act of God. Developments taking place today are as powerful as the upheaval in 1517 during the time of Martin Luther."[1]

In fact what the Holy Spirit wants to do may impact more segments of Christendom than what the Protestant Reformation achieved! From Orthodox to Anabaptist, from Pentecostal to Lutheran, the notion of a cell-driven church is completely reorienting church leaders' understanding of the nature of ministry.

"Pure" Cell Churches

How does the Meta-Church perspective differ from the notion of a "pure cell church"? (By pure cell church I mean a church that is built on cells as the basic unit *and* that calls a small group a cell only if that cell is intentionally trying to be a basic Christian community—an embodiment of all the Bible says about the church.) The distinction is mostly a matter of rigidity. Suppose, for example, you have a headache, and you decide to relieve the pain by taking an aspirin. Will you insist on swallowing a tablet that contains nothing but aspirin, or is it okay to take something that's cherry flavored or orange colored, as long as the proper pain-relieving ingredient is also present? (See figure 62.)

Meta-Church thinking examines the degree to which a church has been "cellularized," and its leadership linked. The pure cell church

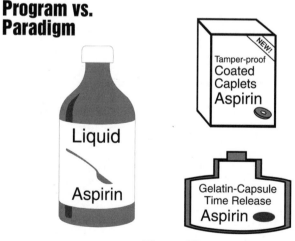

Figure 62

is, in most cases, a bull's-eye on the target; the Meta-Church is a perception of how churches are moving toward that bull's-eye.

Thus the Meta-Church asks what is preferable, but acknowledges that certain inevitable realities don't fit the ideal. It tries to discern the degree to which group leaders are in fact convening their people, and the degree to which coaches are in fact working with group leaders. In the process, it nudges the system toward that optimum.

> The pure cell church is, in most cases, a bull's-eye on the target; the Meta-Church is a perception of how churches are moving toward that goal.

From Church Plant to 100-Year-Old Program-Based Design

The Meta-Church, then, is not a program, nor does it require any particular curriculum. Rather, it's an X ray to help you look at what

---

Parallel Terminology

Prepare Your Church for the Future by Carl F. George	=	*Where Do We Go From Here?* by Ralph W. Neighbour Jr.
Cell, nurture group, or care group	=	Cell, growth group, shepherd group
Apprentice	=	Intern
X (responsible for 10) or cell leader	=	Shepherd servant
L (responsible for 50) or coach	=	Zone servant
D or staff pastor (other than senior)	=	Zone pastor

Bow Valley Christian Church

5300 Fifty-third Avenue N.W.
Calgary, AB T2A 2G8
Phone: (403) 286-5300
FAX: (403) 286-4003
Denomination: Christian Church

Senior Pastor: Allan Dunbar
Contact: Rick Scruggs
Attendance: 550
Total Cell Groups: 35

Becoming a Church That Is Small Groups

"We're not a church that has small groups. We're a church that is small groups," says Allan Dunbar, senior pastor of Bow Valley Christian Church, Calgary, Alberta. "Not that we've arrived. We're very much in transition, sometimes painfully so. But we use the cell model for everything—all age levels, all meetings, all groups, all leadership development."

The church began in 1929. Dunbar came as senior minister in 1973. In the late 1980s he began to place priority on leadership development through small groups.

"We've taken a serious look over a period of several years at how to apply New Testament principles to church life, organization, and administration," he says. "We began to analyze every group in the life of the church, using the Learn-Love-Do-Maintain formula* as a tool for guiding our groups toward a nurture style. Then we repurposed our committees to function more as task groups, making sure the LLDM functions were balanced. Finally we took the same approach with our critical care groups [recovery and support groups]."

In recent years, Dunbar has established a time (currently Sunday evening) to meet twice a month with the church's volunteer leaders. His goal is to impart vision, help the leaders huddle with one another, and provide skill training in response to needs they've voiced. "We see this as a tremendous opportunity to develop leaders. Our staff works harder in prayer and preparation for our VHS leadership meeting than for anything else we do."

The response? "We have 100 percent attendance, which is important both for teamwork and for our esprit de corps," says Dunbar.

Dunbar and his staff constantly keep Meta-Church perspectives before the entire congregation. For example, every issue of the church newsletter in some way focuses attention on small groups. A recent issue featured a cell leader who wrote a column on "Ten Top Reasons to Be Excited about Small Groups!" Another described how the annual report had been structured and color-coded around the Meta-Globe.

"In order to continue the transition, we've got to keep the ideas before the people at all times and in many different ways," says Dunbar. "We're very frank about both our dreams and failures, but something powerful is clearly working. In all my years here, I've never seen the people as excited about ministry as they are now."

* See page 323.

you have in order to figure out what's missing. It can be applied at any level, whether a new mission church or a deeply traditional church (a program-based-design church, to use Dr. Neighbour's phrase).

Similarly, as indicated in chapter 9, Meta-Church philosophy applies equally well for liturgical and nonliturgical, innovative and traditional, seeker-sensitive and open-church style. Why? Because just as an X-ray machine can examine an arm, an ankle, or even a nonhuman, so Meta-Church technology can analyze any kind of church for its vision, standards of care, spans of care, leadership

> In pursuing "best," the Meta-Church doesn't have a need to reject "good" and "better."

connections, system of leadership development, and balance between celebration (the convention of cells) and cells.

According to Meta-Church thinking, function is more important than outward form. As in the aspirin analogy used above, the active ingredient is not its color, flavor, or shape but a certain chemical compound. What makes aspirin effective is not its packaging but its active ingredient. The same analogy can be applied to programs, ministries, curriculums, and "labels" of a church, which may or may not be essential to the underlying vital ingredients discerned with the help of a theory of organizational development.

The Meta-Church, then, is willing to live with irregularities. It doesn't insist on a particular form so much as a preferred result. It suggests ways of increasing a church's effectiveness through accepting with gratitude all that exists, and then solving problems in one of several directions, such as (1) a decentralized ministry through cells, or (2) a ministry within larger groups (congregations and celebrations), which helps people become acquainted with one another, and then sends them to cells.

The Meta-Church remains constantly aware of its purposes and principles, but it also honors history. It asks about what already exists, and then it probes to what extent a higher level of effective-

Mt. Paran Church of God

2055 Mount Paran Road
Atlanta, GA 30327
Phone: (404) 261-0720
FAX: (404) 565-3495
Denomination: Church of God,
    Cleveland, Tennessee

Senior Pastor: Paul Walker
Contact: Jim Chambers
Attendance (main campus): 10,000
Total Cell Groups (main campus): 400

Cell Groups 25 Years Later: A Proven, Essential Foundation

Mt. Paran Church of God, Atlanta, Georgia, has grown from a congregation of about 350 in 1960, when Paul Walker became senior pastor, to today's total worship attendance of more than 10,000 at the two campuses where he preaches each Sunday. In addition, another 3000 people are spread across Mt. Paran's three other metro-Atlanta campuses (each of which have a different preaching pastor).

What tools has the Holy Spirit used to enable the Mt. Paran churches to experience three decades of almost nonstop growth? "We've had a vision to mobilize the people of God to do the work of God," says Dr. Walker.

As such, he has consistently emphasized the need for leadership development and the legitimacy of lay caregiving. "First we've tried to stress the ministry of Christ, since his entire ministry dealt with caring for people. Second, we've always underscored the importance of relationships—that a church is made up of relationships. If people are to grow in the grace and knowledge of Jesus Christ, they need to be in relationships that involve the idea of lay care. Third, we've tried to stress what we call therapeutic preaching—taking biblical truths and helping people apply them to daily life."

The expressions of lay mobilization have been continually refined over the years. "I first got involved with small groups in the 1960s," says Walker. "I went to Seoul, Korea, visited the church led by Dr. David Yonggi Cho, and saw the light, so to speak. I came back, tried to do exactly what he did, and found myself failing."

But he kept experimenting, and with encouraging results. "We moved from the 1960s where our Sunday-school classes were intentionally small and group oriented, into the 1970s and home-fellowship groups, then into the 1980s with support- and recovery-group models, and now into what we call a multiple-group model where we have a little bit of everything," says Walker.

"Our people have bought into small groups," summarizes Walker. "Groups give people a sense of identity. As a church grows larger, people can get lost without a group to help them feel significant, feel a sense of acceptance and belonging, and feel like they're making a contribution to the lives and hurts of others. All those needs are met best in a small group situation."

Predictably, Mt. Paran's goals for the future are shaped through the lenses of small groups. "We are intentionally building group ministries into every facet of our church," says Jim Chambers, director of discipleship development at Mt. Paran Church of God. "Small groups have helped us ensure that we not only continue to grow numerically, but that the quality of life-change, discipleship, and care keeps pace with the numerical growth."

ness is achievable. In pursuing "best," it doesn't have a need to reject "good" and "better."

How Does It Play in Peoria?

Meta-Church thinking, then, offers a church leader a helpful perspective on the everpresent, ongoing process of transition.

First, it affirms the wisdom of working with the people who are ready to work with you. If 50 percent of your church is not interested, leave that 50 percent alone. Salt the oats a little, and pray that God will use you to make people thirsty, but don't beat people up or become angry with them. Cast a vision of a preferred future, run with those who respond, and allow time for God to bring along the others in their season.

Second, approach the churches you serve (or counsel) with a certain respectfulness that says, "I'd really like to understand the work God is already doing here. Then I'd like to ask, 'If this church were growing faster and needed to expand more, which of the elements here are the most able to help in the expansion process? Which kinds of cells can grow most rapidly? What kinds should we leave in place?'" This approach meets much less resistance than a formula of one-size-fits-all. Whenever anyone says, "If you have a cell that doesn't fit this characteristic, you're dead wrong," those who are moving toward that ideal, who haven't arrived yet, feel rejected and looked down on.

Third, the Meta-Church encourages a leader to be prayerfully diagnostic. We want to search for the theories and principles that help us identify what God is blessing. Then we want to learn how to transfer those dynamics from one application to another. In doing so, we can help existing churches (or new churches comprised of inappropriately trained believers) accentuate the principles at the heart of what makes a cell church work.

The Future Is Closer Than We Think

Pure-cell-church and Meta-Church advocates both predict that one day soon North American churches of twenty-five to fifty thousand will appear just as they are already present on most other continents of the world. Where will these churches be?

Most will develop within urban centers and metropolitan sprawls. In fact many of these churches already exist and are currently running between four hundred and three thousand people for worship services.

We're anticipating that those recognized today as "big churches" will, in many instances, be dwarfed by what is to come. Through the *DataMIRROR* project,[2] we are creating a database of North-American churches that are operating at a consistent growth rate of 20 percent or more a year, and are anticipating that their compound growth will soon show some very, very large "conventions of cells."

These are exciting days to partner with the Holy Spirit. I don't believe that God is nearly as interested in our labels—Cell Church or Meta-Church—as he is in our training more and better disciples of the Lord Jesus Christ. To that end, let's continue to press forward.

Questions for Discussion and Application

1. According to this chapter, how is the concept of Meta-Church similar to the concept of pure cell church? How does it differ? Why do those distinctions matter?

2. What are the advantages of pressing for "pure" cells? What are the advantages of being willing to nudge *any* cell toward the ideal?

3. Do you believe that "one day soon North American churches of twenty-five to fifty thousand will appear in every metropolitan area, just as they are already present on most other continents of the world"? Why or why not? What good could such churches do?

18

Sunday School, Meta-Church, and Children

I'm by no means ruling out Sunday school. A Sunday
school is simply a centralized on-premises cell system.

Let me be very clear: Whenever this book speaks of cells and
small groups, I'm by no means ruling out Sunday school—for
adults or children. The phrase "cell groups" refers to an encompassing care system that includes Sunday school. A Sunday school is
simply a centralized, on-premises cell system. Churches should
have as many Sunday schools as they can afford. My only hesita-
tion is that the Great Commission (Matthew 28:18–20) reminds
Jesus' followers not to limit a church's vision to the size of a director of Christian education's office staff, of a parking lot, or of a
Sunday-school wing.

What happens if you build the largest Sunday-school facility in
the world, with the largest parking lot, you fill them up (with adults
and/or children), and Jesus says, "There's still more to feed"? Few,
if any, churches have enough money to build all the classrooms
needed—and the parking lots to support them—to do the job God is
calling for. In that regard, the Sunday school will sooner or later

Vineyard Christian Fellowship

1201 Riverside Avenue
Fort Collins, CO 80524-3218
Phone: (303) 484-5999
FAX: (303) 498-8685
Denomination: Vineyard

Senior Pastor: Rick Olmstead
Contact: Ric Lehman
Attendance: 1300
Total Cell Groups: 80

Youth Don't Take a "Back Seat" Here

The head-banger types now sit on the front row of the Sunday-morning worship services. Their punk hair and pierced body parts catch the eye of many older worshipers. But senior pastor Rick Olmstead doesn't even have to say, "Remember, what counts is not what you look like, but who you are in Christ." Instead, this visual symbol reminds everyone of a much-sought-after goal: a youth ministry well integrated into the life of the church as a whole.

"What we're experiencing started with youth pastor John Furste's vision that teens could do ministry," explains associate pastor Ric Lehman. "The youth program has experienced numerical growth and seen teens accept the challenge to do the ministry themselves. The whole church rejoices in how our kids are making such tremendous strides in affecting their community."

Furste feels the same way. "We've always taught our teens that they're capable of making a high impact on their peers," he says. Four years ago he developed the Rock & Roll Church Service for youth group meetings—a separate high-energy celebration geared for teens. Teens found them to be highly relevant, and attendance soared as friend invited friend. But something more was needed; new kids weren't getting involved beyond this initial entry point.

In 1992, Furste decided to take a more proactive stance on training church kids and getting them to lead. He started with two small groups led by adults. These served both as examples and as a training ground for the development of more groups that would eventually be led by teens. By 1993 five teen groups had been birthed, with pairs of teens leading most of them, and with future leaders being trained.

These teen leaders receive plenty of special stroking and care. Furste meets with them monthly for discipleship, worship, sharing, and prayer. They fill out reports on the weekly activities and attendance of their groups. They also attend a monthly VHS (for Vision, Huddle, and Skill training) meeting for all adult leaders of small groups. At present about 60 percent of the seventy-five teens who attend Sunday's youth group also participate in a weeknight small group. Others take part in a small group, but don't yet attend the youth group or the corporate worship. "We're reaching teens through relationships, not programs," says Furste. "Sooner or later our newcomers feel part of the whole church. When they do, they don't feel pushed into the back row. They join us at the front."

prove to be inadequate as a church's only and perhaps even primary method of nurture, care, discipleship, and evangelism.

> What happens if you build the largest Sunday-school facility in the world and Jesus says, "There's still more to feed"? Few, if any, churches have enough money to build all the classrooms needed to do the job God is calling for.

If I must limit the harvest of souls to the rate at which I can raise building-fund monies, how am I going to tell the Lord of the harvest, "We couldn't win people because we didn't have a bigger Sunday-school wing," when he may well be completely unwilling to accept that kind of excuse? We will never have a large enough budget to build the number of Sunday-school classrooms needed to rebuild a society as sick as ours; it is time to revisit the New Testament, to keep our Sunday schools intact, but to go ten times beyond them in terms of our effectiveness.

My motive is not to criticize Sunday schools; rather I'm trying to shatter some of the limitations we place on obedience to God because of our building budget or because of the limited number of time slots that our church buildings are being used.

The New Testament doesn't say a thing about Sunday school. It does, however, teach a great deal about making disciples. If Sunday school is a tool for making disciples, by all means it has God's blessing. But if we start limiting ourselves to that form, and especially to today's Dewey-philosophy, classroom-style, public-school-copied substitute for Sunday school's original vitality and intent, then we're in danger of offering a puny excuse for disobedience to the Great Commission.

As Elmer Towns, North America's dean of Sunday-school history, purpose, and methodology, has said in one of his more recent books: "Unfortunately, most Sunday schools in America are adrift, foundering or headed in the wrong direction. . . . We need something more than improved teaching methods, extensive teacher preparation or better facilities. . . . Taking Sunday school to the streets will reinforce its original evangelistic purpose."[1]

Prince of Peace Lutheran Church

200 E. Nicollet Boulevard
Burnsville, MN 55337
Phone: (612) 435-8102
FAX: (612) 435-8065
Denomination: Evangelical
   Lutheran Church in America

Senior Pastor: Mike Foss
Contact: Handt Hanson, Director
   of Worship
Attendance: 3000
Total Cell Groups: 150

Welcoming Children into Worship—and the Leading of Worship

"We're vitally interested in the messages we communicate to children about the worship environment," says Handt Hanson, director of worship at Prince of Peace Lutheran in metro Minneapolis. "Unless we're careful, we can give them a negative perception of the public realm. At Prince of Peace we want to dispel the view that children are accepted only if they're quiet, don't move, know how to read notes, enjoy adult music, and don't stand on the pew or chair, even if they're too short to see anything."

Hanson's philosophy is to help children know that they're both special and important. For example:

• Ushers regularly distribute children's versions of the adult bulletin (pink for pre-readers, blue for readers).

• Bags of soft toys are available at each entrance to the sanctuary, designed especially for toddlers and children.

• All public events include a children's sermon that presents the foundational themes of the adult sermon.

• Usher stations contain children's Bibles.

• Children's songs, children's choirs, children's vocal teams, children's Suzuki classes, and children's worship leaders are regular features in worship, not special-occasion events.

• Once a year the sixth graders plan and lead a "children's worship weekend" in which they study, plan, write, and join all worship events that weekend.

Does this emphasis on children require a certain worship style? No, according to Hanson, who plans four different services a week, each of which follows a different worship style. "The issue of inviting, welcoming, and involving children in worship is not a question of style, but of deployment. Liturgy is the work of the people, not a performance or particular mode of expression," he says.

How well is this "child-friendly" environment received? During Hanson's twenty years on staff, the church has become one of the largest in its denomination. And its growth continues. The better judge is the children themselves: When an opening song carries children's voices over the P.A.—because they're the worship leaders this week—the other children in the congregation often break out in noticeable smiles, almost as if to acknowledge, "Children are valuable to God at this church." To the leadership team at Prince of Peace, such expressions are the true sign that children feel welcome in their worship of God.

Differences between Sunday School and Small-Group Systems

Sunday school has been and can be a viable, vital force in most churches across North America. But certain shifts have occurred in society that affect many Sunday-school settings. Notions of scolding ("You ought to have come"), truancy ("Why weren't you there?"), program ("Our top priority is these three points"), and time clocks ("I showed up, put in my hour, and now my duty's done") are being replaced by a focus on one-another ministry and Bible application. To the extent that a Sunday school doesn't join these transitions, it misses a very important quality of life.

Of course, the best tradition of Sunday school has always emphasized that unless the pupil comes first, the lesson is never going to take root in the life. But if we don't specifically guard against it, Sunday schools sometimes do a better job of codifying and programming truth than they do focusing on relationship-based ministry (see chapter 4).

What churches can learn from a Meta-Church perspective is this: The extent to which a Sunday school is actually a small-group system, and whether it is handled like a curriculum-teaching system or a caring system. To the extent that it's a teaching system more than a caring system, it will fall short of being able to deliver the love that children need. In other words, do we see Sunday school as a program for delivering educational topics or as a leader system that attracts followers who commit themselves to doing the truths they discuss?

All the benefits present in a successful home cell system, in terms of touching and loving people, can certainly be emphasized in the Sunday school as well. In fact many healthy and growing Sunday schools, when analyzed according to what they actually accomplish, are more a place to develop relationships than classrooms of doctrinal instruction. They function more as pastoral care than as historic Christian education. If you adopt this perspective for understanding the nature of Sunday school, and of what it could become, you won't see any contradiction between Sunday school and small groups.

New Hope Community Church

11731 SE Stevens Road
Portland, OR 97266-7597
Phone: (503) 659-5683
FAX: (503) 774-1133
Denomination: Independent

Senior Pastor: Dale Galloway
Contact: Church Growth Institute
  at the above address
Attendance: 5500
Total Cell Groups: 500

Seven-Day-a-Week Opportunities for Children

How does Meta-Church thinking impact ministry to children? If the experience of New Hope Community Church, Portland, Oregon, is any indicator, the results are a vast array of ministries designed to meet the needs of boys and girls. Each represents the idea of adult lay pastors (and occasionally teen lay pastors as well) caring for children through the context of small groups.

"My main purpose is to recruit and train leaders," says Clara Olson, the full-time lead pastor for ministries covering birth through sixth grade. "By myself I could maybe effectively minister to ten to fifteen children a week. But for every person I can help to capture a vision for children's ministry, that's ten to fifteen more children who can receive our pastoral care."

Olson came to the church as a staff member in 1986. According to senior pastor Dale Galloway, the children's ministry up until a year or so before Olson's arrival "was one of the worst I've ever seen." Olson was contagious in her enthusiasm, vision, and knack for affirming the talents of those with whom she works. Step by step she saw the birth of new ministries and the cellularizing of large-group ministries. Sunday-school classes, for example, now use learning centers to facilitate small-group interaction. Large children's choirs pause to convene brief Tender Loving Care groups.

During all this growth and transition, the programming has increasingly spilled off campus. "You could say that our children's Sunday schools now go from Sunday morning to the following Saturday night," says staff pastor David Durey.

How does Olson's philosophy of ministry compare with that of traditional churches? "I find the leader and let the leader develop the ministry," she says. "Then our group of workers itself becomes a care group. We watch out for each other's needs, we pray together, we love each other, and then we go out and minister to the kids. We believe love and nurture are frequently more important than the specific content we teach."

New Hope's experience seems to represent the trend of the future. Veteran church consultant Lyle Schaller reports that "the emergence of the seven-day-a-week church as the successor to the big Sunday-morning churches of the 1950s is one of the most significant developments of this century."[*] Pastor Galloway confirms that trend. "Ten years ago, our children's ministries were based on curriculum, teachers, and classrooms that we filled only on Sunday mornings," he says. "Today, not only do we have the finest Sunday-school classes possible, but we have multiple kinds of ministries every day of the week."[**]

[*] Lyle E. Schaller, *The Seven-Day-a-Week Church* (Nashville: Abingdon, 1992), 15.

[**] Clara Olson has compiled her experiences at New Hope and her philosophy of ministry into a three-cassette self-study kit titled *How Do Children Fit into the Meta-Church?* Order from The Charles E. Fuller Institute, 1-MAP-META, or directly from New Hope Community Church.

> Unless we specifically guard against it, Sunday schools
> sometimes do a better job of codifying and programming
> truth than they do focusing on relationship-based ministry.

In many other instances, however, fundamental differences exist between Sunday school and a care system. For example, a Sunday school often starts with an audience and figures out how to make the teacher ingredient work; a small-group system frequently starts with a leader and coaches the leader to form a group. Sunday schools frequently emphasize a content-centered lesson as the most important ingredient of the classroom time; the small-group movement usually insists that the care of people as persons is as important as any truth to be taught in a particular time frame.

Many people find it helpful to understand Sunday school as an on-premises arrangement of small groups: a group system brought into a church building.

Preferred Sizes for Sunday-School Classes

In order to avoid the sociological strangulation that can choke people out and alienate newcomers, churches should prepare for new units before they actually need them, and then organize them as soon as they're needed. Many Sunday schools do not realize that they are actually turning people away. If people feel their church system is not responding to their needs, they can lose motivation or be unenthusiastic about welcoming newcomers.

In your Sunday schools, try to increase the number of events you organize at the level of ten or so people. This change in social architecture will help people build and deepen friendships, and, as a result, will do a better job of meeting needs. Many churches, wanting to be evangelistic, find that their bottleneck is neither lack of evangelistic desire nor an ability to attract newcomers. Instead, it is often the unwillingness of Christians to allow new people into their lives. Thus the issue that's bigger and more important than getting people to come is that of accepting the people who do come, by making time for them in one's day-to-day lifestyle.

Sunday schools that are growing have spans of care not much larger than 1:6 or 1:7. That is, for every five to eight people in a class, someone needs to be deputized as an additional caregiver. Too often, whether the class is fifty or 150, only a handful of people are allowed to have a meaningful role in the ongoing ministry. Most Sunday-school participants are willing to do more than take up space at the coffee line!

If a church says, "We're having a hard time finding volunteer workers," and has several large Sunday-school classes sitting and being fed each week, the problem is often that these potential volunteers are in too large a group to be effectively mobilized for ministry. Try creating smaller settings and telling the leaders, "Nurture your people and find out which ones are gifted in teaching. Then help them take responsibility to develop their teaching gift, and plug them into an assistant position as an apprentice." You'll soon have all the volunteers you need because you have decentralized the search for talent.

The blockage for most churches is not lack of talent. Rather, the choke point occurs with the notion that one person, leading a large group in centralized fashion, can find all the needed personnel. By contrast, if you are continually plugging people into an apprentice slot and if your existing leaders are committed to helping people develop their spiritual gifts, you'll have all the teaching talent that the Holy Spirit wants your church to have.

How to Train Sunday-School Teachers

Virtually all authorities agree that apprenticeship is a superior form of instruction. Most training is lost if it is received prior to taking a job. By contrast, most of the training that you experience while in a job is retained. Put someone underneath the arm of a gifted, veteran teacher, and *then* run him or her through your denominational, curriculum-sponsored, or Teacher Training Association–type training. The apprentice teacher is a motivated learner. Interest and willingness are the keys. "I'm watching carefully," says the leader-in-training, "because I know that you're going to be out of town (or whatever) in two weeks, and I'll be needed to teach the class." No amount of academic-type study can substitute for the learning that occurs when you combine in-service training and education with skillful supervision.

Sunday-school classes frequently don't create apprentice-leader positions. In many cases, not only does an eventual teacher shortage prove that it was unwise to staff so thinly, but part of the joy of teaching a Sunday-school class is meeting with other adults to prepare the lesson. Besides, when adults work in pairs and groups,

> I'm not aware of a "Meta" type of group. Meta-Church thinking is a way of seeing the whole, and then nudging various components of a church toward greater vitality.

they have a lot more fun sustaining themselves, they produce better work, and their morale stays much higher.

The most important thing a Sunday-school teacher (or other small-group leader) can learn is how to prayerfully prioritize your time by spending it with the right people. Who in the class is already caring for others in the class? Who shows a special sensitivity to your class's relationship network? Who watches out for the first-time visitor, the first- or second-time absentee, and the first return of an absentee? Spend time with those people who know how to help sustain and nurture relationships, and your class is bound to grow.

Children in Adult Cells

The term *Meta-Church* is descriptive. Occasionally, someone asks, "How do Meta-Church groups stack up against other kinds of small groups?" My reply is that I don't understand the question fully because I'm not aware of a specifically Meta type of group. Meta-Church thinking is a way of seeing the cell in the context of the whole, and then nudging various components of a church to contribute to its greater vitality. The Meta-Church, like an X-ray machine, helps you describe how a group is connected to the rest of the church, and then goes on to diagnose how to make that group work better.

Meta-Church concepts, for example, examine the extent to which "touching" occurs between pastoral staff, Sunday-school superintendent, and teachers of Sunday-school classes. These concepts help us discover the strong correlation between the person-to-person warmth in a given class and the quality of touch that pastoral supervisors give their Sunday-school teachers. They also help us understand that it's more strategic to celebrate changes in people's lives than it is to cover points in a lesson.

How do children fit into adult cell groups? That decision rests with the parents involved, not with a policy from the pastor or church board.

If you don't make child care a responsibility of the cell, then you are allowing a centralization that may limit cell growth. You don't want groups to say, "We can't hold a cell meeting because the church office hasn't opened the nursery." If the cell leadership says, "Okay, then how do you want us to handle child care issues?" the best answer is, "How do you want to do it?" Give cell groups permission to hold meetings anywhere and anytime that they will organize their own baby-sitting.

You want to wean church adults off a dependency on the pastoral staff or church office. If these same people, as a group, joined a bowling league or went boating, they would no doubt figure out a child care plan without placing any expectations on church staff. The church that mobilizes its care units can do the same thing.

Therefore, some groups involve the children in the meeting. Other groups have the children present in the opening section of the group, and then put the children to bed at the host home (reclaiming them at the end of the meeting). Some groups opt to hire baby-sitters. Others have the parents take turns serving as the sitters for all the families involved in that particular group. Other groups, meeting near the church building, coordinate with similarly located groups and use the church nursery, which is staffed by a group from the church's youth ministry. The possibilities are endless.

Children and Youth in Their Own Cells

The discussion in this chapter has been intended to affirm that most churches manage their children reasonably well (see figure 63). How you handle children in the Meta-Church is not very different from what most churches are doing now, with two exceptions:

1. Churches will want to move in the direction of equipping parents to have family evenings at home; cell groups, as artificially extended family, are designed to strengthen the nuclear and extended family, not to replace it. The responsibility of parents to train their children in the ways of the Lord still stands as an important goal of Christian education (Deuteronomy 6:4–9; Ephesians 6:4). In all likelihood, however, only when adults are trained and resocialized in cell groups will family evenings become a widespread or meaningful practice because without training they simply won't have the skills to pull it off. But when adults participate in a home-cell group where they learn to pray, to express their feelings, to be reverent, to manage an evening without distractions in the company of other adults, they will become capable of replicating that experience for their own kids at home.

2. Children and youth will be far more involved in the production of services through celebration arts. The wave of the future is theater for children and theater by children—where children are the producers of the drama, sometimes mixed with adults and sometimes as a pure children's troupe.

Age-Graded Sunday-School Classes	Children's church (Music, Lessions, Crafts)	Children's Sermons During Adult Worship Service
MidweekClubs (AWANA, Scouts, etc.)	**What about children?**	Theater byChildren (Celebration Arts Clubs)
Family Home Evening (Catechism by Parents)	Christian Day School or Home Schooling	Support or Recovery Groups for Children

Figure 63

This concept stems from the team concept of worship production discussed in chapter 9. I have even seen children as leaders of adult worship events. I was in Capetown, South Africa in 1993 where more than ten thousand people participated in a prayer rally. At one point, a nine-year-old girl led the worship song. What a statement on the importance of children!

Children's and Youth Cells

If I solicit audience questions in the opening minutes of a Meta-Church presentation, more than one person is certain to ask something along the lines of, "How do you do cells for children?" If, however, I wait until the end of the seminar, such questions rarely arise, even if my presentation didn't mention the words *child*, *children*, or *youth*. Why? They've gained new insight into the nature of how to provide leadership, direction, and development in the church, and they've discovered that these perspectives easily apply to children's or youth ministry. Thus the way to develop children's and youth cells is much the same as adult cells—focus on volunteer ministers, increase the nurturative dimension, develop apprentice leaders (usually adults or older teens), and maintain small spans of care.

The progression for understanding and establishing volunteer ministry for children and youth might go as follows:

1. Every church is more than a big, undifferentiated mass of people. Churches are comprised of teams and small groups —whether the church's leaders have had the eyes to "see" them or not.

2. There are basically four things going on in a group, no matter what type of group you're analyzing—Sunday-school class, Christian Service Brigade battalion, multigenerational volleyball league, children's choir, or youth group. Those key functions are:

    • Loving (community building through care)

    • Learning (Bible study, understanding the history of your church, etc.)

- Doing (activity that benefits those outside the meeting, such as painting the church or playing handbells for the main worship service)

- Maintaining (business or process maintenance, such as the sign-up list of who's going to attend the pizza party)[2]

3. The first of these factors—a sense of nurture and community-building—can be increased in any kind of group. The idea, using the Meta-Globe analogy, is to green up as many existing children's and youth ministries as possible and to incorporate a significant role for nurture in every new group that's formed.

4. Children's ministry is neither baby-sitting nor distraction control! Children's and youth cells can support and supplement the role of the family by influencing the moral and spiritual development of these precious gifts of God. When concepts of lay pastoring are applied to children and youth, adults, teens, and children can be profoundly affected.

Children and youth can be pastored, and they can minister to one another as well. Virtually every dimension of Meta-Church care and celebration can be applied, with great effectiveness, to ministry among children and youth.[3]

Questions for Discussion and Application

1. What insights from this chapter were most helpful to you? Why?

2. In what ways are the children in the church you serve receiving lay shepherding?

3. What will your church's ministry to families and children look like five years from now? How cellularized will it be? What's the next step toward getting there?

19

Theological Education
of the Future

Too many pastoral staff members see their job as being the primary, hands-on provider of pastoral care in the church.

Jesus' story about the shepherd with ninety-nine sheep to count, and one to go look for (Luke 15:1–7) has been translated by many Protestant clergy to mean that one trained cleric can provide adequate, quality care for one hundred people. Perhaps that ratio worked in times past, especially if there was only one lost or hurting person in each flock. But in the typical church of one hundred people today, probably twenty-five of them are experiencing some degree of trauma at any one time. The rapid transitions of our mobile society, the decay of our culture, the erosion of commonly accepted Judeo-Christian values, and the dissolution of the family unit have made it impossible for one professional shepherd, even if expert at racing around the parish, to meet the care needs of one hundred people.

That's why we've got to change our method of organization and our system of care. The Bible says, "When the foundations are being destroyed, what can the righteous do?" (Psalm 11:3). The answer is to rebuild the foundations.

> We've got to change our method of organization
> and our system of care.

Other trends are likewise calling for new ways of organizing care. Economics, for example, are determining that smaller churches cannot support full-time pastors.[1] Already many households of smaller-church clergy are partially self-supported by second jobs, working spouses, or generous in-laws. In addition, more and more people who lack the personal leadership skills necessary to amass a growing congregation are going through seminary. If these people work at a comfortable level, their churches will likely reach a maximum attendance of around one hundred, or, if certain more ideal dynamics come into play, around two hundred.

Finally, the Bible itself seems to challenge current notions of the kinds of leaders that are needed for churches. If pastoral leadership doesn't teach volunteer leaders how to develop their leadership abilities by giving them the vehicle of leading a small group, these leaders will probably not learn how to do the "work of the ministry" (Ephesians 4:12). Too many pastoral staff members see their jobs as their being the primary, hands-on provider of pastoral care in the church. The larger the church, the more impossible that expectation seems to be, so the easier it is to shake off. But the smaller the church, the more the pastor is constrained by people's explicit or implicit saying, "We hire you to do our ministry here."

As a church becomes larger and develops more caring units, the pastor and other leaders of the church might consider being in a group together. The idea is not to remain in that one group forever, but to learn the skills of how to manage a small-group meeting so that it can spin off other groups that will likewise have functions of caring, of "speaking the truth in love" (Ephesians 4:25 KJV), of encouragement one to another, and of creating additional leaders who can spin off other cells.

The Challenge Facing Seminaries

Sooner or later the clergy-preparation process boils down to an issue of leadership. As chapter 2 indicated, leadership means the ability to command a following. Leaders have the ability to produce attendance at meetings and are defined as conveners of teams or groups.

Leaders are made from the gifts God gives—the spiritual gifts, the personality, the talents, and the temperament. It is fictitious, therefore, to think that seminaries are able to create leaders. Seminaries can polish leaders; leaders can be identified, improved on, and perfected. But no human seems to have discovered how to make leaders. Even if we could make leaders, chances are that the process would be too expensive. Is it not better stewardship of kingdom resources to start with the people who by and large already have raw leadership?

> Leaders are defined as conveners of teams or groups.

The most practical approach for seminaries is not to let anybody in who doesn't already know how to lead. What if no one were allowed access to ordination-track theology who had not already demonstrated the leadership necessary to grow and build a community of faith? If this were allowed, our institutions of higher learning would be educating only champions because they'd be picking the right people to start with—even if this new perspective means that theological institutions have to downsize to 20 percent of their current enrollments.

Please don't misunderstand me. In many ways, today's theological education has triumphed in the sense that it can produce pulpiteers who make brilliant sermons that are biblically exegeted and sensible. Further, seminaries are helping their students learn to be good counselors. I support the need for graduate schools of theology. I also affirm a need to load the pipeline going to those schools with a higher caliber of leader—one who has a greater ability to get the job done. In other words, wouldn't it be great if theological seminaries could run on the kind of ratio that M.I.T. or Harvard experiences? They pass over ninety applicants to get ten; sometimes ninety-nine to get one. By analogy, wouldn't it be great if the only people who could get into graduate schools of higher theological education were people who could already build churches; who already knew how to do evangelism; rally the troops; plan, and handle in-house politics? All seminaries would need to teach is theology! Anything taught would be practically guaranteed to spread to one hundred or one thousand other people because of the strength of leadership represented by the students.

It's easier to give a theological education to a leader than it is to take a scholar and transform him or her into a leader. If a church's staff are to be effectively used in building a growing, healthy priesthood of believers (1 Peter 2:4–10), the people at the helm must be leaders and leader-producers—whether or not they're scholars. The best of both worlds, of course, is to have leaders who have also been educated. Increasingly, however, people are enrolling in seminary and Bible colleges not to gain the kinds of theological insights that leaders need, or to hone their leadership skills, but to sort out their own personal issues. Or they go because they desire to help others.

Moving toward personal maturity and being a leader are not necessarily the same thing. Likewise, having a God-given compassion for others is wonderful, but it does not necessarily make someone a leader. The sequence that guarantees the greatest fruitfulness is for someone to be recognized within the culture of a church, and then to give that person theological instruction. That is the intent of many denominations and movements, but it is not always their practice.[2]

> Having a God-given compassion for others is wonderful, but it does not necessarily make someone a leader!

Meta-Church Construct

To illustrate these ideas with the jargon of the Meta-Church, nobody could go to seminary without prior in-church evidence of being able to function at the level of L *and* D (which would include proficiency as X or C). By contrast, most seminary candidates today demonstrate the skills of an X or C but not the leading and managing capabilities of an L or a D.

What about pastoral staff who are already serving in churches and who sense that their calling and gifts are primarily those of an X and a C? Perhaps their greatest contribution to the future of their churches will be to bring on some D-L-X-type people and partner with them, so as to multiply themselves. The fact that a clergyperson doesn't know how to do something is irrelevant, as long as that pastor knows what needs to be done and lets somebody else do it.

Why are D- and L-levels so important to have in a church? The purpose of Meta-Church organization is to support the people who are making a difference out in the X-led groups. Healthy X groups feed the church altar and every other ministry of the church.

Suppose someone serves in a small parish? That person will need to wear several hats: X, L, C, and D. There's no danger in doing so initially. The harm occurs when pastors don't know they're wearing four hats. They keep enduring the ongoing strain, and burn out, or become angry because they don't know how to get the ministry done. The secret here is to learn how to give away the lowest-level hat first, and then the next level and the next level, and eventually work oneself out of a job. A pastor, in this case, would develop Xa's (apprentice cell-group leaders), and give away every hat as quickly as possible. Giving away the L hat comes next, and also the C hats wherever possible.

The focus of the Meta-Church perspective is the development of the most common level of talent: the leader of a ten group. A skillful pastor will learn how to reach into every group and identify the leader who is there. A pastor with leadership ability will know how to bring those Xs into a leadership community to give them training in an ongoing way.

> A skillful pastor will learn how to reach into every group and identify the leader who is there.

As leadership is empowered and incubated, the X leaders cultivate multiple generations of apprentice leaders, who in turn further multiply the harvest of need-meeting ministry embodied by the church.

"Virtual" Seminary of the Future

Here's what I believe will happen to seminaries in the not-too-distant future. It appears that increasingly large churches will replace their denominational programs in four cardinal areas: (1) sponsorship of foreign missions, (2) church planting, (3) instruction in practical theology, and (4) mentoring in spiritual formation.

Seminaries, along with perhaps other parachurch institutions, will design new curriculums for in-service practicums. This approach to leadership development will become, in effect, the new Christian-education organizational-development paradigm for the future. Extended training modules will emphasize three fundamental themes: systemics, spirituality, and mentored leadership development. The use of CD-ROM, tutored video, or audiocassette instruction, fax, modem, and other innovations will enable almost any large church to create and house a virtual seminary.

> This approach to leadership development will become, in effect, the new Christian-education organizational-development paradigm for the future.

Other classic seminary emphases, such as biblical, historical, or systematic theology, may be covered in the traditional academic classroom. Or perhaps these virtual seminaries will bring the professors on-site to the host church!

What might these ideas look like? If a seminary—whether real or virtual wants to train people for the leadership tests that arise in the trenches of front-line ministry, it could make this assignment for Evangelism 101: "Bring us a convert." Evangelism 201 says: "Bring us a convert's convert." Evangelism 301 says: "Bring us your whole soul-winning class and let us check the converts of your whole class."

You don't need to leave home to satisfy that kind of assignment. You don't even need a pencil; you need bodies—in particular live, warm, breathing new Christians.

Will there be a seminary without walls? The future is closer than we think.

Questions for Discussion and Application

1. What, in your opinion, is the purpose of a seminary? What should be the qualifications for being admitted?

2. How could seminaries become more effective in preparing church leaders?

3. Which idea most appeals to you in this chapter? Why? Which idea would you modify? How?

PART 4

Sharing the Ministry

20

Don't Settle
for Anything Less!

Rather than inviting them to join the frantic pace of yet another harried ministry opportunity, I'll be beckoning them to join the communion of the Holy Spirit in a fresh way.

In January 1992 I was preparing to board an airplane on my way to give a series of lectures. I began to feel a deep sense of distress. I was sick of being in airports and sleeping in hotel rooms.

I began thinking, spurred by an idea from Peter Drucker's *Managing the Non-Profit Organization,*[1] about how my tombstone would read if I continued traversing the continent to give lectures. Where was the path of my life leading to? If at the end of my time on earth, my ministry played out the way it's been going, what would be left?

I had a vision of this tombstone inscription:

Here lies Carl George. His wife and children made do without him for one-third of his working life so that he could be in airports, hotels, and seminar halls. During that career he gave twenty thousand church growth lectures.

My stomach turned. I realized that I was defining ministry in terms of my activities. Giving twenty thousand church growth lectures (or sermons) is not a reasonable exchange for my life or for one-third of my days with my wife and children. I asked God to help me understand what kind of a tombstone would be worth the sacrifice that my family and I are making and the price we're pay-

> No longer am I examining simply what God gave me strength to do. Now the focus is on what happened as a *result* of what God did through my obedience.

ing. "Does what I'm doing really make a difference?" became a preoccupying question.

For a long time I thought about all the things in Scripture that God calls his children to do and be. Of those, I wondered, which is his priority for me? As I listened to the promptings of the Holy Spirit, I came to a fresh understanding of the things that are worth dying for. In my mind, I developed a new dream for a tombstone statement:

> He helped 20,000 churches release 200,000 volunteer leaders to become evangelistic lay pastors so that 1,000,000 people could be brought into the kingdom of God, and experience his love and salvation.

The standard of measurement is different from my "first" tombstone. No longer am I examining simply what God gave me strength to do. Now the focus is on what happened as a *result* of what God did through my obedience. I would have helped teach twenty thousand pastors how to give away their ministry to at least ten volunteer leaders apiece.

More than Numbers

What does that distinction mean in my day-to-day activities? I will spend more time listening to God in prayer, and then in training other people to take my place. With those I touch, rather than inviting them to join the frantic pace of yet another harried ministry opportunity, I'll be beckoning them to join the communion of the Holy Spirit in a fresh way.

Is there biblical precedent for this dream? Yes. How about the fruitfulness of some ten thousand converts in a one-day revival meeting after a forty-five-second sermon? Those are results! It happened on Mt. Carmel under the ministry of Elijah. The prayer time in preparation, however, was three years. When the right instant came, Elijah proclaimed what God was going to do and waited for God to move in. The result was thousands of conversions (1 Kings 18:1–39).

Is this the kind of thing the Holy Spirit wants to do in our time? I believe the answer is yes. We are living in a time of unprecedented opportunity. God is stirring something mighty in certain churches around the world, and they are reaping phenomenal conversion growth, discipleship growth, and numerical growth as a result. I'm increasingly driven to discover what God is already doing in these churches, and then become a part of it.

I am convinced we are in a time of transition, just like the chrysalis stage between caterpillar and butterfly that I spoke about in chapter 1. When will the future arrive? Perhaps, like the side mirror on a car that says, "Warning, objects are closer than they appear," so the Meta-Church, as the church of the future, may be closer to the North-American horizon than most people suspect. There's no question that churches are recovering in the 1990s the importance of the clergy's spending time developing their volunteer leaders. From Bible times to now, this idea is part of God's plan: 2 Timothy 2:2 speaks of the apostle Paul's training Timothy who, in turn was to train "reliable men who will also be qualified to teach others." Paul had established a number of churches in different locations (Acts 14:23, 16:4), and Timothy was charged with creating the local eldership. Likewise Titus received the same assignment (Titus 1:5). These men did not stay on the scene; they had to leave people in each place who were capable of ministering in their absence.

Similarly, as a church grows larger and the pastor realizes "I can't be present every time ministry takes place," it's very appropriate, using the models of the New Testament, to shift to the role of the bishop—training volunteer worker Tony to facilitate this home-based group and volunteer leader Aliza to work with that home-based group. The heart of the Meta-Church is focusing on leaders and releasing them to do what God has called and gifted them to do. That's ministry as it was meant to be!

More than Small Groups

If you read this book (or, frankly, any of my previous books) and think my primary emphasis is small groups, you've missed my point. If you think the primary need I'm highlighting is that of developing cells, you've missed my point. I love small groups, but I'm really not a small-groups person. My true heartbeat is for leadership development.

> If you read this book and think my primary emphasis is small groups, you've missed my point. My true heartbeat is for leadership development.

I have both led and participated in a wide variety of small groups during the last several decades. Whether meeting bi-weekly with a handful of friends for a prayer breakfast or being part of a weekly couples' Sunday school, small groups have played a vital role in the stages of my journey of faith. My wife, Grace, could affirm the same for many of the chapters in her life.

The most dramatic episodes in our lives involved small groups when we were members of the Lake Avenue Congregational Church in Pasadena. Small groups came about as a result of how our senior pastor at the time, Paul Cedar, announced to us what the game plan for care was to be at that church of more than three thousand. A mother of five had approached my wife (we are parents of six) about being in a small group with us. My wife, with me at her side, had been asked to lead this group, and so we were invited to attend the small-group leaders' training session held on the church premises. At that gathering, Pastor Cedar said, "You and I both know that in a church of three thousand people, I can't even learn everyone's name. If people aren't going to get lost in this church, they've got to be cared for at the smallest possible group level. Since you know these people by face and are caring for them regularly, I want you to know that I consider you to be the pastor of the people in your small group. That's our game plan for care." He continued, "We'll back you up, but you go first. Take care of whatever pastoral needs they have, and tell us what you did. If you need help, call us after you have tried it, and we'll back you up."

That was an amazingly empowering set of instructions. In a previous book, *Prepare Your Church for the Future*, I recount some of the joys and privileges of serving as a volunteer minister to this group of ten or so.[2]

But the bottom line to those experiences is this: When I want to help someone become a leader, what's the best training laboratory that can be found? A small group. I don't mean handing someone a ready-made small group as you would a teacher with a previously established Sunday-school class (as important as Sunday school is). Rather, let's offer a new level of challenge: "If you can pull a small group together, you can lead it. If you can't, even after being trained as an apprentice leader, then you have some serious leadership skill and vision challenges ahead of you."

More than Eager Learners

Once you understand that concept, you've solved the riddle of the leaf and the stem. Does the stem produce the leaf, or does the reverse occur? Do stems appear where leaves are, or vice versa? Answer: You build the stem, and the stem builds the leaf, and then the leaf strengthens that stem. By analogy, you build the leader and the leader builds the group, but the experience of convening the group builds a stronger leader.

Or, to shift the analogy, remember the opening illustration of chapter 5? A person in an airplane had a parachute release cord affixed and an instructor saying, "Next!" As that individual gets closer and closer to action, he or she becomes more and more alert to the clues about how to survive! In like manner let's learn how to invite people into a position where their thinking is consumed with, "My turn is next; I need to be learning."

And thus unfolds the entire Meta-Church construct, with its system-wide focus on leadership development.

More than an Experiment

You may have read this far, and now find yourself so far out on a limb that you're becoming uncomfortable. "So this cell-church paradigm is still in the experimental stage?" you ask. Sort of. In favor of the cell-church paradigm, all we have to show are the largest churches in the world—twenty churches each above twenty thousand—that use some variation of this technology and a host of historically significant occurrences during every era of church history. The Wesleyan class meetings, as one well-documented example, were used of God to sweep the continent of North America, from the first U.S. Wesleyan class meeting in the 1760s[3] to Methodism as America's largest Protestant denomination from 1855[4] until 1967.[5] And having interviewed people from those large churches and studied those historical movements, I'm further convinced that this new perspective is indeed what the Holy Spirit is doing in our era today.

More than Something Korean

Whenever I'm asked about those who have mentored me and those for whom I have the highest respect, I always mention the pastor of the largest church in the history of Christendom: Yoido Full Gospel Church, Seoul, Korea, founded and led by David Yonggi Cho. I can imagine few, if any, people from whom Christendom has more to learn—or who has been more misunderstood and misrepresented by Western believers.

In chapter 6 I told the story of how evangelism, discipleship, and pastoral care in Dr. Cho's church compare to most European and North American models. Perhaps you, like I, have long prayed and pleaded toward heaven, "Oh God, there must be a way for us to see that same level of fruitfulness in our churches." Despite the obvious cultural differences between the Orient and here, as well as some apparent theological differences, I cannot dismiss these Third-World churches by saying, "You know, it's amazing what you can do if you're Korean (or West African, or South American, or whatever)." Suppose the primary blockage on our continent is *our* limited awareness of what is possible: that because we haven't seen enough cell-based churches growing to unprecedented size, we can't believe it would be possible here.

Again, our motive has nothing to do with exalting *bigness*. Rather the issue is one of *"moreness."* Of all the potential mission fields on planet earth, the number of unchurched in the United States puts our nation in the top ten national mission fields in all the world. In that sense, perhaps we should look on North America as a mission field growing within Christendom. Thus our true motive for evangelism and church growth: We want *more* people to know God through Jesus Christ! We want to think in terms of people who voice allegiance to Christ and then demonstrate that commitment through the community of a church.

> We should look on North America as a mission field growing within Christendom.

Dr. Cho and others have shown us that this kind of growth doesn't come by preaching harder so much as it does by working smarter. If pastors will share the ministry with their laity by giving reasonable ministry assignments, the number of ministers could be multiplied, and desperately needed help would become available.

The Heart of the Future

In a nutshell, what is the fundamental active ingredient in the church of the future? Growing cells led by volunteer ministers are the fundamental building block. Everything else can be rationalized around that one concept. The task of church leaders and managers, then, is really rather simple: worship, recruitment, challenge to serve, supervision, specification, and, as needed, recovery therapy. If those things are in place, the cell and its leadership will be able to thrive. If any of those elements isn't in place, the cell will merely limp along.

The more of a handle you have on leadership development, the easier it will be to pull together cell-based ministries in the church. The less a handle, the more unrecognized genius and divine mystery will shape your next steps. Systems thinking allows you to be more deliberate and intentional about strengthening leadership and positioning your church for God to grant it growth and health.

As such, a Meta-Church is utterly dependent on the Holy Spirit. The discerning use of modernity's techniques, marketing tools, management training, or professional skills in no way lessen our reliance on the Holy Spirit. Nor do they allow a "truth decay" that discounts the cost of discipleship or deifies the quick fix instead of seeking durable results that matter for eternity. Nor can they substitute for knowing God, for pursuing his anointing and call, or for seeking him for renewal and revival.

Meta-Church perspectives are a way of seeing what you are up against as God builds a church in which everybody has a chance to be loved and listened to, no matter how many people he sends. By what forms will such a church be recognized? Meta-Church perspectives lead to practices that put priority on developing volunteer leaders who, in turn, multiply the number of cell-size groups. These groups—whether they help produce the vital, celebrative, corporate

> The church of the future will enlarge the kingdom
> of Jesus Christ by a multiplication of care
> through shared ministry with lay pastoral caregivers.

worship services or whether they help fill the pews as worshipers in those services—all become centers of pastoral care, new leader development, and evangelism.

The staff of a Meta-Church, after putting priority on (1) visiting the throne of grace in prayer and (2) nurturing their own spouse and/or children, have only three primary jobs: (3) training producers of worship events, (4) training producers of get-acquainted events, and (5) training leaders of cells. Their vision is to release the people of God to do the work of God, using their various spiritual gifts.

Dare I say, "That's it—everything else is secondary"? Could such a new perspective and priority encourage warehouses of untapped volunteer energy to be released as a result? Could the quality of disciples and the number of new lives being touched in most churches experience a quantum leap as a result? The church of the future will enlarge the kingdom of Jesus Christ by a multiplication of care through shared ministry with volunteer caregivers. That's the heartbeat of the Meta-Church.

"How Blessed Are The Feet of Those . . ."

The most durable thing that can happen as a result of your reading this book is for you, perhaps accompanied by others in your church, to enter the throne room of God and emerge, after much prayer, with an unshakable confidence that you understand his plan for your church with greater clarity than ever before. Followers of Christ are ever learning the ways of God. We make continual discoveries of how our own fallenness, brokenness, and lack of faith are crippling us. In short, we sometimes don't realize how much we're getting in our own way.

We, like the veteran Christian in the oft-recounted sermon illustration, sometimes lose hope because of the squalor of sin that surrounds us. This particular saint, after a most discouraging day, walked home exhausted, feeling overwhelmed by the brokenness and human need he encountered day after day. As he walked past a man, obviously drunk, wretching in the gutter, he prayed, "Dear God, if you're really so concerned about the plight of mankind, why are you allowing that man, unattended, to vomit in the gutter and lie in his own filth? Why are you permitting his suffering to continue without your intervention?" Perhaps for the first time in his life, this religious man heard an audible response to his prayer. God said, "I did something about that man's misery, suffering, and separation from me. I called him to your attention."

Such is the challenge you and I face. We have been given the privilege of standing here on earth, in the very place of Jesus Christ, animated by his Spirit, agents in his operation, and able, by modeling, to share his love in the flesh on earth until he comes.

May God's compassion so fill your church that you settle for nothing less than a revolution in leadership, where the training and releasing of volunteer leaders multiplies your church into a larger, more loving and more caring future.

Questions for Discussion and Application

1. What is the "heartbeat" message of this chapter? In what ways do you agree with it?

2. Why would God want the church you serve to become like this description: "The church of the future will enlarge the kingdom of Jesus Christ by a multiplication of care through shared pastoral lay ministry"?

3. What is your next move?

21

Resources, Networks, and Lists

Resources

Many of the books cited in the footnotes as well as dozens of other resources—seminars, books, cassette clubs, videos, extended training modules, self-study kits—that undergird Meta-Church technology can be obtained by contacting:

The Charles E. Fuller Institute
P.O. Box 90095
Pasadena, CA 91109-5095
phone: 1-800-MAP-META
FAX: 1-818-449-6129

Information on *DataMIRROR* and the Electronic District of the Future can be obtained by contacting:

DataMIRROR Service Center
P.O. Box 5407
Diamond Bar, CA 91765
phone: 909-396-6843
FAX: 909-396-6845

Postscript to Readers of *Prepare Your Church for the Future*

During the two and a half years since the publication of *Prepare Your Church for the Future,* ongoing feedback has affirmed the principles and observations outlined in that book. Hundreds of testimonials have documented the idea that small groups are the way ministry is done in most churches (whether these tiny social units are acknowledged or not). Numerous case studies have also confirmed *Prepare Your Church for the Future*'s premise that ministries develop best only as leaders are developed. As a result, *The Coming Church Revolution: Empowering Leaders for the Future* insists even more emphatically that leadership development is the most strategic activity of the professional ministry.

My colleagues and I are continually learning, however. All knowledge, save what is divinely revealed in Scripture, is subject to obsolescence as we learn to describe reality more accurately.

If we're wrong today, we're committed to being right tomorrow. The whole Meta-Church construct has been built on responding to ideas and testing them. We want to understand the "best practices" that the Holy Spirit seems to be inspiring and accomplishing in pacesetting churches in North America and around the world.

Here then are the most significant refinements since the writing of *Prepare Your Church for the Future.* They are listed not by priority but in the order discussed in this book:

1. Churches of All Sizes. Early research indicated that beyond-huge churches could be built only if small groups (cells) were used. We now have adequate documentation that any size church, including new church missions, can enlarge both their harvest and their health through a system of staff-coached, volunteer-led, cell-based care. (See chapter 1 in this book.)

2. Paradigm Name. We now downplay the term *Meta-Church model* because of how the word *model* tends to be overly identified with curriculums, programs, or techniques. (See chapters 1 and 4 in this book.)

3. Birthing New Groups. The Turbo Launch method is a significant and distinctive protocol for birthing new groups. (See chapter 2 in this book.)

4. Meta-Globe Zones. We no longer recommend a Gray Zone for highlighting finance-related issues. (See chapters 10 and 14 in this book.)

5. Orange Zone. The Orange Zone has developed and matured, and there are no longer negative connotations if a group is assigned to this zone because its function is not clearly understood. (See chapter 10 in this book.)

6. Yellow Zone. Previously we had suggested that medium-size groups might be replaced by celebration-size and cell-size groups. We have learned that some medium-size events are necessary due to socialization needs, especially among youth ministries and singles ministries. (See chapter 11 in this book.)

7. Blue Zone. We now recommend the label ECR (Extra Care Required person) as preferable to EGR (Extra Grace Required person). This lessens the sense of stigma. An ECR is simply someone whose neediness is sometimes difficult to accommodate in a cell group. (See chapter 12 in this book.)

8. Coaches. We've discovered the concept of "acting L" to be a distinct role from that of "apprentice L." (See chapter 12 in this book.)

9. Role Notation. For years we used parentheses to designate a rising leader and double parentheses for a leader who is yet to be identified. That annotation method proved unworkable when we began to use optical scanners to computer-generate a Meta-Globe. We now increasingly use the letter "R" to indicate a rising leader and "U" to show that a new occupant is needed for a particular role. (See chapter 13 in this book.)

10. Function of Any Cell. The acronym LLDD is now voiced as LLD*M*. We found that people interpreted the fourth component, "*D*ecide," to signify board and committee activity, rather than the *M*aintenance needs of the group itself. (See chapter 18 in this book.)

11. Members of the Body. We now advocate the term *volunteer* leader as preferable to *lay* leader because it communicates a higher level of dignity and a greater sense of empowerment. After all, the word *layman* or *layperson* is not found in Scripture!

Glossary of "Meta" Terms and Emphases

"Meta" Definitions

metanoia—a New Testament (Greek) word translated "repentance" or "change of mind."

metamorphosis—a Greek word transliterated into English, indicating a transformation or change of form, such as from caterpillar to butterfly.

Meta-Church—a growing, usually changing, local church committed to a joyous corporate worship of God (celebration), to the formation of nurture groups and ministry teams (cells) led by volunteer ministers, and to an organization of professionals and volunteers that focuses on development of leadership for ministry.

Meta-Globe—a way of visualizing Meta-Church concepts, based on a model of planet Earth.

Meta-Map—a way of using visual objects to represent the group meetings in a church, proportional to the number of people involved.

Meta-Zones—the six color-coded regions on a Meta-Globe.

Meta-Zoo—a series of animal analogies designed as a mnemonic device for understanding the qualities of variously sized churches. The church-size categories (worship attendance—adults and children) and Meta-Zoo animal analogies (as detailed in *Prepare Your Church for the Future*, 42–54) are listed here:

1. House church (5–35), mouse

2. Small church (35–75), cat

3. Medium church (75–200), lap dog

4. Large church (200–1000), yard dog

5. Superchurch (1000–3000), horse

6. Megachurch (3000–10,000), elephant

7. Beyond-huge church (10,000+), dinosaur or convention of mice

Note: Early research indicated that beyond-huge churches could only be built if small groups (cells) were used. We now know that any size church, including new church missions, can benefit from cell methodology.

Meta-Globe Color Zones (and Corresponding Globe Region)

1. **Purple** (north polar and axis)—governance, such as church board, pastoral staff, policy-making subcommittee, etc.

2. **Red** (main body of the northern hemisphere)—celebration events involving 100s and worship arts groups (task groups) involved in producing these events.

3. **Orange** (northern tropical zone)—new church development, cross-cultural missions, and auxiliary.

4. **Yellow** (southern tropical zone)—bridge and mezzanine events involving congregation-size groups and their cell-size leadership teams.

5. **Green** (main body of the southern hemisphere)—nurture groups and ministry teams of approximately ten people.

6. **Blue** (south polar)—classical pastoral care including crisis care and psychologically intensive ministry.

Roles

IN-GROUP ROLES.

Senior X—a cell leader who has birthed several groups, which, in turn, have themselves birthed new groups (X is the Roman numeral for 10).

X—leader of a small group (X is the Roman numeral for 10).

Xa—leader apprentice (X is the Roman numeral for 10).

H—Host/ess, member of the leadership nucleus of a small group who takes responsibility for group meeting site, refreshments, etc.

B—baby-sitter or child care coordinator for a group, if necessary.

I—an individual in a group (I is the Roman numeral for 1).

G—a growing disciple, someone in gift-discovery and ministry-finding mode.

S—a seeker, someone who has not yet made a commitment to the group and/or to Christ.

EGR—Extra Grace Required person (former label). One whose neediness is sometimes difficult to accommodate in a cell group.

ECR—Extra Care Required person (preferred, more sensitive description).

GROUP-SURROUND ROLES
(ALSO CALLED JETHRO II TERMINOLOGY)

D—professional staff status, with L, X, and C under supervision (D is the Roman numeral for 500).

Da—volunteer staff, or assistant D, or apprentice D.

L—coach who supervises approximately five cell leaders (L is the Roman numeral for 50).

aL—an acting L; a role carried until an L is developed.

La—an L apprentice; a role carried while still functioning as an X.

C—leader or teacher of a middle-size group (C is the Roman numeral for 100).

Other Acronyms

ABF—Adult Bible Fellowships: large adult Sunday schools.

AMP—Acquaintance Making Place: opportunities within larger meetings to meet people face to face.

FPR—Financial Performance Review: a governance function dealing with budgets, financial accountability, and ministry results.

GTF—Guilds, Troupes, Forums: an ensemble incubator concept involving Guilds (gatherings for artistic skills development, such as music lessons or drama training), Troupes (ensemble of performers or a team of artists or technicians, such as a choir, quartet, film crew, or banner-making group), and Forums (settings in which an audience may view the troupe, such as a dress rehearsal or a final performance).

LLDM—Love, Learn, Do, Maintain: the components of every group, differing in proportion. Love (nurture, care), Learn (common interest or activity), Do (group service to people beyond its membership), and Maintain (management of group life, social contracting, "housekeeping"). Formerly referred to as LLDD (Learn, Love, Do, Decide).

LRPC—Long Range Planning Committee: usually a governance function.

MCIF—Marketing, Calendar, Interpretation, Facilities.

PC/P—Pastoral Care/Psychology: encompassing most Blue Zone functions.

SIF—System Interface Function: a description of how a group contributes to the whole and also what it needs or derives from the whole.

VHS—Vision, Huddle, Skill: vital components in those meetings designed to develop a leadership community.

Other Specialized Terms

Ad Hoc Groups—short-term groups.

Age- or Life-Stage Divisions—a way of segmenting a general population, or a church membership, based on various stages of life, from infants through senior adults.

Apprentice Community—the meetings and training offered to leader apprentices, designed to assure their rapid development in Bible knowledge and application.

Auxiliary—usually an Orange Zone function, such as certain in-house adult Bible courses, bookstores, cassette ministries, radio/television ministries, and church-sponsored schools.

Bridge Events—fellowship-size events primarily designed to attract outsiders; usually a Yellow Zone function.

Career Pathway Assumptions—the progression from I to Xa to X, and so forth, that rising leaders may follow.

Celebration—a large gathering for worship and praise, usually a Red Zone function.

Cell—a group of approximately ten people, embodying many of the following characteristics: nurture, intimacy, accountability, gift development, pastoral care, assimilation, evangelism, and discipleship.

Cell Life Cycle—the process of group formation, maturity, and birthing of new groups.

Cho Model—a lay-pastored, cell-driven, systems approach to small-group evangelism, pastoral care, and leadership development used by David Yonggi Cho.

Clericalism—a clergy-centered paradigm of ministry.

Closed Groups—groups that do not admit newcomers, being closed either for an extended season or for the life of the group.

Congregation—a mid-size group, often represented by the Yellow Zone, of approximately 25 to 175 people.

Crisis Response Teams—usually a Blue Zone function, dispatched on the basis of information from Telecare Teams; they sometimes represent a modified deacon program.

DataMIRROR—a data transformation tool that enables a church to see, as in a mirror, its progress against its own history and goals and against those of comparable churches.

Debriefing—a report-taking function common during "huddling."

Docent Network—a strategy for multiplying the influence of growing churches through a program of systemic mentoring. The word *Docent* indicates a learner who teaches not just with words but by showing and demonstrating. A *Docent Quartet* is a team of *four* growth-minded partners who give peer support as they each take on Docent roles. A *Docent Cluster* occurs when each member of a Docent Quartet recruits up to five Learning Partners, who then become *Apprentice Docents* as they recruit Learning Partners of their own.

Dysfunctional Family—a medical and psychological term, popularized by various self-help writers, indicating a family that is not emotionally healthy.

Empty Chair. See *Open Chair.*

Ensemble Incubator—a worship production structure, placed on the axis of the northern hemisphere.

Feeder-Receptor—a pattern of Christians leaving smaller churches to become involved in a larger church, typically of

400 or more people. In this phenomenon, a large percentage of the larger church's growth may be traced to this pattern.

Fishing Pools—mid-size groups that provide opportunities for cell leaders and apprentices to meet newcomers.

Front Door Entry—a term to describe the experience of people whose initial attendance at a worship service does *not* involve a prior relationship with someone in the church. (See also *Side Door Entry.*)

Geographic Districts—a way of grouping a church's groups (usually in a very large church) according to ZIP code areas or other map-identifiable boundaries.

Gift Finding—the ongoing process of discovering and using the gifts that the Holy Spirit has given to every believer.

Grand Home Visitation—an intensive series of house-to-house visits, typically involving an X, L, and/or D visiting participants in a cell-group ministry. David Yonggi Cho has popularized this idea.

Hats—an indication of how many different roles a person has in a church (Bible study leader, choir member, etc.).

Huddles—meetings, whether formal or informal, involving ministry supervision, such as a D-L huddle or an L-X huddle.

Iceberg Analogy—an illustration indicating that, in a Meta-Church, the celebrations on premises are but the "tip of the iceberg" compared to the number of cells meeting off premises.

Jethro I Model—the appellate judicial system proposed by Moses' father-in-law in Exodus 18.

Jethro II Model—an adaptation of Jethro I, designed to maintain reasonable spans of care in a pastoral care structure.

Leadership Community. See *Ministry Community.*

Leadership Training "Food Groups"—vision, huddling, and microskill training.

Linking/Linkages—the "wiring" that connects various groups and leaders to one another.

Listening Prayer—the kind of prayer that spends less time talking to God and more time listening for his perspective.

Meta-Mapping—a visual way of diagramming and analyzing the meetings of a church, according to size, purpose, and leadership needs.

Mezzanine—a fellowship-size group (or subcongregation) from which people can move into either smaller groups or larger events.

Migration, Migration Pathways—an understanding of how and why people go from one group to another, such as from celebration to congregation to cell.

Ministry Community—the leadership cadre of a church (typically the Xs, Ls, Cs, Ds, and occasionally apprentices for each).

Ministry Team—a small group focused on a task, whether preparing the Communion altar (Red Zone), planning a high-visibility event (Yellow Zone), doing repair projects on the church building (Green Zone), or systematically phoning the church (Blue Zone).

Mutual Pastoral Care—the peer-to-peer ministry that typically occurs among members of a small group.

Nurture Groups—small groups whose primary purpose is to care for one another.

Open Chair—the intentional use of an available chair in a small group as a symbol that the group is seeking and desiring newcomers to join them. This concept was first popularized by Lyman Coleman.

Paradigm—a model for understanding and interpreting reality, such as a "clergy-centered paradigm of ministry."

Push and Pull Analogy—two understandings of how to fill a worship celebration, based on the question of how to raise a submerged boat: Use big-talent muscle to "pull" and attract newcomers, or use small-group leadership to "push" (or "float") people toward the large service.

Quaker Questions—discussion questions designed to engender relational bonding between two or more people. Dale Galloway and Lyman Coleman have popularized many examples of these questions.

Repurposing—a strategy and process for reshaping an existing ministry.

Re-seating—the process of helping a cell-group member find a different, more suitable group.

Reunion—a collection of cells for fellowship or ministry-team purposes. A reunion is sometimes called a zone event.

Seeker Services—a philosophy of ministry, popularized by Willow Creek Community Church (S. Barrington, Ill.), that intentionally targets people who are not yet committed to Christ and/or to a particular church and produces large meetings strategized to make baby boomers rave about the meetings' attractiveness and relevance.

Shepherding Movement—a controversial movement, now largely defunct, mainly within the charismatic and Pentecostal community, which stressed a high degree of control by lay shepherds over their groups.

Side Door Entry—a term to describe the experience of people whose initial attendance at a worship service involves a prior relationship with someone or some group in the church. (See also *Front Door Entry*.)

Span of Care—a concept, highlighted by the Jethro II model, which measures how many people are receiving direct, primary care from the same person.

Telecare—a safety-net concept in which teams routinely phone each household of the church to offer prayer support and care.

Turbo Group—A group made up almost exclusively of apprentice leaders, each of who plans to launch a new group in the near future. The term was coined by Jim Dethmer.

Vision Casting—the inspiring communication of a preferred future for a church or ministry; vision casting typically involves game plan, party line, and hero making. (See *How to Break Growth Barriers* by Carl F. George with Warren Bird, chapters 2 and 3.)

Notes

Introduction

1. In most cases I use the word *church* to refer to people, not a building. When referring to the latter, I most often use: "church facility," "church property," etc. Similarly, I use the word *congregation* to refer to a particular size of gathering (as in "celebration," "congregation," or "cell"), rather than as a straight synonym for the word *church*.

2. Carl F. George with Warren Bird, *How to Break Growth Barriers* (Grand Rapids: Baker, 1993), 130–31.

3. Among Christian writers, a broad range of ministry technologies are compatible with Meta-Church perspectives—some of which use the term *Meta-Church* and some of which do not. In addition to noting the twenty-five "People to Watch," beginning on page 339, see also the various endnote citations in this book, especially chapter 10 (Orange Zone), chapter 11 (Yellow Zone), and chapter 12 (Green Zone). From time to time, The Charles E. Fuller Institute has compiled a "Meta-Church Resources" catalog, or section in its regular catalog (P.O. Box 90095, Pasadena, CA 91109, 1-800-MAP-META).

4. George with Bird, *How to Break Growth Barriers*, 189.

Chapter 1

1. The idea of a pastor as a "producer of lay ministers" is developed in great detail in George with Bird, *How to Break Growth Barriers*.

2. Elmer L. Towns, *Ten Sunday Schools That Dared to Change: How Churches Are Changing Paradigms to Reach a New Generation* (Ventura: Gospel Light, 1993), 12.

3. John Vaughan has written several books that examine and profile the large church. He reviews much of the literature in the field in his *Megachurches and American Cities* (Grand Rapids: Baker, 1993), 17–28. He provides close-up examinations in *The Large Church* (Grand Rapids: Baker, 1985) and *The World's Twenty Largest Churches* (Grand Rapids: Baker, 1984).

330

Some of Ralph Neighbour's findings are published in "A Note from the Publisher," *Cell Church Magazine* 2, no.1 (1992): 3. See also Jim Egli, "Where Do We Go from Here?" *Cell Church Magazine* 2, no. 1 (1992): 23–27, and Egli, "A Bird's-Eye View of the Global Cell Church Movement," *Cell Church Magazine* 2, no. 3 (1993): 5.

C. Peter Wagner's *Stop the World, I Want to Get On* (Glendale: Regal, 1974) and *Spiritual Power and Church Growth* (Altamente Springs, Fla.: Creation House, 1986) are also worth noting.

4. C. Peter Wagner, "Church Growth," in *Dictionary of Pentecostal and Charismatic Movements*, ed. Stanley M. Burgess and Gary B. McGee (Grand Rapids: Baker, 1988), 187. Vaughan, *Megachurches and American Cities*, 33–37, 53–57.

5. For information on the seminars, cassette clubs, and other resources supplied by the Charles E. Fuller Institute, phone their customer service helpline at 1-800-MAP-META or 1-800-999-9578, fax them at 1-818-449-6129, or write to them at P.O. Box 90095, Pasadena, CA 91109–5095.

6. This feeder-receptor pattern is explained further in George, *Prepare Your Church for the Future*, 31–34, 44, and George with Bird, *How to Break Growth Barriers*, 60–63, 65, 174, 187.

Chapter 2

1. A number of writers, both Christian and secular, emphasize the idea of constantly developing new leaders at the grassroots level. Some of these authors use the term *apprentice* and some do not. Among the more particularly significant books are Robert E. Coleman, *The Master Plan of Evangelism* (Grand Rapids: Revell, 1988); Ralph W. Neighbour Jr., *The Shepherd's Guidebook* (Houston: Touch Outreach Publications, 1988); three by Bill Hull: *The Disciple Making Pastor* (Grand Rapids: Revell, 1988), *The Disciple Making Church* (Grand Rapids: Revell, 1990), and *Jesus Christ, Disciple Maker* (Grand Rapids: Revell, 1990); and two books by J. Robert Clinton and Laura Raab: *Barnabas—The Encouraging Exhorter: A Study in Mentoring* (Altadena, Calif.: Barnabas Resources, 1985), and *The Mentor Handbook: Detailed Guidelines and Helps for Christian Mentors and Mentorees* (Altadena, Calif.: Barnabas Resources, 1991). Other valuable resources are David A. Womack, *The Pyramid Principle* (Minneapolis: Bethany House, 1977); O. J. Bryson, *Networking the Kingdom* (Waco: Word, 1990); Gordon MacDonald, *Ordering Your Private World, Expanded Edition* (Nashville: Oliver-Nelson, 1985); Peter M. Senge, *The Fifth Discipline: The Art and Practice of the Learning Organization* (New York: Doubleday Currency, 1990); and Michael E. Gerber, *The E Myth: Why Most Small Businesses Don't Work and What to Do About It* (New York: HarperBusiness, 1986).

Chapter 3

1. George, *Prepare Your Church for the Future*, 121–25.
2. See chapter 12 for further discussion on how coaches [Ls] typically emerge.

Chapter 4

1. A. Paul Hare, *Handbook of Small Group Research*, 2d ed. (New York: Free Press, 1976); Richard Hackman, *Perspectives on Behavior and Organizations*, 2d ed., ed. Patricia S. Nave (New York: McGraw, 1983); Richard Hackman, *Groups That Work and Those That Don't: Creating Conditions for Effective Teamwork* (San Francisco: Jossey-Bass, 1990).

2. Robert Wuthnow, *Sharing the Journey: Support Groups and America's New Quest for Community* (New York: Free Press, 1994).

3. Frank R. Tillapaugh, *Unleashing the Church: Getting People out of the Fortress and into Ministry* (Ventura: Regal, 1982).

Chapter 5

1. Knowles' view of adult learning, called andragogy, is explained in his *Modern Practice of Adult Education: From Pedagogy to Andragogy* (Chicago: Follet, 1980), 43-44, and is cited approvingly in Stanley, Paul D. and J. Robert Clinton, *Connecting: The Mentoring Relationships You Need to Succeed in Life* (Colorado Springs, Colo.: NavPress, 1992), 231–32.

2. Juan Carlos Ortiz, *Disciple* (Carol Stream, Ill.: Creation House, 1975), describes how he tried this approach to teaching about tithing.

3. For further background on this story, see Carl F. George and Robert E. Logan, *Leading and Managing Your Church* (Grand Rapids: Revell, 1987), 19–20.

Chapter 6

1. "Yonggi Cho Changes His Name," *Charisma & Christian Life* 18, no. 4, (November 1992): 80.

2. As one example, in his book, *The Fourth Dimension* (Plainfield, N.J.: Logos, 1979), Cho explains that in the corporate worship services at the Yoido church, "We make our announcements very short, with the Word of God taking preeminence. . . . The Word of God is always uppermost" (p. 25). Further, he urges followers of Christ that "your desire must be screened through the Scripture" (p. 109). You must "feed your mind with Scripture, for the Word of God is full of positive life" (p. 123). You must "expand your thinking life according to Scripture. Then God can have absolute freedom to express Himself through your thoughts" (p. 124). You must "study the Word of God; this is the textbook with which you can renew your mind" (p. 147). And you must "fill your thinking with the Word of God. Then God can have a free approach to your life and flow out to do mighty things for the glory of God through you" (p. 150).

3. Most Cho titles are distributed in North America through David Cho Ministries, P.O. Box 69420, Seattle, WA 98168, phone 206-946-5672, FAX 206-946-8461. *Caught in the Web,* a biography of Cho's earlier years, written in 1981 by missionary John Hurston, who served at Cho's church for a number of years, is out of print. Dr.

Cho's only authorized English biography to date is: Nell Kennedy, *Dream Your Way to Success* (S. Plainfield, N.J.: Bridge Publishing, 2500 Hamilton Blvd. 07080, phone 908-754-0745, FAX 908-754-0613, 1980). A summary of the development of the Yoido Full Gospel Church from its start through 1982 is included in John N. Vaughan, *The World's 20 Largest Churches* (Grand Rapids: Baker, 1984). See also the chapter, "Biggest Little Church in the World," by John Stetz in Towns, Vaughan, and Seifert, *The Complete Book of Church Growth* (Wheaton: Tyndale, 1981), 61–68.

4. George with Bird, *How to Break Growth Barriers*, 36–42.

5. George, *Prepare Your Church for the Future*, 52, 129–35.

6. Cho's authorized biography also suggests ten factors that help explain the growth experienced at the Yoido Central Full Gospel Church: 1. Holy Spirit, 2. Prayer, 3. Fasting, 4. Delegating leadership of lay people, especially mobilizing women, 5. Daring to dream a clear-cut goal, 6. Speaking the Word with boldness, 7. Obedience to the Lord, 8. Clear confession of faults before God, 9. Success-mindedness with success-oriented fruits, 10. Receptivity. Kennedy, *Dream Your Way to Success,* 230.

7. If you, the reader, are aware of other churches using Meta-Church technology and experiencing increased conversion growth, reaching 70 percent or more, please drop a note to: Electronic District of the Future, P.O. Box 5407, Diamond Bar, CA 91765, phone 909-396-6843, FAX 909-396-6845. Also, a new data-tracking resource, called *DataMIRROR,* now in a testing stage, is designed to compare churches of "similar ministry circumstances" so that they may learn from one another's growth patterns. For further information, write to the same address.

Chapter 7

1. George, *Prepare Your Church for the Future*, 153–80.

2. See chapter 13 for a definition and discussion of telecare.

Chapter 8

1. George with Bird, *How to Break Growth Barriers*, 85–100, 145–63.

2. VHS is an acronym for Vision, Huddling, and Skill-building. See "Structured Leadership Training" in this chapter and chapter 12 for further explanation.

3. This list is by no means exhaustive! One reviewer of this manuscript also suggested Acts 20:20; Hebrews 10:25; Ephesians 4:16; 1 Peter 1:5; and 2 Corinthians 3:3.

4. I am especially indebted to the work of Robert Clinton for this perspective. Some of his writings are cited in chapter 2, footnote 1, and chapter 5, footnote 1.

Chapter 9

1. George with Bird, *How to Break Growth Barriers*, 109–25.

Chapter 10

1. Donald A. McGavran and Winfield C. Arn, *Ten Steps for Church Growth* (San Francisco: Harper and Row, 1977), 47. Lyle E. Schaller, in *44 Questions for Church Planters* (Nashville: Abingdon, 1991), 20, says that church planting "continues to be the most useful and productive component of any denominational church growth strategy." C. Peter Wagner, *Church Planting for a Greater Harvest* (Ventura: Regal Books, 1990), says "The single most effective evangelistic methodology under heaven is planting new churches" (p. 11); "Without exception, the growing denominations have been those that stress church planting" (p. 13); and "Church planting develops new leadership. Many studies have confirmed the fact that the most important institutional variable for the growth and expansion of the local church is leadership" (p. 20). Robert E. Logan, *Beyond Church Growth* (Grand Rapids: Revell, 1989), says "We never will fulfill the Great Commission without the multiplication of churches" (p. 194) and "There are no better ways [to fulfill the Great Commission] than by planting new churches" (p. 192). See also Charles L. Chaney, *Church Planting at the End of the Twentieth Century* (Wheaton: Tyndale House, 1982); Jack Redford, *Planting New Churches* (Nashville: Broadman, 1978); and David J. Hesselgrave, *Planting Churches Cross-Culturally: A Guide for Home and Foreign Missions* (Grand Rapids: Baker, 1980).

2. John N. Vaughan, in *The Large Church,* 47, demonstrates how John Wesley created "a fully developed network of mission chapels" across England.

3. Vaughan, *The Large Church,* 49.

4. Elmer L. Towns, *The Ten Largest Sunday Schools and What Makes Them Grow* (Grand Rapids: Baker, 1969), 16.

5. Vaughan, *The Large Church,* 34. See also John N. Vaughan, *The World's Twenty Largest Churches,* 269-71. According to Vaughan, "As early as 1984, the [Cho] congregation reported having 115 foreign missionaries ministering in sixteen different countries." *(Megachurches and America's Cities,* 18), and "The Yoido church starts new daughter churches throughout Korea in five new locations each year" (p. 19). According to Nell Kennedy, *Dream Your Way to Success,* 219, in 1975 Cho sent missionaries to Japan, Europe, and the U.S. In 1979 he started fifty churches "in other areas too distant for the people to travel to Yoido." In Cho's own words, "From the beginning of any church, missions should be a priority" (David Yonggi Cho, [*Answers to Your Questions.* Seoul: Church Growth International, 1984], 35).

6. One of the larger demographic information organizations is Percept/CIDS (Church Information and Development Services), 151 Kalmus Dr. Ste. A104, Costa Mesa, CA 92626-9793, phone 800-422-6277 or 714-957-1282, FAX 914-957-1924.

7. One organization that uses Meta-Church thinking and continually produces new cutting edge resources (seminars, training kits, and others) on themes related to church planting is: Church Resource Ministries, P.O. Box 1354, Alta Loma, CA 91701, phone and FAX 909-989-3599, attn: Dr. Robert E. Logan, Vice President.

8. For a state-by-state list, see George Barna, *Church Marketing: Breaking Ground for the Harvest* (Ventura, Calif.: Regal, 1992), 248-49.

9. For religiously oriented demographics, see footnote 6. For other general demographics, numerous books, computer software, and commercial vendors are available. For example, see Diane Crispell, *Insider's Guide to Demographic Know-How* (Chicago: Probus Publishing, 1990); and Penelope Wickham, *Demographic Know-How* (Chicago: Probus Publishing, 1988). Also many commercial software packages, such as *Map Expert* and *PC-Census,* offer ways to research the demographics of a targeted geographic area. Among the largest commercial marketing information services are Claritas/NPDC Business Information Services, 1-800-234-5973; and Demographics on Call, Donnelley Marketing Information Services, c/o Dunn and Bradstreet, 70 Seaview Ave., P.O. Box 10250, Stamford, CT 06904, 1-800-866-2255.

Chapter 11

1. George, *Prepare Your Church for the Future,* 57-67.

2. Lyman Coleman, c/o Serendipity, P.O. Box 1012, Littleton, CO 80160-1012, customer service: 1-800-525-9563, FAX: 303-798-8102.

3. George, *Prepare Your Church for the Future,* 162–64, 171.

4. Howard A. Snyder in *The Radical Wesley and Patterns for Church Renewal* (Downers Grove, Ill.: InterVarsity Press, 1980), 63, says, for example, "Wesley put one in ten, perhaps one in five, to work in significant ministry and leadership."

5. Arthur Flake, *Building a Standard Sunday School* (Nashville: Sunday School Board, 1934) and *True Functions of the Sunday School* (Nashville: Sunday School Board, 1936).

6. Louis Entzminger, *How to Organize and Administer a Great Sunday School* (Fort Worth: Manney, 1949).

7. Elmer L. Towns, *Ten Sunday Schools That Dared to Change*; *10 of Today's Most Innovative Churches* (Ventura, Calif.: Regal, 1990); *154 Steps to Revitalize Your Sunday School and Keep Your Church Growing* (Wheaton: Scripture Press, 1988); *The Ten Largest Sunday Schools, and What Makes Them Grow; The Successful Sunday School and Teachers Guidebook* (Carol Stream, Ill.: Creation House, 1976).

8. Lyle E. Schaller, *The Pastor and the People* (Nashville: Abingdon, 1973), 80–86.

9. C. Peter Wagner, *Your Church Can Grow*, rev. ed. (Ventura, Calif.: Regal, 1984), 111–26. See also my discussion in *Prepare Your Church for the Future,* 57–69.

Chapter 12

1. For more background on vision and vision casting see George with Bird, *How to Break Growth Barriers,* 27-55.

2. For a list of resources, including many of those published by Dale Galloway, contact The Charles E. Fuller Institute, P.O. Box 90095, Pasadena, CA 91109, or phone 1-800-MAP-META.

3. For background on my development of the EGR idea, see my book, *Prepare Your Church for the Future*, 105, 110–11, 126, 128, 195.

4. David Johnson and Jeff VanVonderen, *The Subtle Power of Spiritual Abuse* (Minneapolis: Bethany House, 1991); Ron Enroth, *Churches That Abuse* (Grand Rapids: Zondervan, 1992); and Flavil Yeakley, *Disciplining Dilemma* (Nashville: Gospel Advocate Company, 1988).

Chapter 14

1. For a more detailed explanation of the Ensemble Incubator, see chapter 9; for the Vision-Huddle-Skill concept, see chapter 12.

2. For a catalog or information on Charles E. Fuller Institute seminars that offer training in Meta-Church perspectives, call 1-800-MAP-META, FAX at 1-818-449-6129, or write to P.O. Box 90095, Pasadena, CA 91109-5095. For information on a new data-tracking resource, called *DataMIRROR,* now in a testing stage, which uses Meta-mapping to link churches of "similar ministry circumstances" so that they may learn from one another, write: *DataMIRROR,* P.O. Box 5407, Diamond Bar, CA 91765, phone 909-396-6843, FAX 909-396-6845.

Chapter 15

1. Lyle E. Schaller, *Strategies for Change* (Nashville: Abingdon, 1993), 10. In one of his earlier books on change, Schaller says, "Anyone seriously interested in planned social change would be well advised to recognize two facts of life. First, despite the claims of many, relatively little is known about how to achieve predictable change. Second, much of what is known will not work" (*The Change Agent* [Nashville: Abingdon, 1972], 11). Schaller also has written a two other books on change: *Getting Things Done* (Nashville: Abingdon, 1986), which focuses on the leadership role and style of individuals, and *Create Your Own Future* (Nashville: Abingdon, 1991), which focuses on members of long-range planning committees.

2. George with Bird, *How to Break Growth Barriers*, 85–108.

3. The "Berry Bucket Theory" is a tool for understanding the various responses to a pastor's age or number of years at a church. Different presentations of the "Berry Bucket Theory," each with a different slant and application, appear in Carl F. George and Robert E. Logan, *Leading and Managing Your Church* (Grand Rapids: Revell, 1987), 147-64; and George with Bird, *How to Break Growth Barriers*, 111–16.

Chapter 16

1. Several training manuals are available commercially, including Dale Galloway's *Lay Pastor Training Manual for Successful Home Group Meetings* (Portland, Ore.: New Hope Community Church, 1986). Such resources are carried by The Charles E. Fuller Institute, 1-800-MAP-META.

Chapter 17

1. Ralph W. Neighbour, Jr., *Where Do We Go From Here? A Guidebook for the Cell Group Church* (Houston: Touch Publications, 1990). P.O. Box 19888, Houston, TX 77224, 1-800-735-5865.

2. For further information on *DataMIRROR*, write: *DataMIRROR*, P.O. Box 5407, Diamond Bar, CA 91765, phone 909-396-6843, FAX 909-396-6845.

Chapter 18

1. Towns, *Ten Sunday Schools That Dared to Change,* 12, 15, 18. Here are some other significant quotes from that book and the changes that should be made in North American Sunday schools:

• Emphasizing relationships—"people bond to the church through relationships" (p. 17).

• Changing the title of teacher to leader—"This book suggests that we no longer call them teachers but leaders" (p. 18). "This title moves the focus from talking, speeches, and someone up front lecturing. . . . The role of the Bible study leader must change to provide spiritual care to everyone in the class. The leader must follow up on absentees, help people solve their problems, and bond people into adult Bible fellowships" (p. 77). "People do not prefer another school experience that may remind them of an unpleasant past. The term 'teacher' implies school. It also implies that his or her work begins when the class begins and terminates when the class ends. However, the title 'leader' suggests being an example, giving care, and protecting followers. . . . Whether they are called 'class leaders' or 'shepherds,' new titles for teachers give new expectations to class members" (p. 143).

• Sunday school as leader centered—"The message of the 10 Sunday schools discussed in this book is that the teacher must cast a vision in the hearts of pupils. . . . The power of Sunday school is still in the teacher who influences students" (p. 10).

• Dropping the term Sunday school—"Change the name from Sunday school to adult Bible fellowship. The focus is no longer on education or an academic environment. Focus on fellowship. Call the class an adult Bible fellowship because fellowship by itself is not enough. It should be fellowship based on the Word of God" (pp. 77–78).

• Meeting anytime or anywhere—"The church of the future must be a cafeteria, not a plate lunch, which symbolizes that time, topic, and systems of ministry have been predetermined and controlled. . . . In the future, the church must be a cafeteria by offering choices and variety to its people . . . because peoples' schedules demand more choices and variety to meet their varied needs" (p. 145).

• No formulas—"This book . . . suggests many models for revitalizing the Sunday schools of the '90s. No one prescription will work in every situation" (p. 18).

2. For more background on this "LLDM" configuration (formerly voiced as LLDD), see the appendix of this book and George, *Prepare Your Church for the Future*, 89–90.

3. Additional resources include "How Do Children Fit into the Meta-Church Model?" a self-study kit (cassettes and notes) by Dale Galloway and Clara Olson, and four chapters on children's and teen cell groups, by Lorna Jenkins, in Neighbour's, *Where Do We Go From Here?*

Chapter 19

1. According to the 1992 Church Compensation Report by John C. LaRue Jr., sold by *Christianity Today* (800-866-6464) and summarized in "Church Staffing Levels and Expenses," *Your Church,* November/December 1993: four out of ten churches with budgets under $50,000 have a part-time person, typically a pastor. Churches with attendance under fifty average just $22,300 annually on either one part-time or one full-time person (this costs $892 per attendee annually).

2. For more background on these changes, see the opening chapter, "The Changing Face of American Christianity," in Lyle E. Schaller, *The Seven-Day-a-Week Church* (Nashville: Abingdon, 1992), 17–36.

Chapter 20

1. Peter Drucker, *Managing the Non-Profit Organization* (New York: HarperBusiness, 1992), 195–202.

2. George, *Prepare Your Church for the Future*, 137–39.

3. Tim Dowley ed., *Eerdmans' Handbook to the History of Christianity* (Grand Rapids: Eerdmans, 1977), 451–52.

4. Ibid., 534-35.

5. Dean M. Kelly, *Why Conservative Churches Are Growing: A Study in the Sociology of Religion* (New York: Harper & Row, 1972), 5, 21.

Key Leaders and Authors

Twenty-Five Key Christian Leaders and Writers to Watch

Anderson, Leith—pastor of Wooddale Church in greater Minneapolis and author of *Dying for Change* and *A Church for the 21st Century.*

Arn, Win (father) and Charles (son)—pioneering researchers and observers in the tradition of Donald McGavran, authors of thirty-seven videos and thirteen books including *The Master's Plan for Making Disciples* and *The Pastor's Manual for Effective Ministry: A Compilation of Outstanding Articles, Research, and Insights from The Win Arn Growth Report.*

Barna, George—trend researcher and author of such books as *The Power of Vision* and *A Step-by-Step Guide to Church Marketing: Breaking Ground for the Harvest.*

Callahan, Kennon L.—pastor, theologian, and consultant; author of *Twelve Keys to an Effective Church* and other titles.

Cho, David Yonggi—pastor of largest church in Christendom, author of several books including *Successful Home Cell Groups* and *More than Numbers.*

Coleman, Lyman—author of Serendipity materials, creator of numerous questions and conversational games designed to enhance relationship-building skills in small groups.

Dethmer, Jim—church planter; former teaching pastor at Willow Creek Community Church responsible for implementing a leadership-development system at that church.

Galloway, Dale—founding pastor of a large and thriving Cho-model church in Portland, Oregon; author of numerous resources and books, including *20/20 Vision*.

Haugk, Kenneth C.—pastor and clinical psychologist who created the Stephen Series of lay ministry training.

Hurston, Karen—missionary whose family served with David Yonggi Cho in Korea; small-group consultant; author, with her father John W. Hurston, of *Caught in the Web*.

Hybels, Bill—founding pastor of Willow Creek Community Church in metro Chicago, the church with the largest week-to-week attendance in North America, and author of several books including *Too Busy NOT to Pray*.

Logan, Robert (and team)—founding pastor of a fast-growing church that was helped by Meta-Church technology; researcher; author of *Beyond Church Growth* and other resources.

Luecke, David—author of *Evangelical Style, Lutheran Substance* and co-author of *The Courageous Church*.

Murren, Doug—founding pastor of Eastside Foursquare Church in greater Seattle; author of several books, including *Baby Boomerang*.

Neighbour, Ralph—author of scores of books, including the paradigm-challenging book *Where Do We Go from Here?* and an adapter of the Cho model in the U.S. and Singapore.

Ogden, Greg—pastor; author of *The New Reformation.*

Schaller, Lyle—church consultant, seminal thinker, author or editor of more than eighty books on the subject of church health.

Schuller, Robert A. (son)—church planter who is using Meta-Church technology as foundational for the church.

Schuller, Robert H. (father)—founder of the Crystal Cathedral in Los Angeles, and developer of many innovative approaches to preevangelism.

Snyder, Howard—pioneering thinker; author of *The Problem with Wineskins, The Radical Wesley and Patterns for Church Renewal,* and other books.

Tillapaugh, Frank—author of *Unleashing the Church: Getting People out of the Fortress and into Ministry;* his pastoral ability to release volunteers into ministry task forces is unequalled.

Towns, Elmer—pioneering writer and researcher, especially on the topic of Sunday school growth; creator of a highly influential series of lists that documented North America's largest Sunday schools.

Vaughan, John—leading researcher of large churches worldwide, and author of *The Large Church, The World's Twenty Largest Churches,* and *Megachurches and America's Cities.*

Wagner, C. Peter—missionary strategist; professor at Fuller Theological Seminary School of World Missions; leading spokesperson in current prayer movements; author of many books and articles on church growth.

Warren, Rick—innovative, founding pastor of Saddleback Community Church, Mission Viejo, California; popular seminar speaker; founder of The Encouraging Word cassette ministry; author of several books.

Ten Authors on Related Topics to Watch

(Most have authored far more titles than the ones listed below.)

Barker, Joel, *Paradigms: The Business of Discovering the Future* (New York: HarperBusiness, 1993) and *Future Edge: Discovering the New Paradigms of Success* (New York: William Morrow, 1992).

Bennis, Warren, *On Becoming a Leader* (Reading, Mass.: Addison-Wesley, 1989); *Why Leaders Can't Lead* (San Francisco: Jossey-Bass, 1989); *An Invented Life* (Reading, Mass.: Addison-Wesley, 1993); and with Bert Nanus, *Leaders: Strategies for Taking Charge* (New York: Harper & Row, 1985).

Covey, Stephen, *Reflections for Highly Effective People* (New York: Simon and Schuster, 1994) and *The 7 Habits of Highly Effective People* (New York: Simon and Schuster, 1989).

Drucker, Peter F., father of the management-science movement; author of numerous books including *Managing the Non-Profit Organization* (New York: HarperBusiness, 1992) and *Post-Capitalist Society* (New York: HarperBusiness, 1993).

Gerber, Michael, *The E Myth: Why Most Small Businesses Don't Work, and What to Do about It* (New York: HarperBusiness, 1986).

Handy, Charles, *The Age of Unreason* (Boston: Harvard Business School Press, 1989).

Kotler, Philip, author of more than a dozen books on marketing; coauthor, with Norman Shawchuck, Bruce Wrenn, and Gustave Rath, of *Marketing for Congregations: Choosing to Serve People More Effectively* (Nashville: Abingdon, 1992).

McGinnis, Alan Loy, *Bringing Out the Best in People* (Minneapolis: Augsburg, 1985) and *The Friendship Factor* (Minneapolis: Augsburg, 1979).

Peters, Thomas J., *In Search of Excellence* (San Francisco: HarperCollins, 1982) and *Thriving on Chaos* (New York: Knopf, 1987).

Senge, Peter M., *The Fifth Discipline: The Arts and Practice of the Learning Organization* (New York: Doubleday Currency, 1990).

Subject Index

Figures are noted in *italics*.

Denominational Index

Scripture Index

349